The Day Before America

BOOKS BY WILLIAM H. MACLEISH

Oil and Water
The Gulf Stream
The Day Before America

THE
DAY BEFORE
AMERICA

William H. MacLeish

Illustrated by Will Bryant

A Richard Todd Book
HOUGHTON MIFFLIN COMPANY
Boston • New York

For Marion W. and Ida E. Boggs
Friends in Law, Friends in Love

———————

For information about permission to reproduce selections from
this book, write to Permissions, Houghton Mifflin Company,
215 Park Avenue South, New York, New York 10003.

Library of Congress Cataloging-in-Publication Data
MacLeish, William H., date.
The day before America / William H. MacLeish
p.   cm.
ISBN 0-395-46882-5
ISBN 0-395-74014-2 (pbk.)
1. Indians of North America — History. 2. Hunting and
gathering societies — North America. 3. Indians of North
America — Philosophy. 4. Natural history — North America.
5. Human ecology — North America.   1. Title
E77.M1144   1994   94-9504
970.01 — dc20   CIP

Printed in the United States of America

Book design by Robert Overholtzer

MP 10 9 8 7 6 5 4 3 2 1

Some of the material in this book has appeared, in slightly different form,
in *Eco*, the *New York Times Magazine*, *Smithsonian*, and *World Monitor*.

ACKNOWLEDGMENTS

Many of the people and institutions of help to me on this journey are named in the text or the notes section at the end of the book. Those who are not, and to whom I owe a great deal, are Robie Macauley, my editor before his retirement; Richard Todd, who actually edited *The Day Before America* and who saw its shape long before I did; Will Bryant, my old friend, whose illustrations grace these pages; Jane Cushman, my agent, who had the faith I sometimes lacked; and the poet Elizabeth Libbey, my wife, who so often eased the hard going. I am also grateful to the Merrill Lynch and Co. Foundation, Inc., of New York City, and Mrs. Alexander Campbell, late of Geneva, New York, for their financial assistance.

I want to give special thanks to Dena Dincauze, a leading American archaeologist, who teaches at the University of Massachusetts. We talked together often about ideas and sources, and she had the kindness, and perseverance, to read an early draft. William Cronon, an environmental historian formerly of Yale and now at the University of Wisconsin, gave me the right advice on framing the book. Russell Graham and his colleagues at the Illinois State Museum in Springfield showed me what the Midwest was like deep in prehistory. Dean Snow, of the State University of New York at Albany, and George Hamell, of the New York State Museum in that city, introduced me to the Iroquois, and Ron LaFrance, of Cornell University, opened my eyes to their way of thinking. Dennis Stanford and Pegi Jodry, of the Smithsonian Institution, taught me about early hunters in the West, and Richard Ford, of the University of Michigan, showed me the basics of plant domestication in North America. Thompson Webb III, of Brown University, and Margaret Davis, of the University of Minnesota, helped me see that change is something of a constant, that oaks and elderberries and prairie grasses are not the sessile beings I once took them to be.

In considering modern human impacts in the United States, I had the great good luck to hear the plant geneticist Wes Jackson, the writer Wendell Berry, and the environmental analyst Donnella Meadows in conversation at Jackson's Land Institute in Salina, Kansas. In the evenings there, I walked and talked with F. Herbert Bormann, an ecologist I had come to know years before at Yale. There followed visits to George Woodwell at his Woods Hole Research Center on Cape Cod, Hunter and Amory Lovins at their Rocky Mountain Institute in Colorado, and Thomas Lovejoy at the Smithsonian Institution in Washington, and, in that city, an afternoon with Garrett Hardin, human ecologist emeritus at the University of California, Santa Barbara.

It is my hope that these interactions have taken some of the glare out of my authorial errors. I know they have left me beset by a need to travel further, to see, in the day *of* America, how the Red Queen runs her race.

CONTENTS

1

Existence in Reality

TRAVEL WORRIES ME. But the actuality of passage is so often wonderful, so often an experience that brings all my senses into resonance, that I rarely can turn away from it. Even in my dreams and nightmares, on empty roads, in huge rooms full of strangers, I am, despite myself, a wayfarer.

Travel brought me this book. It was the fall of 1986, and I was aboard the topsail schooner *Welcome* as she sailed from Portugal to Madeira and the Canary Islands and then across to the Caribbean. My intent was to get as close as I could to the track of the voyage that opened the Americas to Europe. I had with me reports of that westering. Off watch, I would read of long-tailed white birds and brilliant bull dolphins playing around *Santa Maria* as they were playing around *Welcome*. I would read that the Admiral had fine weather, the air "soft and refreshing," that he wanted for nothing "but the singing of a nightingale," and I would look down the moon track and hear the trades in *Welcome*'s rigging and compare contentments.

I had other histories of the European conquest of the Americas with me and in one read a passage selected for the Admiral by his son Fernando. It is part of a myth recorded by the Roman writer Seneca: "An age will come after many years when Oceanus will loose the chain of things, and a huge land lie revealed; when Tiphys will disclose new worlds and Thule be no more the ultimate." Fernando wrote, "This prophecy was fulfilled by my father . . . in the year 1492." It was a boast but not a blind one. Tiphys had been pilot to Jason and the Argonauts. Christopher Columbus was pilot to all Europe.

I was at *Welcome*'s helm one night when my watchmate, a Cornish sailor with years of experience in Atlantic crossings, remarked on a certain odor on the wind. It reminded me of bacon frying. What you're smelling, he said, is dust from the Sahara drifting west. I thought of the specks of desert trapped in our sails. In my reverie, everything around me seemed to be moving toward Seneca's huge land: my ship, the ghost ships a couple of hundred miles to our north, the very soil of Africa. The myth said the land was beyond Thule, itself the symbol of the unimaginably remote. Anything at that remove must have seemed beyond time, a place without a past. Distance would have guarded it as dragons guarded other mythical beauty, and it could have been brought back to the world only by the hero's touch.

It seemed possible to me, musing at the helm, that the first Europeans to cross the Atlantic might have sensed something of the myth. If they did, they would have looked at the land rising where the sun set and they would have called the ancient land they saw the New World, new because strange, but new also by virtue of their seeing it, releasing it in their minds from its strangeness, its isolation. Even a modern Euro-American could take comfort from the fallacy of 1492. I found myself thinking of my much used homeland, a thousand miles distant beyond the bow, as somehow still fresh, still new.

The dry hiss of bow slicing water brought me back to *Welcome* and my watch. I was struck by the power of Fernando's selection, angry that for a moment I had succumbed to it. With the anger came purpose: I would go looking for the past that Seneca's myth had done so much to diminish. I suddenly needed that past — to travel in it, to learn about the ways in which my homeland acquired its aspect, its landscapes, its assemblages of life. I needed to understand what I could of its changing: ice to raging flood, to river; parklands to grass-lands, tundra to forest; a country without people to a country changed by the fires and settlements and clearings of people.

I wanted to link that long past with the short one I was born into, the day *of* America. To do that, I would need to learn how Europeans lived on their lands; how their livestock and their ideas and their energies, transported west in the caravels of the Spanish and the brigs of the English, transformed my homeland in ways glacier and flood and first people never did. I would need to learn something of what my society has lost in its gaining.

Might as well get started, said the wayfarer in me.

I hesitated, I worried, but I did start — five years ago. Al-most immediately it became apparent that I was unprepared for my purpose. For one thing, my culture kept getting in the way. I was beset by stereotypes. I pass one every time I drive to the nearest big town. It is a statue of a native American, all twenty-eight fiberglassed feet of him, in front of a tourist place on the Mohawk Trail, the road that runs along the Deer-field River at the foot of our hill and on west across the Berk-shires of Massachusetts. On his pedestal are the words "Big Indian Shop." His owners advertise him as the biggest Indian chief in the state, yet he is pure Plains, with a feathered head-dress that would have impressed Buffalo Bill. There is a pretty good version of a grizzly bear around the side of the shop, and a couple of tepees. When I asked why the Western motif on a road named for one of the most famous of Eastern tribes, I was told, "People think of one thing when they think of Indian."

I did, from boyhood until I stood in the shadow of the Big Indian and asked my simple question. Efficient conquerors increase the efficiencies of their conquests by redefining the

conquered. Calling the place the New World was a good start. So was what Europeans called the people who lived here. *Indian* is generally thought to have arisen from the Admiral's notion that he had made landfall in the fabled Indies of the Orient. (There is a saying among the Iroquois of today, the descendants of those who traveled the real Mohawk trail: Thank God Columbus wasn't looking for Turkey!) When the Indian presence dwindled in the East, it was only natural to capitalize on the public's fascination with the Indian West by bringing war bonnets and silvertip bears to the tourist trade along the Deerfield.

Current stereotypes carry more than Buffalo Bill hokum. In 1990, during the run-up to our second Earth Day, a commercial for plastic garbage bags showed children picking up refuse left in a meadow by some careless consumer while ghostly but pleased tribesmen smiled at them. Today we dance with wolves and visit tribes of equestrian saints. We hear that Indians, by nature and heritage, are environmentalists and ecologists without equal. If you are going to dehumanize someone, it may be better manners to do so with canonization than with calumny. But manners don't alter the consequence.

There were other problems to contend with. I am trained to the pursuits of individualism and material advancement. When I first read of the subsistence of ancient peoples in this country, I shied from the word. *Subsistence* to me meant poverty, underdevelopment, things un-American. Even after Webster's informed me of its primary meaning — "existence in reality" — the idea of sending my imagination among foragers, among people who lived communally in and by the natural world, was frightening.

My fancy would have to sally forth from the security of its landscape. It would have to accept the disappearance of my town of Charlemont, of New York, St. Louis, San Francisco, 1.5 million square miles of farmland, 87,377 square miles of urban development, 2.2 million miles of paved roads, and close to 200 million motor vehicles. I had to subtract some grasses and all honeybees, along with starlings, wheat, rye, brown rats and house mice, and all domesticated animals except dogs and turkeys. There would go the eucalyptus and the apple tree, the wine grape and the chickpea, and the constant conversations of our machines. And, most terrifying of all, there would go some 250 million people and with them my America.

Mythologists gave me some comfort by introducing me to the notion that there may be in all of us a sense deep beneath memory of having lived in new lands, of having been first people. But my people were not first people *here*. I am descended, through my father's mother, from William Brewster, Elder Brewster of the Plymouth colony. We came here eighteen generations ago and in time broke the cultures of those who had been here for perhaps six hundred generations. By those yardsticks, I thought, I am a stranger in my own land.

I accumulated scores of books and papers and stacks of recorded interviews. I began the research in full agreement with Alexander Pope that "the proper study of mankind is man," but it wasn't long before I fell in with companions whose ideas changed my mind. They were ecologists and other scientists who in the past couple of decades have found new ways to examine and interpret what modern society, arrogant in its literacy, calls prehistory. The tiniest bits of organic matter can now be dated and identified fairly well. Palynologists recover seeds and pollen from lake bottoms or, lacking lakes, from the urine-preserved middens of pack rats, and evoke landscapes as they evolved through millennia. Climatologists study cores from the bottom of the sea or the innards of a glacier and use what they find to model the cycles of temperature and precipitation. Health specialists can estimate how a certain people were faring at a certain time by looking at what is left of their bones. These researchers talk a lot to each other. They have learned not to departmentalize the past. From them, I learned that the full and proper study of mankind, womankind, or any other kind of kind is neither the individual nor the species but the whole of life, seen in all its combinations, habitats, niches. What I was looking for was not people but land, lakes, streams, and seacoasts, all inhabited by plants and by animals, including that strange being with big feet, not much fur, grasping hands, and an exuberance of curiosity and cleverness.

Scientists and shamans I met on the page or in person spoke again and again of that inclusiveness. Dena Dincauze, an archaeologist who teaches at the Amherst campus of the University of Massachusetts, wrote that "it is folly to think of separating human evolution from the history of the environment; neither can be understood without the other." I determined that no matter where I found myself in telling the stories of the American land, as it was without us and as it has been and may be with us, I would not forget those words.

Ecologists told me of a character out of Lewis Carroll they have borrowed as a metaphor for change. She is the Red Queen, whom Carroll described as "the concentrated essence of all governesses!" "Now, *here*, you see," the Queen tells Alice, "it takes all the running you can do, to keep in the same place. If you want to get somewhere else, you must run at least twice as fast as that!" From large scale to small and back again, existence is in movement, reacting to the behavior of clouds, landforms, water tables, nutrients, predators, prey. Populations of all species fluctuate, as do assemblages of species. Each being has at least some way to monitor what is going on and to make at least some response. Whether or not an individual response is adequate to preserve an organism's place in the order of things, the sum of responses is enough to produce further environmental changes, which demand additional responses, which produce . . . the Red Queen effect.

There are, obviously, many intervenors in such a system. Some beings affect a whole landscape, as the elephant and, I gather, a porcupine work to maintain African savannas. But as a species we seem addicted to alteration. Even hundreds of millennia ago, when our numbers were insignificant, our promise was evident. We would try one adaptation and then another, applying tools and techniques to offset a given hardship. When an adaptation worked, it made our lives more secure, and our populations tended to increase somewhat. When hardship returned, whether or not as a consequence of these actions and reactions, we would again adapt. It is difficult to argue that our choices were inevitable or that they followed any long-term strategies. Humans are sprinters. We do run twice as fast, and true to the Red Queen's words, we have traveled everywhere in the world, doing what we thought best at the time to improve our opportunities. That is all we have had to do to win the success of survival. Up till now.

Now, I came to think, we must ask ourselves whether we can survive our successes. Can Americans, still the richest society of the species, continue in our way of life, and can others who wish to emulate our wealth do so, without eventually degrading existence? I found that the more I read and listened, the less I thought that we could. It was not an easy admission, for I was, and am, still entranced by our attainments. Besides, if I *were* to address our penetrations beyond what international leaders now choose to call "sustainable development," I might find myself drawn into accepting some responsibility for my society's actions and reactions. With that acceptance, I would then have to accept that whatever else we may be — special in divine eyes, sublime in our artistry — humans have become the master meddlers of the planet.

I read, I made notes, I thought, and I became a prisoner of the wall of work I had built around me. For weeks I sat and stared at it. It diminished me. I felt like the immured wretch in Poe's "The Cask of Amontillado." I knew where I wanted to go — first back to the time of what scholars call Contact or the Encounter, the meetings between white and brown that in this country began on a scrubby beach in Florida and ended more than three centuries later in the scrub and scree of the mountainous West. Once I had thus made two pasts one, I could travel back to the ice and my story's true beginning. But how to escape? How to get past the lowering authorities on my shelves?

The key lay in the prison. My eyes fell on the book that first turned me toward the consideration of humanity and its home. It was long and dense, the proceedings of a scientific symposium called *Man's Role in Changing the Face of the Earth.* But for me it was an introduction to the writings and conversations of some of the finest natural philosophers of the century — Marston Bates, Carl Sauer, Lewis Mumford, Fairfield Osborn, Kenneth Boulding, F. Fraser Darling, so many others. I have never recovered from reading it.

Toward the end of the symposium, the participants sat around jawing about anything that came to mind. When they started in on techniques of learning and their fit with reality, a man named Edgar Anderson, who headed the Missouri Botanical Garden in St. Louis at the time, launched into a story about workaholic graduate students. Anderson recalled one whom I could sympathize with entirely. Anderson said he "had this inherited feeling that, if one is happy and having a good time, it is not quite right. . . . One is paid to be miserable about his lifework; the easy thing is not the thing to do."

The student submitted to Anderson a long memorandum about how he proposed to study the bejesus out of his chosen plant, the clematis, during summer fieldwork. Anderson blue-penciled most of the items and returned the memo to the student with a letter I wish I had received in my twenties, before I had set about fashioning the inner drill sergeant who has given me marching orders just about every morning for the past forty years. Anderson wrote:

> These are all good ideas, but I've got something else that is very much more important. Every time you get where there is one of these populations of plants, find a large, flat rock, in the shade if necessary; sit down upon it for at least fifteen minutes by your wristwatch; and do not try to think about your clematises. Just think what a nice day it is, how pretty the flowers are, and the blue sky. Think how lucky you are to be doing this kind

of work when the rest of the world is doing all the awful things they do not want to do. Just let your mind alone. Now I am not joking. Please do this, by the clock if necessary.

A few weeks later, Anderson said, the student told him he had tried the flat-rock trick. "Now it is probably just coincidence," he said, "but when I got up from the rocks the first time and started down across the hillside, I noticed . . ."

I said silent thanks to Dr. Anderson. Then I walked down to the Deerfield and lay down on a slant of warm ledge. I listened to the purl of the river, to the keening of a hawk. My will gave way to what lay under it, and I was gone. The song of the Deerfield became the soughing of the open sea. I saw from some height three specks of sail bearing off to the southwest and recognized them. The Admiral, I could see, had decided to follow flocks of migrating birds. He had heard that the Portuguese had found new lands for themselves in this manner.

I wanted to follow him down into the Bahamas. But my intent lay west, across the Gulf Stream, in a country Columbus would never see. I was after cultures as they existed before the first European boots, soggy with the Atlantic, left the first heeled tracks on its beaches. I was after lineages that were heir to the *first* encounter, that of people with an unpeopled land — all, no matter what their station, gifted with a sense of having lived here since the time when the ice still lay thick in the north.

2

Across the Border

AT SUNSET on the day before America, diversity lay at every hand. People spoke in more than a hundred tongues. They lived by every possible combination of hunting, fishing, gathering, gardening, and farming open to them. The quality of soils and the effort required to open and tend them determined some of their choices of how to live. Cultural and social biases determined others. Surpluses of fish or grain or garden plants or meats helped create powerful, tiered societies here but not there. Some cultures had endured for millennia. The ruins of others lay in the earth or silent by some river or canyon, the power of their design enough to stun any stranger who stumbled upon them. Climate often had something to do with their rise and fall, but so too did the ways in which people lived, their demands on their fellow beings.

This was an old land at its discovery. No chapter, no book, can convey the reality of such dynamics, of such a confusion of lives lived so long ago. I have chosen to write sketches of five cultures and to comment briefly on a transformation of others. Two of the cultures were coastal, one on the Gulf of Mexico, another on the Pacific. One was in the Northeast, one in the Southwest, one in the heartland. Two remain today, vastly altered. Two had disappeared by 1492 but only a few centuries before had wielded the influence of empires.

The Calusa, the Fierce People, probably knew about the Admiral within weeks of his arrival in the Bahamas. They paddled out into the Straits of Florida occasionally and traded with the islanders on the other side, so they would have heard the news. And when the first European, an irascible Spaniard named Juan Ponce de León, entered their territory a couple of decades later, they showed him something of their prowess as archers, sending arrows through breastplates, pinning armored horsemen to their mounts.

Their base was in rich country, estuaries fed by the Caloosahatchie River and two other streams debouching near what is now Fort Myers. Fresh water mixed with salt over miles of shallow flats, to the contentment of multitudes of shellfish, and brought in enough nutrients to supply carpets of sea grass. The surface shimmied as sea trout and jack worked over schools of pinfish, grunt, and silver perch. The commotion often drew sharks, which ran in through channels between the barrier islands to the west that served, most of the time, to keep the sea in its place.

Canoes were everywhere, out in open water or working the edge of the mangroves, plying among the islands. Dwellings lay hazed by the smoke of buttonwood and mangrove burning in hearths and the smudge fires that kept down the mosquitoes. Black mangrove was the best kind of fuel. The more they chopped it, the better it grew.

Hammers clattered in the dooryards. Stone was scarce, and the material of choice was shell. The dense and heavy central column of the whelk made a fine hammer or chisel, and a big clam a serviceable anvil. The Calusa were a populous people — perhaps 4,000 of them were living around these estuaries in 1492 — and their fondness for shellfish as food and tool had created quite a trash problem over the centuries. Some of their dumps were twenty or thirty feet high. Whelk shells by the thousands faced a moated cemetery mound — moated to keep the spirits of the dead from wandering.

What looked from a ways offshore like creek mouths in the mangroves could be the beginnings of Calusa canals. The average one was something like thirty feet wide, up to eight feet deep. One ran for more than seven miles to connect with a creek that flowed into the Caloosahatchie. It could handle the largest canoes — giant dugouts, fashioned with fire and adze out of huge pine butts, capable of carrying forty people or their weight in cargo. The craft could start their run out in the flats and, following this channel, end up in the Okeechobee basin, out of the wind most of the way.

A canal bisected an island close to the mainland, south of the Caloosahatchie. A huge building stood on a mound there, covering at least a couple of thousand square feet. Wooden masks and effigies carved with art of great power were placed near the entrance. Hundreds of men and women gathered to sing and dance in and around the structure. The island was Calos, the central place of this people and the home of their ruler. He had at his call a force of men known across the whole Florida peninsula and down through its chain of keys for their skill at arms. He received tributes of food and feathers and captives from towns up to five hundred miles away. His might not have been a state, as the Aztec complex in the Valley of Mexico was a state. But it was on the verge. And unlike the Aztec and most other prehistoric high cultures, it was building its sophistication on an economic base that did not include agriculture. Seafood, yes, and some deer and raccoon and alligator and snake, and wild plants like sea grape and heart of palm and wild potato. But there was no significant reliance on crops.

Hunters and gatherers usually don't go in much for kings and nobles. For much of the first 2,000 years of their occupancy, the Calusa didn't either. Their environment was rich enough to give them more than a satisfactory return on their investment of time and effort. By sticking to their estuaries and making foraging trips inland, they provided themselves with the means for settling down. Settlement and surplus eventually may have increased their numbers enough to cause some competition and stress. They also may have had to make sure that when one source of food ran thin, if even for a season or two, other sources, often at increasing distances from the center, could be tapped. Hierarchy may have developed as a way of dealing with such complexity.

Whatever the agencies of its growth, the Calusa, on the eve of the Spanish *entrada*, had built what a Florida archaeologist calls "one of the most complex fishing-gathering-hunting societies known in the history of humankind." It did not long remain so. Alien pathogens came down the Caloosahatchie, and an alien and economically aggressive culture. The kingdom by the sea weakened and eventually faded before the attacks of the whites and of people from the north, who would come to be called Creek and Seminole.

Why mounds? From Alabama and Georgia to Ohio, tourists ask this question. Why did those people go to all that trouble? On any sunny summer day, a few American families on vacation climb up grassy terraces and stand looking at other terraces and ask these questions. Those who look west, over the roof of an auto body shop to the city of St. Louis and its single McDonald's arch, see part of an answer: given the chance, we all take the trouble to build mounds.

The sites of more than a hundred mounds have been found here, scattered across about six square miles at the edge of the Mississippi's floodplain. At least a score have been leveled in the interests of agriculture and urbanization. Even under grass, the structures and the great plaza they surround reach for the imagination, as their architects intended them to do in their days under the sun. There is a certain sadness to their power. These are the bones of the largest ceremonial center to develop in the country before the coming of the Europeans and *their* mounds, and not one of us living today knows its true name. Whites came to call it Cahokia, but that was derived from a group that was living around the mounds when we started filtering in sometime around the middle of the eighteenth century.

In the flush of conquest, few whites could bring themselves to believe that the builders of Cahokia had any connection whatever with the pesky savages. The president of Yale figured the Canaanites had had a hand in the construction. Ben Franklin said no, it was the Spanish, and other luminaries voted for Romans, giants, and the lost tribes of Israel. Now whites are willing to believe what archaeologists tell them: Cahokia was indigenous. By A.D. 900 or so, human occupation was already altering the landscape. Clearings pocked the floodplain and the land back toward the bluff. People were growing plants in them, plants they had tamed to one degree or another — goosefoot, knotweed, and maygrass for their greens or starchy seeds, and sunflower and marsh elder for their oily ones. Some gardeners were experimenting with a new crop, a domesticated grass from Mexico that now feeds billions of humans and their livestock around the world. Some of us call it maize. Some call it corn.

The communities that would become Cahokia were sited, deliberately, near bottoms where the Mississippi jumped its banks almost every year, laying down new sediments on the floodplain, leaving lakes and fish in the low spots. If the flooding became too severe, there were always bulges of higher and drier land on the plain to farm. There were also acorns and hickory nuts and wild berries and fruits to be had from the bottoms and the highland forests to the east, along with deer and turkey and waterfowl, perhaps even an occasional bison killed and butchered on the far shore of the river. The people here clearly had something similar to what the Calusa had —

a solid subsistence base that could produce storable and exchangeable surplus. Again similarly, the organization that developed here to manage all this was becoming increasingly hierarchical.

The great mounds rose in fits and starts. People filled their baskets with sixty pounds or so of earth, walked up a hill of their own making, dumped their loads at designated spots, returned. Fifteen million round trips would be required for the largest mound. That, spread across, say, three centuries, is not prodigious. Assuming the project was in operation only half the time, three hundred loads a day would suffice. Three dozen people could do the job and still take some of the afternoon off. When they were finished, workers built large, steep-roofed buildings on some of the terraces. These seem to have been temples, places as close to the sun as Cahokians wanted or were able to get them.

In time, a great circle of stakes as big as telephone poles appeared on the flats near the largest temple mound. They were sited in such a way that those in charge of such mysteries could have used them to determine equinoxes and solstices, the better to plan the cycles of ritual and horticulture. Maize had become a staple now, a necessity as population and prosperity and consumer demand increased. Exchange along the trails and river systems brought in chert from distant quarries to be knapped into efficient hoes, copper from the Great Lakes for ornaments and points, hematite for paints, whelks from the Gulf shores — perhaps even from a Calusa diver — for the gorgets and other ornaments so prized by those in control. Exchange had been a part of life in this country for thousands of years, but the leaders of these people were giving it new dimensions. A man of high rank was laid to rest in a mound on a bed of more than 20,000 imported shell disks. Another leader succumbed and took with him hundreds of projectile points knapped from exotic stone, along with a dozen or more relatives and retainers sacrificed to mark his passing.

Cahokia reached its cultural peak about A.D. 1100. Round about the countryside were smaller mound-towns, each with its kilted elite presiding over spiritual and commercial life, over the supplies of stored corn that fed economic growth. Gathering and producing food became the job of many, but not of all. Artisans knapped flint and other stones. Traders came and went in the lanes between hundreds of small huts of poles and thatch. Women made clay pots, flensed stretched deerskins. Men, in from lakes and forests, repaired their dwellings and bartered — a bow for clothing woven of strips of rabbit skin, a dart point for a bit of copper jewelry. It is possible that on days of special ceremony, perhaps 40,000 people came in from the hinterlands to see their leader, the embodiment of the sun, conduct his rituals on the great mound. That would have matched the population of London at that time. The resident population was more on the order of 10,000, remarkable enough for the middle of the "New World."

Chiefdoms tend toward instability over time. The competition for power can be intense among the elite, and alliances are forever forming and fading. It might be fear of dissension from within that explains the stockade that appeared in the very center of Cahokia. It ran right through communities, without regard for boundaries, as if erected under pressure.

Land and water may have been less bountiful, less resilient after A.D. 1100. Climatic change might have had something to do with that. Rivers swollen with heavier rains may have reshaped the floodplain, eating away at the best farmland. Human hands also contributed to the decline. Each year Cahokian hearths could have consumed the limbs and twigs of trees covering roughly six square miles of forest. The nearest bluffs had been denuded to such an extent that they were gullying badly. Whatever the many causes of degradation, life got harder. By 1300 Cahokians were moving out, and by 1500 they were gone, some to the southeast into lands that in historic times were held for a time by the Natchez. Left behind were stunning accomplishments in a place that had no people, no name.

The land of northwestern New Mexico is unforgiving and has been for a long time. There is a dry wash there, broad, with sandstone cliffs on the northeast side and talus slopes on the southwest. It is Chaco Canyon, and in a good year it doesn't get much more than eight inches of precipitation. In 1492, there might have been a few humans passing through this high country. If so, they probably were Athapaskans, recently arrived emigrants from what is now northwestern Canada on their way to becoming Navajos or Apaches. The first of them through the canyon must have gotten a jolt. The designs on the rocks were strange enough. On one cliff someone had pecked mountain goats, spirals, dancers, a woman with triplets. I saw them a few years ago, and below them some modern stockman had written, "Jean: I cannot get no feed. I cannot wait for you." In the protection of an overhang were pictograms of a great comet or exploding supernova, a moon, a hand.

Sooner or later the Athapaskans would have seen what makes Chaco so important to this story. They would have come around an outcropping on a cliff face and seen a half-dozen huge edifices on the valley floor, empty, sounding in the wind. Several more ruins lay on the mesa above, each containing hundreds of rooms. On the south side of the wash were dozens of small stone structures.

The Navajos later poked around and decided that the people who had built at Chaco were Anasazi, ancient and alien ones. What the Anasazi called themselves are words in the wind.

They appear to have been masters of the dry life, farming at first by the grace of moisture that collected along the bottoms of dunes and alluvial fans. They were doing that in Chaco by A.D. 500. Three centuries later, the first of their great houses went up, each near breaks in the cliff where water from the thunderstorms of July and August ran down off the mesa. There is evidence that the Anasazi knew their hydraulics. When a storm hit, water sheeted off the cliffs and ran in flumes down side canyons. Teams of people ran to stations along an ingenious irrigation system. A side canyon would dump into an Anasazi ditch, which would carry the water up the wash for a while to slow it down and then deliver it to stone-lined distribution boxes. The teams must have worked frantically to keep passages clear, lifting gates that led the water and its rich muds on to grids of small garden plots farther out on the flats. By the time a storm had gone muttering off toward the Rio Grande Valley, a hundred miles to the east, the corn and other plants in the gardens were drinking deep. Snowmelt in the spring was usually sufficient for them to germinate. With this intricate catch-as-catchment-can irrigation, they stood a good chance of getting enough summer storm runoff to insure good tasseling and full ears.

These people delighted in stonework. They built their great houses with care and forethought, laying out most of them in D-shaped floorplans, often building close to the cliffs to take advantage of the warmth the rock absorbed from the winter sun. But they were not above scrapping a whole wing and starting again with a new design. They overengineered. Their walls belonged in fortresses. They went to the trouble of facing them with exquisite stone veneers and then hid that art behind mud plaster.

Everywhere, they made their architectural statements. They built walls across windy mesas; laid out roads — more than four hundred miles of them — on the land with a ruler; dug huge round rooms in the earth for ritual, storage, social doings. They built shrines and left offerings in them of bowls filled with turquoise. They built or influenced others in the building of outlying settlements, scores of them, over at least 57,000 square miles of mostly dry land. They had the will to do it and, in a sufficient number of years, the water. Seeps and shallow wells, small reservoirs carved in cliff rocks, even the semisaline Chaco, gave them cooking and drinking water and mud for construction. Nature and the engineers did the rest. The result gave Chacoans a measure of safety and storage, shelter and social congress, efficiencies of scale in maintaining systems of exchange reaching as far as the Pacific coast. The long walls kept out the unknown, the enemy, and, in high-country winters, when the temperature sank below zero, some of the cold.

It is likely that quite a few of the children playing in the great-house plazas had the swollen bellies that indicate parasites, unbalanced diets, perhaps gastroenteritis — a disease that, along with tuberculosis, does well in crowded conditions. Some of the adults were anemic. Many suffered from dental cavities caused by the sugars in the maize they ate and by the shortage of rougher food. Others were bent with arthritis aggravated by heavy labor. The great houses demanded quantities of timbers for beams, something like 200,000 matched stems of ponderosa pine in all. After local trees were cut, young men went farther and farther to find more. In time, they were carrying in pine they had cut on mountain slopes more than fifty miles away. Each log weighed at least six hundred pounds.

The years of the twelfth century were downslope ones for the Chaco stoneworkers. They had come into the wash in wetter times, but then drought began to bite down again. As at Cahokia, the demands of a technologically advanced society started to degrade surrounding life. There had been deer on the mesa earlier, and some antelope, along with piñon and its nutritional seeds, but their numbers were fast dwindling. The flats of the wash had long since been stripped of bushes and grasses for fuel.

Again as at Cahokia, people began to leave, calmly, purposefully. Abandonment seems not to have been particularly tragic. Rather, it was ordinary, ongoing, one of the costs of living in much of the pre-Columbian world. Societies of the time built their communities to a certain density and left them when dwindling rainfall or failing resources or cultural pressures dictated. The survivors lived more simply for a time and, where and when they could, started over. Some emigrants from Chaco moved down to the Rio Grande Valley, where there was more water and it took less ingenuity to get it. Big pueblos went up there shortly and shortly faded. But the people themselves abided. The blood of many who now live in native communities around Santa Fe is undoubtedly mixed with some that is ancient and alien.

The People of the Cape built seagoing craft with sleeker bows than the Calusa dugouts. By 1492, they had been using them for centuries to hunt whales. Each canoe was around forty feet long and carried eight men. They were beautifully built, with high stems and sterns and plenty of freeboard to handle the big Pacific swells. At the start of a hunt the crews would chant, keeping the beat for the stroke. But when they closed, they were still. One canoe would take the lead and the others would swing in behind. Not a sound. They kept their paddles in the water. Even when one lifted out, the dagger point of the blade kept the drip small and silent.

They were after gray whales, animals that could run to fifty feet. The lead canoe would lunge forward, six paddlers digging water to put their boat close to a huge shape moving just under the surface. The steersman aft would guide them in and almost over the black shadow. Then the hunter in the bow would stand, balance eighteen feet of heavy harpoon, and drive it down with his arms and shoulders. The head and its barbs usually sank well into the animal. The hunter would retrieve his shaft. Others made sure that the line paid out, that the big floats of sealskin attached to it were ready to go overboard, that the boat veered off properly.

Other canoes would dart in, strike, fall back. Toward the
end there might be a dozen floats for the whale to fight
against. He or she would weaken fast, faster if a harpoon had
struck a lung or an artery. Then the first canoe would return,
the hunter waiting until he had the angle he wanted for his
killing lance.

Within minutes, men were stabbing small harpoons into
the head. Their barbs were attached by short tethers to skin
bladders that would buoy the animal. One paddler might dive
overboard and rig a line to close the animal's great mouth so
he wouldn't take on water.

Sometimes the whalers were lucky and made their kill
within sight of shore. On occasion, they struck their prey far
offshore and followed him miles west into truly deep water.
Then they would spend a day or more towing him home.
They would head eastward toward the mouth of the strait that

would be named Juan de Fuca, separating what would be the state of Washington from the province of British Columbia. A rich sea, this. The great Japan Current, the Gulf Stream of the Pacific, brings warm water to these coasts, gentling the extremes of climate. Winds and the earth's rotation force surface waters away from the coast, replacing them with cold water, high in nutrients, that wells up from the depths and over the lip of the continental shelf. That lip and its biotic concentrations are only ten miles offshore, closer than anywhere else on the northwest coast. That is why the grays and humpbacks, the fur seals and other pelagics of fine flavor, like to linger.

Many boats hunted out of a tuck in the coast about fifteen miles south of the headland on the southern shore of the entrance to the strait. It seemed a hostile place, rocky and brutal in foul weather. But there were islands close by to protect the rows of houses that paralleled the shore for a half-mile or more. The whalers' settlement was one of five main villages raised by the People of the Cape. The word for this village, as it has come to be spoken today, is Ozette.

Behind the houses, the land angled up steeply and then rolled away in riotous forest. Wet air from the sea rose to clear the mountains to the east here, and rain fell in feet — eight a year or more. Vegetation erupted. On the coast, Sitka spruce grew to over 250 feet and lived for the better part of a millennium. Giant hemlock and western red cedar stood a little inland. Ferns and mosses fought for space. The ground, where it was visible, was shot with clay and tended to break loose on a slope. Around A.D. 1700 something, quite possibly a big earthquake, sent a mudslide thundering into Ozette, burying houses intact just as ash buried Pompeii.

The Calusa spent some time at sea, but theirs was essentially an estuarine life. The People of the Cape — and their relatives across the strait on Vancouver Island — were truly marine. They drew their life from the whaling grounds, the sealing grounds, the shoals where they took great halibut in the summer, the choice spots where they trolled for salmon in summer and early fall, the line tied to the paddle hand so the stroke would give appealing action to bait or lure. Their hooks were masterpieces of wood and shell. They made sharp rakes to take herring. They took fish eggs from reefs made of submerged shrubs.

These mariners were expert woodsmen. They knew what each tree would do for them. A hemlock hung up in the forest would produce a kind of compressed wood ideal for wedges. Yew had the strength and resiliency for bows and paddles. Cherry bark was best for wrapping harpoon heads, and red cedar bark made good woven raingear. Cedar lent itself to the carving of masks that rivaled those of the Calusa. It split beautifully and lasted well in the wet, so houses, multifamily dwellings up to sixty feet long, were built of cedar. They were designed so that planks on roofs and walls could be removed and transferred to another frame in another camp, saving time and labor as the households moved through their seasonal rounds of sea and river fishing, hunting, gathering.

South of Ozette, along parts of the California shore where acorns and marine resources supported prehistoric population densities that were probably higher than anywhere else in the country, the mean size of some favored shellfish had been decreasing, signaling overexploitation. No such signals of stress appeared at Ozette. One reason might have been that control of access to food resources rested with individual households. This was a ranked society, more hierarchical, like those at Chaco and Cahokia, than others in the America of 1492. The elite ate higher on the halibut than the commoners or the slaves. But the system kept the entire community from descending on the nearest beach and putting more pressure on the local steamer clams than the clams could handle.

Yew for whaling and sealing harpoons. Red cedar, adzed and smoothed and oiled, for canoes. Cedar bark for seagoing storage baskets and for fathoms upon fathoms of line. Hemlock for halibut hooks. The forest gave these people the sea. It had been doing so, with only insignificant changes in technology and subsistence strategies, for 2,000 or 3,000 years, perhaps more. It continued to do so after the "houses moving on the water," the windships of the Europeans, showed up in the late 1700s. Even in our day, these people, who call themselves Makah, do what they can to keep the covenant. They run fishing boats at their main settlement, at Neah Bay. They have built a museum for the proper study of things excavated from houses buried by the slide at Ozette. But to maintain themselves in the money economy of the twentieth century, they have found they need to make a great sacrifice. With sadness, they have opened their forests to the clear-cutters.

The high grasslands of North America were apt to offend the European eye. There was always too much wind, too much space, too little rain. The place yawned. White explorers took to calling it the Great American Desert. White archaeologists of the nineteenth century argued that few natives could have lived there before they acquired the necessary amenities from the conquering culture.

Now there is enough evidence to suggest that the plains and basins of the West may have been one of the first regions settled by humans. They lived ingeniously from the time of their first appearance 10,000 or more years ago, collecting plants and seeds, nuts of pine and deciduous trees, insects, animals of all sorts, and shifting their range, as did all of life around them, to stay within the envelope of optimal moisture.

By 1492, farming was established along the floodplains of the Missouri and other big rivers flowing through the plains. Like the Cahokians, the prairie peoples took every advantage of riverine cycles, planting and harvesting corn and other crops between floods. They lived, many of them in earth lodges, on the terraces and moved to the bottoms when winters bit too deeply.

Farmer or forager, most grasslanders developed a bond with one being, the dominant animal of the plains: the bison. They spoke with reverence of the bison, danced for them, studied them all their lives. They became bison, dressing in hides and horns, pawing the ground, bawling. And they took bison, decoying them, using the animals' own habits against them. They drove them over cliffs. They stalked them with bows. On foot.

These were the true ancestors of the Big Indian. There was not a horse among them. The horse as we know it evolved as a native of North America. It spread west into Asia, but died out here about 10,000 years ago, probably because of climatic change and perhaps hunting pressure as well. It is an illustration of the powers of chance that an animal that disappeared from one continent should survive in another only to escape a similar fate through domestication. The grasslanders of 1492 had to await the coming of the Spanish before they could acquaint themselves with an animal their ancestors saw and quite possibly ate.

Coronado could have been the first provider as he searched for Cíbola on the prairies in the 1540s, but the main initial supply seems to have been the Spanish horse herds around the town of Santa Fe. The horse culture developed rapidly during the seventeenth and early eighteenth centuries, spreading from the southern Apaches up to the Blackfoot in the north. And along with it came the trade in firearms, first from French fur traders and later from American traders.

The horse gave grasslanders the ability to go after small groups of bison and to carry more of the meat back to the settlements. The horse and the gun together made possible the rise of a different sort of plainsman, the mounted warrior, the chevalier of the Big Sky. Raiding became a calling, and taking the assets of others a shortcut to social stature. People fled from one violence and fell before another. Long before the first white easterners went west, much of the West was at war with itself. On horseback.

Like most other beings, people have a penchant for living on the edge. They like estuaries and floodplains and bluffs. With good reason: food and other good things often abound where one ecosystem abuts another. Even at sea, at the boundaries of currents or in places like the shelf break off Ozette, there is an edge effect.

So too along a limestone escarpment trending from west to east across central New York, passing just south of Syracuse. To the north lie marshy plains, and to the south highlands traversed longitudinally by valleys broadened by glacial ice. The climate of the flatlands is mild, tempered by winds off the Great Lakes. The hills have harsher weather, and in 1492 a traveler in the woodlands around the escarpment would notice the effects. Stretching north to Lake Ontario, thirty miles away, was a confusion of oak, hickory, chestnut, even trees usually found farther south, such as dogwood and sassafras. Up on the higher ground, it was mostly maple and beech and hemlock.

A group of people lived near a high spot on the ridge and took their name from it. They called themselves Onondaga, People of the Great Hill. Their fields were down in a magnificent valley a couple of ridges east of the Great Hill. To a modern farmer, the land would look untidy. Trees lay about like jackstraws. Stone axes had felled the smaller ones. Those of greater girth had been girdled, the bark sliced right around the trunk, the skeletons left to stand until winds and rot could topple branches and stems. Maize grew well among the rubble, and beans, squash, and sunflowers. The system worked. In a way, it was a forerunner of the modern "no-plow" farming methods.

There was little, if any, forest primeval to be seen, except on inaccessible ground. By 1492, people had been using and managing the woods for thousands of years, for firewood, for construction. Ever since agriculture had taken hold strongly, five or six centuries before, they had been clearing land more or less continuously. Every fifteen or twenty years, when soils tired and pests became insufferable and it took too long to find firewood in decent quantities, they had moved a few miles and started over. The woods were full of their old fields and the scars of the fires they had set to provide more forage for deer, more open lanes in which to shoot them, and more blueberries and blackberries for themselves. Regrowth had created mosaics of trees, most of which were less than a foot through, and that is the way these people liked them — eminently choppable, about the right size for posts to support their longhouses.

The term is apt. The Onondaga may hold the record for length: four hundred feet, enough to shelter at least one hundred people. The lodges in the average village were a bit over two hundred feet long, but at twenty feet in both height and width, they were still imposing. They were sheathed in elm bark, tight enough to keep out the winter, tough enough to last until it was moving time again.

There appeared to be enough sustenance for everyone. Population densities were fairly low in the region. Fish, both resident and anadromous, were there for the seasonal taking. So were game, wild plants, and, of course, the crops. And yet the village was palisaded.

Every so often, small groups of men appeared at the edge of the clearing around the settlement. They hallooed and waited for a response. Some changed their attire so their friends and relatives would recognize them more easily. Spirits were known to live in the forest, and it was wise to establish one's identity when emerging from the trees. The men often had captives with them. Some of the warriors carried scalps. The captives were destined for adoption or for torture and death.

Violence had been growing for decades, not only around the Great Hill but among other Iroquoian speakers, whose settlements spread across New York and, in Canada, around the Great Lakes and up the St. Lawrence Valley. The Little Ice Age, the general cooling that would last into the nineteenth century, had made its effects felt in the Northeast early in the fifteenth, decades before Columbus's arrival in the Bahamas. It is possible that growing seasons had shortened enough to cause the People of the Great Hill to switch from one principal food resource to another. Even with plenty of open land left, such switching might have been sufficient to cause friction. So might overhunting of deer in some places; the ani-mals were valued not only for their meat but for their hides. So might resource pressure from Mississippian centers, to the west.

Gender roles also could have been playing a hand. Women had long been gardeners. When corn came in, they tended it. As a result, they were now prime food producers, with enhanced social power. In addition, villages were large enough that the hunting, constructing, and general providing that men had once done by themselves were now more communal efforts. How then did the males do what males seem endlessly condemned to do — prove themselves? Certainly by pressuring other communities, by raiding. Possibly by hunting the most dangerous game, another male.

Whatever the reasons, blood feuds and vendettas had reached a level not often seen in a country where violence was usually limited and intermittent. Men might be spending more time in the summers trying to manipulate other settlements for the best deals in exchange or alliance — and attacking those same settlements when that seemed feasible — than they spent in the fishing camps. The stories that Iroquois of today remember of those times are full of dragons of discord, of great serpents lying across the trails, of fear and horror in the settlements.

Every once in a while, when people have had enough, they reshape their own culture. Villages near the Great Hill seemed to be passing through that process. One was a recent amalgam of two groups who were willing to give up competition for the sake of cooperation. Another small settlement had sprung up close by, and it too coalesced with the larger settlement. A century later, the process begun here would take hold strongly among the Seneca, to the west.

Some focal point, some leader, is usually associated with such a drastic social change of course. In the Iroquois stories, the Peacemaker and his lieutenant, Hiawatha, convinced warring groups to come together in consensus and work out ways to obtain and maintain peace. Their efforts eventually produced a confederacy, whose symbol was the longhouse. The Mohawk were at the eastern door, and next to them the Oneida. The Seneca were at the western door, and next to them the Cayuga. In the center, the keepers of the council fires, the keepers of the wampum belts that commemorate the alliance, were the People of the Great Hill, pioneers of the peace. Today, though their lands no longer reach to the escarpment, though they struggle to keep their nation together within sight of affluent suburbs, they still hold the center.

3

A Land Without Us

I HAVE NEVER BEEN close to big ice. I've flown over robes of it that masked the spears of the Andes. I've walked up to where it has been: a cup of rock, a holdfast for a prong of the stuff that more than once has gone rooting down the valleys of the Pyrenees. But none of that prepared me for conjuring up the ice that stood in ramparts across this and other northern continents, controlling what went on under it and for great distances beyond it, for fifty millennia before the arrival of the first human beings.

We are children of that ice. That may sound odd, given that we are now living through some of the warmest years I can remember. But as a species, we did most of our growing up in the Pleistocene, an epoch that began more than 2 million years ago and ended with the turn into the Holocene, or recent, epoch 10,000 years ago. Ten or so major glaciations and ten or fifteen smaller ones occurred during the Pleistocene. The cold of the latest pulse, which on this continent is generally referred to as the Wisconsinan glaciation, abated from 14,000 to 8,000 years ago. This move into what is called an interglacial period — a time between advances — might have occurred in sharp steps here and there; analysis of cores from

Greenland's ice sheet indicate that temperatures over the world's largest island may have risen some seven degrees Celsius (the equivalent of thirteen degrees Fahrenheit) in only twenty to fifty years.

What the data tell us, says George Jacobson, a paleoecologist at the University of Maine, "is that the plants and animals alive today are essentially adapted to the glacial conditions that have prevailed for 90 percent of the past several million years. We are so adapted ourselves. Several major branches in human evolution, splits within *Australopithecus* and *Homo*, occurred around 2.4 million years ago and may well have been related to changes in global climate associated with the onset of Northern Hemisphere glaciation." We are relicts, then, creatures of the cold living in a respite from the cold. The last several interglacials have lasted roughly as long as ours has — about 10,000 years. We may indeed be engineering our very own warming period over the next centuries, but once, and if, that runs its course, we will probably find ourselves on our way back to yet another long freeze.

The end of the Wisconsinan, a time preceding the arrival of the first people in what is now the lower forty-eight states, was to be my next temporal destination. To prepare for the journey, I went to the University of Massachusetts in the town of Amherst, near my home on the Deerfield, and asked a glacial geologist there named Julie Brigham-Grette to show me pictures of contemporary cold.

She did. She put on a slide show that forever changed my ideas of serious ice. I found myself flying low over glacial margins in Greenland and Alaska, standing on the baldest ground I have ever seen and staring up at a thick lip of something I could not immediately identify, steep bluffs from 30 to 150 feet high faced with cobbles, dirt, sediment of every sizing. Only occasionally did I see what my limited experience had prepared me to look for — the mystic white-blue clarity of clean ice, the kind of radiance I had once looked down on from a Coast Guard plane on iceberg patrol off the coast of Newfoundland. I had only glimpses of it now, in the wide mouths of meltwater tunnels emerging from the base of dirty walls. I wondered what it smelled like back in those culverts. Perhaps like icebergs; I've been told they can give off an aroma like cucumbers.

Meltwater, I learned, was the key to this landscape. It came from sun cups, depressions on the summer surface of the glacier, and from the depths where pressure formed it and forced it through endless systems of capillaries, veins, and arteries. Rock flour, as fine as a baker's, mixed with it. Gravel, cobbles, and boulders bounced along with it through the black tunnels and spewed out into the light. There, great streams of meltwater, fiery cold and the color of lead, smoked and shouted in front of the ice margins. Water often shot from under the ice with such force that it leaped in fountains as high as a two-story house. But as that energy left it, the meltwater began to drop its sediment along the outwash system, the coarsest closest to the glacier, the rock flour dozens of miles downstream. Streams slowed and began to move through a shifting weave of channels down a plain of raw sediments, a braid plain.

In many places, the ground in front of the glacier was permanently frozen. Bulbs of ice grew in that ground, fed by water migrating to the freezing zone. As they grew, these "pingos" pushed up the surface as a carbuncle pushes against skin and, like a carbuncle, eventually erupted and, as their ice cores melted, collapsed into cratered mounds.

Brigham-Grette put away her slides, and I collected my impressions and walked out into a fall day, chuckling at the thought of trying to walk anywhere near Amherst in the earliest years of the time that concerns me in this book. The ice would have stood many hundreds of feet thick over the campus. I would have been instantly encased, radically altered, and moved inch by inch in a southerly direction. I would have become part of the Laurentide ice sheet at or near its maximal extent.

It is hard to talk with any certainty about the height and behavior of that sheet, since glaciers, particularly great glaciers, obey rhythms as complex and interactive as those in my body. Cold, we all know, is good for a glacier. Yet too much cold can dry out the air, cutting the supply of snow, which glaciers need to grow. Ice masses can stall or shrink until things warm up and wetten up enough for it to snow again.

Most glaciologists are in agreement that the Laurentide per se was at its mightiest roughly twenty millennia ago in most places, though an errant tongue of it probed down into Iowa only 14,000 years ago. And mighty it was. The ice sheets of North America were larger by half than the combined glaciers of Europe and Asia. They covered an area of Canada and the northern United States about the size of Antarctica. The eastern edge of the maximum Laurentide stood out on what are now the coastal shallows of the North Atlantic and were then dry land. From there, the southern margin snaked away across the continent, through northern Pennsylvania and the central portions of Ohio and Indiana and Illinois, then up into Wisconsin, east of the Mississippi, then across and back down south in Minnesota. It curved west into Iowa, then headed off to the northwest, generally along what became the Missouri drainage, on into the Dakotas and Montana and then finally up across Alberta toward the Yukon. During that last leg it lay against the eastern lip of the Cordilleran ice sheet, smaller but no less complex, covering much of the mountainous and coastal West in a series of lobes and independent icecaps.

It was once thought that the Laurentide operated out of a single massive ice dome located close to Hudson Bay. Now, though, the argument favors multiple domes, some of them quite small but each weighty enough to force ice out from under it like plastic. The thickest domes may have been more than two miles high.

That was more than enough to bend winds and generally influence atmospheric goings-on. Today, a greatly simplified diagram of summer circulation over North America would have a jet stream cutting across the north and, in the interior, a counterclockwise flow of winds moving into a great low as air rises over the baking land. Precipitation is most notable in the south and east. A similar diagram prepared recently by climatologists for the period 18,000–15,000 years ago shows a more powerful jet stream split by the glacier. The northern one lay close to the ice domes. The southern one curved over the middle of the continent, calving cyclonic storms (in which winds circle counterclockwise around their lows), and joined its brother over a North Atlantic choked with bergs. Winds sliding down the surface of the continental ice sheet ran clockwise along its southern edge, often in gales that picked up silts from the braid plains and deposited them in layers of loess dozens of feet thick. Things were moderately dry on that margin and wetter than today in many parts of the Southwest. On a continental scale, climates were moister and cooler, but not necessarily much colder than they are now. The ice sent its breath hundreds of miles to the south. But its great domes penned arctic air in its place and may have kept the blue northers that modern westerners fear to a minimum. Even close in to the glacial front, winds were often less than glacial. They came from the high ice, and in descending, their air took on greater density and temperature.

The play of ice and water was as frenetic during the Wisconsinan maximum as it had been during earlier glaciations. The Laurentide sheet came grinding upslope from what is now the Hudson Bay region, extirpating and rerouting streams and pushing a bow wave of meltwater ponds and lakes in front of it. But once it had gained the higher lands overlooking the Mississippi and Atlantic drainages, much of that effluence escaped to the sea. At one point toward the end of its stay, water and sediment from about 2,000 miles of glacial margin were at work redecorating the valleys of the Missouri, Ohio, and Mississippi on their way to the Gulf.

A different Gulf, a smaller one. So much water was locked up in ice that the sea off some coasts lay well below current levels. How much is hard to say, since the weight of the glaciers had depressed some littorals and counterforces had raised up others, but 400 feet is a fair guess — enough to push the shoreline roughly 30 miles to the west on the northwest coast of the United States and to make a dry trough out of what is now Puget Sound. In New England, the ice lip of 18,000 years ago lay along a line running up the spine of Long Island and over Martha's Vineyard and Nantucket. The Nantucket shoals and Georges Bank were proud capes or islands. Water ran out on the flats of the exposed continental shelf, cut slots where the shelf steepened into slope, and shot into the North Atlantic.

There was ice of a sort out in front of the margin: buried blocks of the stuff, relics of earlier marginal stands; pingos and ice wedges and strange polygonal frost marks on the surface. Ground here was frozen at some depth throughout the year. Where it melted, the flats were boggy and the hillsides wrinkled with creeping muck. Permafrost invaded mountain soils in northern New Mexico and left signatures in the uplands of the Carolinas. It ran, spotty or fully developed, in a band fronting the glacial margin, thickest along the western boundary of the Dakotas and in Illinois and Wisconsin and again from just north of Washington, D.C., up to the New York line. Mosses and lichens probably grew where they found conditions conducive, and so did some conifers and forbs, or broad-leaved herbs, shrubs, and dwarf versions of willow and perhaps some birch.

The Wisconsinan ice sheets functioned as biotic displacers. Plants and animals 18,000 years ago lived ten or more degrees of latitude south of their modern ranges. The vegetational maps of eastern North America that hang on the wall behind my writing desk show a large lateral band where spruces grew in open woodland together with sedges, sages, and other herbs. These assemblages, like many others of the late Pleistocene, would be hard or impossible to find today.

In the Southeast, northern instead of today's southern pine

flourished in woodland or true forest. Today northern pine shows a marked preference for sandy soil, but back then it evidently tolerated heavy loams as well. Spruce mixed with the pine in the South. Its large cones indicate a species that may now be extinct. Along the Gulf Coast, in Florida and Alabama, there may have been some broad-leaved trees such as oak, ironwood, hickory, and beech scattered about or living in small concentrations on slopes and good bottomland. Grass did well in some spots. The climate might have been similar to that of modern Maine.

The Southwest seems to have been mostly moister and cooler than today, perhaps by as much as 6°C (11°F) in the summers. True desert persisted in spots like the head of the Gulf of California, but elsewhere conifers spread downward from higher elevations to grow where none grow now. In Rocky Mountain and Great Basin regions, such plants as big sagebrush, limber pine, and blue spruce had larger ranges than they do today, while saguaro cactus and ponderosa pine lived in cramped quarters.

Storm systems from the Pacific didn't penetrate far into the Northwest coastal areas. Strong easterly winds coming in along the front of the Cordilleran ice sheet helped keep a good deal of precipitation west of the coastal mountains, and the absence of the sea from Puget Sound deprived the interior of a prime water source. The Columbia Basin was steppeland, cold and desiccated. Beyond the mountains, sere grasslands continued east in the northern Great Plains, but spruce forest, sometimes speckled with hardwoods, covered central portions and extended on through eastern lowlands. Up in what are now the luxuriantly wooded Appalachians, sedges dominated. But on the flatlands, the spruces grew not much more than sixty miles from the ice in Pennsylvania. And in Ohio, there are signs that glacial lobes occasionally lumbered forward and sheared off stands of conifers.

Animals thrived in these times. Perhaps they liked the

equable climates that prevailed, the absence of strong seasonal contrasts. Cool, moist or dry, what they got was what they would get: few extreme turns of weather. The vegetation of the late Pleistocene, the plant assemblages we've just been talking about, had something to do with the general contentment. There was plenty for the herbivores, the beasts that sustain the mammalian food chain, to chew on, even where conifers grew.

To have seen them! To have walked out on the continent and seen animals none of us have ever seen, ambling in herds, walking alone. There, on the Texas plains, a small group of mammoths, the largest bull standing eleven feet high at the shoulder, his head domed, his back sloping sharply to the hindquarters, his enormous tusks sweeping forward like the arms of a lyre. He is a grazer, an animal dependent on expanses of grass and herbs. Where they are, he is — from the American West across to the open lands of Florida and out on what is now ocean floor. During a decade spent at the Woods Hole Oceanographic Institution, I used to hear reports of huge teeth brought back to port by local scallopers. They had found them in their rakes, the molars of mammoths and their more solitary relative, the mastodon.

The New York State Museum in Albany has a sequence of beautifully created dioramas depicting the prehistory of the region. The first one shows the country around Storm King Mountain late on a winter afternoon toward the end of the Pleistocene. A mastodon and her calf are coming up from the river, through black spruce growing on the lowlands, moving toward white spruce on the uplands. Before them, sedges poke through the snow. The animal is small for her species. The big ones weren't as tall as mammoths, but they were more huskily built.

Peering in at the diorama, I learned that a snippet of carbonized mastodon underfur had been found in the Midwest. It was as fine as that of the otter. A sign suggested that I refer to the animal as "mastodont." That would give full meaning to its name: nipple-tooth. I demurred, but the suggestion made it easy to remember that the mastodon had cusped cheek teeth shaped for tearing up twigs and rough foliage, even spruce needles. The animal was a browser, like the modern moose, and like the moose a loner. It roamed woods and wetlands from upstate New York on out to Missouri and beyond.

Herds of caribou worked the tundra and conifer forests close to the ice sheets for lichen, often in sight of musk ox. Herds of camels, larger versions of the modern dromedary, shared warmer western grasslands with mammoths, a small-ish variety of horse, two types of bison, and, in the foothills, heavily behorned shrub oxen. Sloths the size of a good Jersey bull poked through woodlands in the East and along the Pacific coast. Flat-headed peccaries ran everywhere. Tapirs rooted for soft southern vegetation. An ambulatory hat rack called a moose-elk hid away in eastern bogs. The southern parts of Illinois, Ohio, and surrounding territory were favored by the largest rodent of the times, the giant beaver, which could go to 350 pounds, the heft of a good black bear today. These animals evidently acted more like muskrats than beavers; there is no evidence that they were woodworkers of any special skill. If sketches based on their bones are at all accurate, they looked like something out of *Alice in Wonderland*, oversized marmots with mumps.

Judging by their diversity, the carnivores were delighted with these landscapes. Consider *Smilodon*, the aptly named saber-toothed cats. They were leonine in size but heavier up front and probably slower than the modern lion. They could open their mouths about as far as you have opened this book, and once they had their gape where they wanted, they killed the weak and the young of the largest herbivores. The smaller scimitar cats boasted canines with serrated edges. Milk teeth found with their bones indicate that the children of mammoths were among their favorite foods. Cheetahs and jaguars

went after peccaries and other animals of middling size. Birds such as the "walking eagle," a raptor on stilts, fed well, as did carrion eaters such as the huge, thick-bodied teratorn.

I have in my notes a quotation ascribed to a contemporary native American elder. "I have noticed," he says, "that all men have a liking for some special animal, tree, plant, or spot of earth. If men would pay more attention to these preferences and seek what is best to do in order to make themselves worthy of that toward which they are so attracted, they might have dreams which would purify their lives."

The bear has become such an animal for me. I dream often of bears, black and shot with silver, standing quietly over me, suddenly wheeling among the stars. Bears did well in the late Pleistocene. I read of bears larger than any I have seen or dreamed of, roaming this continent back then. One in particular remains with me, the short-faced bear. The animal was close-coupled and tall, as tall at the shoulder as a moose. The muzzle was blunt enough to put a disquieting number of teeth on line. Both sexes were fast and, in the way of bears, often ferocious. They were among the most effective predators in all North America.

These stories of a younger continent are all very well, but they are static. They are snapshots, lacking the dynamics that inform true existence. To see landscapes alive, we must turn the key; we must bring on what scientists think are the main agents of change, including those that control where the ice domes lie.

Onsets of ice times may have something to do with the patterns of continents as they creep about on their crustal plates. When the continents are positioned so as to restrict the flow of equatorial seawater toward the poles, glaciations may ensue. The amount of snowfall is not as important as the extent of the summer melt. Where it is not complete, leftover drifts eventually will turn to snowfields, snow to ice, ice to ice domes.

The rhythms of individual glaciations appear to have strong solar connections. Variations in the sun's radiation may turn out to affect climate. At this point, though, more is known about the eccentricities in the way we sail around our star. The ellipse of our orbit lengthens and shortens in a cycle of a bit more than 100,000 years. The angle at which we are tilted away from a plane perpendicular to that ellipse varies by a bit less than three degrees within the compass of 41,000 years, affecting seasonal temperature swings at high latitudes. And the time when we pass closest to the sun runs around the calendar every 22,000 years or so, advancing a day every six decades. Rudyard Kipling, in his *Just So Stories*, refers to this curiosity as the precession of the equinoxes "preceding according to precedent."

The net effects during the late Pleistocene of these wheels moving within wheels are still open to question. The most lucid interpretation I've seen uses computer models and data provided by cores from glacial ice, sea bottoms, and lake sediments to give an idea of what things may have been like from

18,000 years ago to the present. Curiously, the earth's orbital position back at glacial maximum was very much like what it is today. Perihelion, the point at which we are closest to the sun, occurred then, and occurs now, in January. The angle of tilt was the same, 23.5 degrees — the difference being that then the angle was increasing, whereas now it is decreasing.

Simulated climates at the beginning of the computer run approximated those I've touched on. Cold and generally dry air persisted in the northwest of the continent while storms dropped precipitation along tracks running across the southwest, south, and east. Conditions close to the ice margins, particularly those in the western United States, were apt to be dry, with silt-laden winds blustering in from the east.

Running forward to 9,000 years ago, the models show that perihelion advanced to July and that the tilt grew to its maximum of 24.5 degrees (it will reach its minimum of 21.8 degrees about 10,000 years from now). What this meant in simplest terms for the Northern Hemisphere was more incoming solar energy, or insolation, during those summers — perhaps as much as 7 percent more than today — whereas winter insolation was a bit less. (The reverse would have been true for the Southern Hemisphere.) Overall, though, average annual temperatures could have been quite close to modern ones.

The seas, with their grand ability to absorb and redistribute heat, would have experienced only mild swings of surface temperature during the higher seasonality period of 12,000 to 6,000 years ago. Land lacks that capacity. In midsummer, the center of the North American continent might have been two to five degrees warmer than at present. And that differential would have bolstered the normal summer monsoon as hot air rose in the dry interior and moist oceanic air came in low to replace it, bringing precipitation to regions near the coasts. The winter monsoon, in which sinking cold air from the interior flows outward, warms, and rises to shower the coastal seas, might have been marginally stronger.

The glaciers aged slowly and erratically under the stronger summers, pulling back here toward their mother domes, regaining vigor there to readvance. By 13,500 years ago, the lid of ice over New England was gone from Connecticut and from my hill in western Massachusetts. In another 1,500 years, its margin had crossed to the northern edge of the St. Lawrence Valley. Ten thousand years ago, at the beginning of the Holocene, glaciation was for the most part a Canadian problem. The Laurentide had retreated from its junction with the Cordilleran sheet, and its southern lip lay across the northeastern tip of Saskatchewan, down through southern Ontario to the upper reaches of the Great Lakes, and up along the littorals of Quebec and Labrador. The Cordilleran mass had shrunk to essentially montane sheets and caps. And by 7,000 years ago, the continent's ice quotient — with the exception of the remains of some domes near Hudson Bay — was similar to what we now have.

If the North American glaciers in their prime restrained outbreaks of bitter arctic air, they acted in their aging to cool the brow of high seasonality summers. It wasn't until a couple of millennia after the peak of summer insolation, as the climatic models I've been talking about indicate, that true monsoonal effects appeared. Only then did the Midwest sizzle, while surrounding areas — particularly the Southeast — received the pluvial benefits of the sea air.

What was solid turned liquid, and the liquids reworked the landscapes. The Laurentide represented more than a third of the world's glacial ice in the late Pleistocene. Its southern margins went stagnant 17,000 years ago as the balance between ice formation and decay throughout the glacial system faltered and began to reverse. Meltwater coursed down the Mississippi, dropping more sediment along the braided system, helping to raise the level of the Gulf of Mexico from its full glacial lows while freshening its surface waters by some 10 percent. Drainage patterns shifted radically as the ice moved back. When the St. Lawrence Valley came out from under the sheets, water that had gone down to the Gulf went east to the ocean, in such quantities that it may have interfered with North Atlantic circulation patterns enough to lower temperatures in Europe.

Lakes multiplied. Some, like Lake Bonneville in and around Utah, had formed millennia before glacial maximum. But many were creatures of the melt. The weight of the ice depressed the earth, and in the lag between glacial retreat and rebound, lakes formed in the Hudson River (Lake Albany) and the Connecticut River (Lake Hitchcock — actually two lakes which together stretched from a detritus dam near Middletown, Connecticut, up to St. Johnsbury, Vermont). Even my own river, the Deerfield, had its standing water, near the little rise in Shelburne Falls where the Big Indian now smiles his small smile at the tourists coming in off Route 2 to see "Live Deer Free." The valley was pretty choked with sediment then, and it wasn't until Lake Hitchcock drained, more than 13,000 years ago, that the Deerfield started serious work on cleaning out the mess.

Proglacial lakes, those close to or bounded by the ice, came to cover most of the newly deglaciated land from modern Lake Ontario to modern Great Slave Lake in northwest Canada. Glaciers calved into many of them, and icebergs scored their bottoms. The largest in North America was Lake Agassiz, five times bigger than Lake Superior, about the size of modern Hudson Bay, a great compilation of water that at its maximum lay over most of southern Manitoba and spiked down along the Minnesota-Dakotas line.

Dependent on the ice, the lakes were nothing more than ponded instabilities. Agassiz water drained down the Mississippi for a while, and on at least one occasion, when an ice or debris dam let go, sent a pulse down the river sufficient to divert it into another valley. Then the lake found an eastern exit through and around the Great Lakes, themselves almost free of the ice, and doubled that aforementioned flow of meltwater tumbling down the St. Lawrence.

I would have liked to have seen Agassiz at play. But the prize for cataclysm goes to the Columbia River system in the Northwest. On several occasions, from 18,000 to 12,000 years ago or so, proglacial Lake Missoula broke through a snout of ice from the Cordilleran sheet and tore up the country. Lake Bonneville too, before it succumbed to the desiccating winds of a moderating climate, seems to have sent a bore, around 14,000 years ago, down the Snake River into the Columbia system. That was a freshet by comparison. The flows from Lake Missoula reached an estimated 28 million cubic yards per second. The average annual flow at the mouth of the Mississippi today is 675,000 cubic yards per second.

The floods may have lasted only a few hours, but they moonscaped a good deal of eastern Washington. They left giant ripple marks across the terrain, some of them fifteen feet high. They carved the bedrock in their channels into potholes, grooves, and cataracts. Where they met a serious obstacle, they built up bars of rock great and small. In the 1920s a student of rivers took a look at what was left and called it the Channeled Scabland.

By the beginning of the Holocene, roughly half of the ice sheets had melted. Meltwater and slowly rising ocean temperatures (heat expands volume) contributed to a general rise in sea level — to about 90 feet below present levels on the Atlantic coast of North America, as much as 120 along the Gulf of Mexico, and 180 along the Pacific. Coasts freed of glacial weight began to rebound at different times and rates. Some western coasts submerged in response to movements of continental plates unrelated to glaciation.

Deep-river valleys were invaded by Holocene saltwater. The parent streams then slowed, dropped their sediment loads early, and buried much of what they had excavated. In muddy shallows like those of the Atlantic, marshes formed and moved shoreward with the river mouths.

The sea itself went scouting inland to fill depressions still caught in the lag between glacial retreat and rebound. The Pacific filled Puget Sound. An arm of the Atlantic reached in toward Ottawa and down into Vermont to form the Champlain Sea. It gradually freshened and diminished as the earth rose beneath it and was mostly gone by 10,000 years ago. I take both wonder and comfort in the thought that Champlain, now a finger of sweet water just a couple of hours north of my house, was once home to porpoises, walruses, seals, and some whales.

We live through our seasons now. We gave up living with them, moving with them, millennia ago. The migrating plover that come to my neighbor's cornfields remind me that a good many of the world's mobile creatures hanker to be in the right place at the right time of year — and that I do not. My domestication is so advanced, my culture so intrusive, that I bear but the scantest witness to what animals are where, except to wonder whether a summer's shortage of bluebirds is due to climatic conditions, loss of habitat, or the discovery in some distant field of a better class of bug.

Given the impact on the natural world of our material culture, it is hard to hear the signals of shifting climates in the record of environmental change. But they are there, even at small scales. Temperatures in the Northern Hemisphere, above the tropics, rose a bit more than half a degree Centigrade from 1880 to 1950 and then dropped by half that amount before starting their recent and worrisome ascent a few years ago.

An insignificant shift, by lay standards. Yet flora and fauna responded to it, seeking and jockeying for their main chance. Animals, whose populations are apt to be more quickly affected by climatic shifts than most plants, reacted fastest. In Britain, the range of barnacles more tolerant of warm water moved north up the coasts within a couple of years of the warming. Herring gulls, which were in the habit of visiting Iceland, began to breed there. European blackbirds continued moving north after 1950, when cooling set in. Others, like the osprey, which clearly pay more attention to temperature, moved south. In the United States, where the warming contributed to the droughts of the Dust Bowl, jackrabbit populations soared in Kansas, and cotton rats swarmed in.

The floral world is not so reactive, particularly at the centenary scale. Many plants can dry up or be burned or frostbitten and still recover within a given habitat. Even at the edges of their ranges, trees can hold out against temperature extremes of some duration by changing their vital habits. Black spruce stops producing seeds when conditions are too harsh and survives by layering — sending out roots from branches touching the ground — and mountain ashes on high Scandinavian slopes grow from seeds brought by birds from lower elevations, where the tree can flower.

The Dust Bowl was severe enough to alter local plant assemblages. But Margaret Bryan Davis, from whose writings much of this information comes, says that the response of forests to climatic change is on another scale. Davis, based at the University of Minnesota, did some computer modeling with another ecologist, Daniel Botkin, of the University of California at Santa Barbara. The two simulated a forest dominated by sugar maple. Then they dropped the temperature by a couple of degrees. Sure enough, spruce took over as the forest dominant. What particularly interested Davis and Botkin, though, was the time required for the takeover — one or two centuries. The temperature drop, Davis writes, "caused the large maple trees to grow more slowly, but had little effect on longevity." Spruce, shaded by the canopy maples, also grew more slowly, even though the lowered temperatures were more to its liking. Since both maple and spruce can live for four hundred years or more, the climatically favored competitor had to bide its time until enough of the great maples died to open the canopy and give the conifers their place in the sun.

By these tenets, whatever stressed our forests in the past hundred years won't produce much in the way of sylvan reaction until well into the next century, at the earliest. Temperature variations over such paltry scales of time and magnitude are eddies in the meandering flows of climate. Even a couple of decades of respectable drought may not show up in the records that palynologists like Margaret Davis build out of fossil pollen grains and plant parts recovered from lake bottoms and bogs. To cause appreciable disturbances along those lines usually requires millennia, the scale of climatic flexing that marked the passage from Pleistocene into Holocene — a transition that some scientists believe was one of the most traumatic to life in the history of the planet.

It was customary only a few decades ago to think of plant and animal communities as strongly cohesive. Come an amelioration of climate, living things shifted their ranges away from the ice — as communities. The story most researchers tell now is one of disconnection, of each species tending to its own needs, reacting to its own luck. In the turmoil of the late Pleistocene, ponderosa pine, whose range had been reduced by the cold to small refuges in the south, spread north up the Rockies. Prairie plants took an increasingly strong hold in the broad spruce band paralleling the ice. Around 10,000 years ago, the conifer gave up. In some parts of the Midwest, perhaps those where Holocene warming was most pervasive, spruce collapsed in less than a century, taking up its modern ranges in upper Canada. Deciduous trees crisscrossed as they moved into higher latitudes. Hickories went north to the Midwest and then east. Oak and maple trended toward the northeast from the Mississippi Valley; hemlock and white pine extended to the northwest.

I am used to seeing beech and hemlock growing together on the hills above the Deerfield River. Yet hemlock arrived in this part of Massachusetts roughly 9,000 years ago, two millennia before the beech. Hickory arrived in Michigan 10,000 years ago but didn't get to Connecticut for another five millennia. Chestnut, a champion dawdler, showed up in northern New England only 2,000 years ago and flourished until disease struck it early in this century.

In addition to altering climates, a number of facts could explain why range extension has been such a many-gaited marathon early in this and, evidence indicates, preceding interglacial periods. Soil maturation is one. Recently deglaciated surfaces are apt to be high in minerals and fairly low in nutrients. Some plants, such as big sagebrush and sedges, move right in, whereas grasses do better in what was unglaciated tundra. Poplar and alder don't seem to mind ice-plowed ground, but spruce may have some difficulties. Davis has found that tundra persisted for 2,000 years in northern New England before spruce showed up.

Available space is another factor to consider. If you are a plant that needs a certain acidity of soil or slant of sunlight, you may not be very successful in extending your range into areas densely occupied by other species with the same requirements. Not, that is, until fire, storm, pathogen, or the workings of mortality open things up a bit for you.

Seed dispersal also affects rates of advance. A good many species, such as hemlock, poplar, birch, and maple, loose their seeds on the wind. Others, such as oak, beech, and chestnut, must rely on gravity, the occasional river, and animate intermediaries. Squirrels cache nuts, though usually not far from the source tree. Deer and other browsers eat them, but few nuts make it through their digestive systems intact. Nut-eating birds, such as turkeys and ducks and the late lamented passenger pigeons, are apt to be equipped with gizzards powerful enough to crush the meats. (The pigeons must still be considered as possible agents. The sound seeds they excreted would have lain exposed to rot and predation on the ground. But their flocks were so huge that at least some nuts must have survived and taken root.) The prime candidates for avian transport may well have been the radiant, strapping beings now on the feeder below the windows of my writing room — the blue jays.

The jay seems to have developed an evolutionary relationship with certain nut trees. It has a bill shaped just right to pierce thin shells and extract the contents, feet that can keep slippery nuts steady, and a throat that can expand to carry up to three white oak acorns at a time to store in the ground. No one knows how far the jays will fly from tree to cache, but distances of well over a mile have been logged. The caches are apt to be concentrated in forest edges and openings, places with more than enough sunlight for oak seedlings. Each bird can theoretically cache thousands of nuts annually, enough to maintain the migration rates for oaks of the late Pleistocene or early Holocene, about 1,000 feet per year. Jays and passenger pigeons could also carry seeds across alien terrain. They may easily have facilitated the spread of beech westward across — over — Lake Michigan.

A thousand feet a year, fast for a nut tree, isn't much in the way of progress. But it adds up to almost two hundred miles in a millennium, more than enough to change North American environments in radical ways. That change is part of what Margaret Davis and others call disequilibrium. The term irritates some of her colleagues. "A lot of theoretical ecologists don't assume that a system is at an equilibrium," Davis says, "but they do assume it is heading toward an equilibrium." And, she adds, "they think they can predict the direction in which it will move." She agrees with their approach but argues that if species are trending toward equilibrium at different rates — and her early work provided some of the most elegant evidence that they are — then they'll never reach their destination. To her, equilibrium is a moving target.

More than thirty genera of mammals in North America, including the clan of my ravening short-faced bear, didn't make it through the end of the Pleistocene. Many mammals did, but few *in situ*. Paleontologists, trained to distinguish between the skeletal remains of the singing vole and the arctic shrew and to recognize the milk tooth of a bison when they see one, can attest to all this. And their story is the same as that set forth by the climatologists and the palynologists: what was bears little resemblance to what is.

When the ice of the Wisconsinan was at its maximum, things simply weren't as polarized as they are now. The country, or most of it, was a land not of monotones but of ecotones, of unending edges between treeland and grassland, wetland and dry, where life is apt to be most exuberant. It was an ark of a world, where saiga antelopes, moose, and lions from Eurasia might mix with indigenous bears and camels and horses. In unglaciated parts of Alaska, you'd find grama grass, badgers, and bison, all associated in the modern mind with terrain far to the south.

One tally of animal remains is a fair indication of what could be found in the Appalachians of Pennsylvania, West Virginia, and adjacent highlands. It runs from three species of mole to one, possibly two, of mammoth. There are three species of bear (grizzly, short-faced, and perhaps the Florida cave bear), five deerlike creatures (including stag-moose and caribou), four bovids (two of musk ox and two of bison), plus tapir, peccary, ground sloth, armadillo, and mastodon. The total for the area exceeded seventy-five species of mammal. By contrast, the number of mid-Appalachian species in the late Holocene came to about fifty. Of these, only six could be called large animals, as against twenty during the late Pleistocene.

A number of mammals moved out of the tally area at the end of the Pleistocene, mostly to the north (musk ox, caribou) and west (grizzly bear, bison). Many of those who stayed experienced a reduction in their ranges. Some shrank in size, a few grew, some went extinct. What was left was sufficient to dazzle the first European eyes to see it. The fact that it represented a biological impoverishment, when set against the life of the last ice time, did not become apparent until the advent of those who could divine antiquity from the bones of the singing vole.

The language of science is apt to be as dense as adamant. Yet every once in a while a word or phrase glints from the heavy page. *Vagility*, for instance. The word derives from one meaning "to wander." Its full definition is "the capacity of an organism to compete successfully for existence."

Scientists, the natural heirs to philosophy, like to jump on an issue that will withstand decades of philosophical scrum. A popular one for prehistorians is, what happened to vagility at the end of the Pleistocene? Why, they ask, did something like two thirds of the big mammals in North America — mammoth, mastodon, horse, camel, ground sloth, giant beaver, short-faced bear, saber-tooth, and the rest — vanish, most of them in the scientifically short space of 12,000 to 10,000 years ago? A few players will take the time to mention that some smaller mammals went too, along with a number of birds (including the teratorn, the hawk-eagle, and the walking eagle). But the big beasts, the megafauna, are more fun to ponder. They were so impressive. They went so quickly.

A number of extinction scenarios have been offered by students of climatic and environmental change in the late Pleistocene and early Holocene. One has it that the hospitable spruce parklands of glacial times were replaced in the wink of a geologic eye by relatively closed deciduous forests of less than middling interest to large grazers in the East. Toward the west, the Pleistocene environments, which may have looked just a bit like the Serengeti and other high savannas of East Africa, became just plain prairie. Mosaics of plant and animal species were replaced by polarized ecosystems. The prairies divided into bands of long-grass, mid-grass, and short-grass growth. Everywhere, to use the felicitous phrase of a paleontologist working in Alaska, things went "from plaids to stripes."

The paleontologist I am most familiar with is a friendly

bearded man named Russell Graham, who spends much of his nonfield time in a long and low building close to the railroad tracks running south out of Springfield, Illinois. Graham, part of a group of prehistorians gathered by the Illinois State Museum, has only to walk down a corridor to visit the loves of his professional life — shelves and shelves of the impossibly large cheek teeth of mammoths and mastodons or the improbable incisors of giant beavers that he and others have excavated, received as gifts, or, only rarely, managed to extract from the clutches of fossil hunters. When I met him, he was putting dated fossil finds from around the country into a computer model that would produce a picture of what mammals went where over time.

For Graham, "habitat destruction is probably the primary ecological cause of the Pleistocene extinction." He thinks that climate probably was the prime agent of that destruction — the shift from equability to the extremes of continentality, particularly the seasonal extremes that so altered patterns of growth, range limits, and vagility itself.

Species of plants and animals that had lived together for millennia began to shuffle and reshuffle along the gradients of radically changing ecosystems. This desertion of plaids for stripes had the effect of reducing diversity. That was fine for animals such as bison or antelopes or other ungulates who don't mind monocultural menus; they began to appear in prodigious numbers. But the big grazers and browsers had increasing trouble. Things were changing too fast for them to adapt biologically. They couldn't migrate, for there was no longer anyplace to go where they might find their old homes on the range. So they went extinct.

The phrase glistens with precision. And yet we can only guess at the sequence of stresses burdening these animals. In places where warming and drying was pronounced, the nutrition of the plants they ate peaked rapidly earlier in the year and rapidly fell away. Like any other prey, plants are not without their defenses. Many grasses respond to heavy grazing by developing tough stems or secreting substances such as silica that make them less digestible. Forbs, shrubs, and trees have their own antiherbivory tricks. I've mentioned that spruces produce terpenes, chemicals that do not always lie easy in the predatory stomach, all their lives. Other flora turn defensive only in certain growth stages or under certain predatory pressures, producing alkaloids, cyanogens, and other compounds that can seriously affect metabolisms. So it is possible, Graham and others agree, that at least some of the Pleistocene megafauna inadvertently, and possibly in desperation, poisoned themselves. And as increasing seasonality altered growing seasons, the simple availability of quality food must have had its effects. Where winters are severe, animals, particularly big animals, must have autumnal access to whatever best fattens them. Otherwise, many of them will not see spring.

Of course, as one species declined in importance, its niche opened to competitors. The short-faced bears may have been discomfited by the dwindling supplies of horse and camel, but they were also being outmatched in their home territories by brown bears. The dire wolf, massive jaws and all, was slow and probably more of a carrion eater than anything else. Carrion became scarce as other slow carnivores, such as the sabertooth, deprived of young mammoths and other slow prey, went for it. Meantime, the timber wolf, able to catch meat on the run, moved in on the slower dire.

There are those who differ with scientists like Graham who argue for environmental change as the proximate cause of the depauperation of North American animal life. Something else was going on, they say. Something else was moving in. A small animal, no match for a mammoth by itself. But such a clever animal, they say. Look, they have a mammoth surrounded. They are after him with stone-pointed sticks. They have him. They have them all.

4

Children of the Ice

THERE IS MORE than one way to think about the appearance of people on the American continents.

Greig Arnold, blood to those who once lived in the fishing village of Ozette on the Washington coast, agreed to talk with me about his people, the Makah. Arnold is a museologist, yet he seemed uncomfortable describing the old way of life in a building built specifically to house displays of artifacts from Ozette. Finally he led me out the museum door, into his pickup. We drove through cutover forest up a steep knob overlooking the mouth of Juan de Fuca Strait. Arnold pointed out a nuclear submarine heading out to sea through quartering swells. Then he turned in a slow circle, there in the wind, telling me about halibut banks and places good for salmon and herring and how the Makah had once used the forests out to the horizon and beyond. I understood why we had come. We were talking about place, you see, and we could not do that within walls. Not properly.

I asked Arnold how long he thought his people had lived on this cape. He thought and said, "From the beginning of time. That's what the elders say. We have been here forever, since the first day of light."

Ron LaFrance, a Mohawk raised up to be a leader of the Iroquois, recently headed the native American studies program at Cornell. The Iroquois are famous through history and late prehistory for their way with the club and the word. I can't attest to LaFrance's skill in a scrap. But he is very good when he wants to be at tweaking the Euro-American, at pinning the tail on the honky. For most American scholars, he says with a grin, "Civilization *had* to start in the Mesopotamian valley; it *had* to start in the Garden of Eden with two nice white people." He tells about going to a conference of native Americans up in Canada, where he joined in poking some serious fun at the conventional view that the first humans in North America came in via the Beringian land bridge linking Siberia and Alaska. "We got into a discussion of whether any of us had ever heard any stories of extreme cold that our people had experienced. No one could recollect any." There are many variants of the legends telling of sky people falling to earth to bring forth men and women or of ancestors coming from a world below through a vertical tunnel to live in sunlight (symbolic exits, *sipapus*, are built into the floors of the great kivas, or round rooms, at places like Chaco Canyon), but no legends, at least at the meeting in question, that would signal an arctic experience.

Vine Deloria, Jr., is a Standing Rock Sioux, a teacher, and a writer (*Custer Died for Your Sins*). "The Bering Strait theory," he wrote in a recent essay,

> is tenaciously held by white scholars against the varied migration traditions of the natives and is an example of the triumph of doctrine over facts. Excavating ancient fireplaces and campsites may be exciting, but there are no well-worn paths which clearly show migratory patterns from Asia to North America, and if there were such paths, there would be no indication anywhere which way the footprints were heading. We can be certain of only one thing: the Bering Strait theory is *preferred* by the whites and consequently becomes accepted as scientific

fact. If the universities were controlled by the Indians, we would have an entirely different explanation of the peopling of the New World, and it would be just as respectable for the scholarly establishment to support it.

LaFrance is an anthropologist. A good friend of his, an archaeologist of Yankee stock, told me only half jokingly that he thinks LaFrance took that turn because he got so tired of answering questions about the Mohawks put to him by white social scientists. Whatever his reasons, LaFrance now finds himself caught in two cultures. He is trying desperately to help keep his traditions from disappearing; there were, when we talked a few years ago, only two men left in the Mohawk nation who could perform the hours of recitation required by one of the nation's most essential ceremonies. But he is also in the midst of academe, where oral memory on that demanding scale doesn't count for much, where he must be "reasonable."

I was brought up on reason and, when pressed, can be counted on to fall back on it. Construct your premises "correctly," and your deductions will be unassailable — as if assault and defense were the noblest function of thought. I was also brought up in the midst of poetry and myth, including the myths my brother, eleven years older than I, brought back from summer fieldwork among the Hopis in Arizona. Reason, I found, gave me a sense of power, but myth gave me a sense of place — something I yearned for.

Perhaps because of that upbringing, I have found myself increasingly drawn to seeking out similarities between myth and reason — or rather, reason's most loyal servant, science. Both, I think, are explanations of existence, though myth aims for entireties and science for discrete and seemingly ever smaller parts of the whole. Both arise from powers of observation that, be the observer a hunter of deer or of DNA, are exceptionally well focused on the matters at hand. Both change. And both work through stories, but work differently. Traditional societies receive theirs from the generational flow, accept them in all their complexity and paradox, learn from them, act on them, and pass them on. Scientists dissect theirs, reject some parts, refine others. Their chant is argument.

The traditionalists seek their identity through continuity. The scientists seek theirs through discovery. And yet, now that what is left of myth appears about to drown beneath floods of information, infotainment, and just plain data, the servant of reason appears ready to take on some bardic responsibilities. As the scholar of stories, Joseph Campbell, put it, "Science itself is now the only field through which the dimensions of mythology can be revealed."

If Campbell is correct, then archaeology and the other disciplines of prehistory should be the sciences that ultimately will reveal to us the mythic dimensions of our origins. Remarkable things can now be said about a tiny chip of exotic flint found several feet below the surface of the ground or a bit of plant material embedded in the ancient, urine-soaked nest of a pack rat. The care taken in the excavation and recording of these objects is often beyond lay understanding. But the country is huge, there are only a few thousand prehistorians to work it, and an inadequate and unpredictable funding system exists to support them. Like biologists a few decades ago, archaeologists are still collecting their data, site by site. But they see the time coming when their stories will be far more encompassing, more revelatory of past human conditions and their influence on the modern. Takeoff for a more thorough study of early people in America, many of them believe, will come, if they can maintain their pace, not long after the millennium turns.

Right now, for many parts and time periods of the continent, the data simply aren't dense enough to provide an acceptable or accepted pattern. A new discovery can and often does affect scientific kilter. In no area of inquiry is the wrangling more vociferous than in that addressing the essential question: when did we get here? One investigator got so carried away recently by what he believes is a discovery that will prove his own unconventional answer that he announced to the press, "This is the one that's going to finish off the skeptics."

Archaeologists usually talk to one another with reasonable civility about matters of the past twelve millennia. If you drop "when" from the conversation, you'll find agreement of sorts about "how." The consensus, the one LaFrance and his friends were having on, is that the first immigrants came out of northeastern Asia. They had enough technological skills and adaptability to subsist on cold steppes and tundras. In time they moved across a broad stretch of land, Beringia, that now lies under the Bering and Chukchi seas and entered the unglaciated part of coastal Alaska. And at some point thereafter they moved south, probably along a corridor between the Laurentide and Cordilleran ice sheets, and came into this country east of the Rockies. From there they moved south, west, and east, ranging across lands that appealed to them throughout the Americas.

Early in this century, there was only enough evidence to support arguments that humans entered North America about 4,000 years ago. But in 1908 a black cowboy with a Gaelic name, McJunkin, was riding a section of range that ran along an arroyo near the little town of Folsom, New Mexico. McJunkin dismounted and went over to look at some bones sticking out of the ground, big bones, of a sort he'd never seen before. Buried with them was a more familar object, part of a small, finely made stone weapon point like the ones a sharp eye could spot occasionally here and there on open ground. As so often happens, years passed before McJunkin's find ended up in an archaeological lab. It wasn't until 1926 that excavators returned to the arroyo, dug, and found more points in association with more bone, the remains of extinct bison. Within a couple of years, it was clear that the bottom had fallen out of the currently accepted, and fiercely defended, peopling theory. Judging by the bison and the stone points, there were hunters at Folsom not 4,000 but perhaps as much as 10,000 years ago.

In 1932, a little shy of two hundred miles south of Folsom, a couple of nonprofessional excavators unwittingly pushed man's estimated time of arrival back another thousand years or so. Digging into what had been lakeshore near Clovis, New Mexico, they found even larger mammal bones, later identified as mammoth. They also found points considerably larger than those to the north, some of them lying between mammoth ribs.

The argument then turned into one of determining the relative age of what became known as the Clovis and Folsom cultures (though I think it would have been nice to have named the latter, the pioneer find, after McJunkin). Further digging in a number of spots showed that Clovis underlay Folsom in the strata of the earth and was therefore older. But fixing chronological age had to await a discovery in the late 1940s by a chemist at the University of Chicago named Willard Libby, who was doing work on isotopes that furthered development of the atomic bomb.

Libby's discovery, which earned him a Nobel prize, concerned properties of carbon 14, a radioactive isotope of carbon produced when nitrogen, by far the most plentiful gas in our atmosphere, is bombarded by cosmic rays. The newly formed carbon circulates as carbon dioxide, and some of it is taken up by plants and animals. Living things maintain a fairly constant amount of carbon 14 in their systems up to the point of death. But when they die, the process stops and the amount of the isotope begins to decline in a wonderfully predictable fashion. Half is gone in 5,700 years, half of the remainder in another 5,700. Measuring the radiocarbon in charcoal (the most reliable) or bone, shell, or horn (not so reliable) yields a spread of years within which the age of the tested object probably

falls. All sorts of things can go wrong: coal in the sediments can stretch the assumed age of a stratum, and a root working its way down through the soil can shrink it. The process isn't of much use in dating objects more than 40,000 years old. But at least Dr. Libby's discovery has brought appreciable and increasing order to what had been mostly a game of chance.

Folsom fell fairly close to the original estimate of 10,000 years. Clovis came in at about 11,500. And from the time in the fifties when that news surfaced until the present, the most commonly accepted bottom line for human occupation has been 12,000 years ago. Fluted points like those at Clovis have been found in just about every state in the contiguous country and in Canada. Despite this spread, the artifacts have been remarkably uniform — though, oddly enough, it has been hard to demonstrate association of points with extinct mammal bones east of the Mississippi. The strength of the evidence has led to the idea that the Clovis people were among the most active pioneers in the Americas.

A number of archaeologists holding this opinion are willing to tack on a millennium or two to their entry date to allow for the possible development of the Clovis culture *in situ* prior to the diaspora. But of these, few will push their horizon back past 15,000 years ago. To do so would run counter to recent studies, among them findings that suggest that the Alberta corridor, the proposed avenue of entry, never was passable along its full 1,200-mile length during the full press of glaciation and became so only after warming began, say, 12,000 years ago.

There have been plenty of early birds around to question the conservatives, before and after Mr. McJunkin took his ride. The earliest ones told stories of Atlantis and the lost tribes of Israel in America, of Celts and Egyptians. More recently, scientists have made claims of great antiquity for human skeletons that turned out to be modern and for stone "tools" whose dating didn't hold up or whose shaping could just as easily have been produced by natural forces.

To be taken seriously, a site's inventory — objects of stone, bone (including skeletal remains, if any), ivory, vegetable matter, wood; things that appear to be storage pits, hearths (including fire-cracked rocks and charcoal), or footprints or coprolites (fossilized feces) — must be shown convincingly to have been the work of humans. The strata in which they lie must make chronological sense. Older layers should be encountered below younger ones, and all should be free from evidence of disturbance by streams, frost heaving, or other forces that can reshuffle the sedimentary deck and thus ruin the record. The sense of skepticism ingrained in most archaeologists is considerably reduced if the site is found to have companions, enough to show recurrent patterns.

A fairly strong argument can be made that, if for no other reason than relative population sizes, truly ancient sites can be expected to be fewer in number than, say, the sites of Clovis, Folsom, and other groupings that collectively reflect what is called the Paleo-Indian tradition. That has often been the case elsewhere in the world, where evidence has been found of bands that lived in a region well before the development of such a successful way of life. Perhaps so. In any event, of the hundred or so sites around North America for which unusual antiquity has been claimed, about a half-dozen are still attracting rigorous attention.

Up in the Yukon, that is, north of the ice barrier and therefore directly accessible to those crossing the land bridge, the 15,000-year limit to occupation doesn't really apply. Two sites show signs of being considerably older. One is out on the tundra of the Old Crow Basin, where what appear to be worked mammoth bones have been found. The sedimentary setting is unstable, however. Some of the altered bone has been dated within the range of 25,000 to 40,000 years ago. Not far away lie the Bluefish Caves, where stone tools have been found, including tiny chipped blades that might have been set into bone or antler projectile points, a technique well known in Eurasia before Clovis (and later practiced by Eskimos on this continent). Bones piled nearby were dated to 12,000 to 15,000 years ago. A mammoth bone and matching flake went to 24,000 years ago, just about matching the recent end of the Old Crow range. Flaking or otherwise shaping mammoth and other large mammal bones was common in Asia, but whether human hands worked the bone at Bluefish has yet to be established beyond doubt. Rock, water, ice, and the passage of large animals could produce roughly similar effects.

In the lower forty-eight states, sites in Washington and Oregon and a few other western states appear to push the first peopling a few millennia beyond the 12,000-year limit. And in Pennsylvania, overlooking a small tributary of the Ohio River, a rock shelter called Meadowcroft remains a reference point for early birds. Excavators dug some fifteen feet, through layers of what appears to be undisturbed sediment laid down under the overhang, past beer cans on the surface to colonial liquor bottles to stone implements and hearths to a strip of bark thought to have been used for basketry and dating to between 16,200 and 19,000 years before the present. Stone points were found at several levels. Some of the deepest ones were quite similar to those used in eastern Asia well before the twelfth millennium.

It can take years, decades, before a site's age and interpretations run the long scholarly — and not so scholarly — gauntlet of criticisms and counterinterpretations. Meadowcroft is very much still on its feet. Behind it, another site, in a cave near Orogrande, New Mexico, has just begun the process. It has produced a pointed bone fragment jammed into a toebone of an extinct horse and what appear to be hearths, some with large, burnt logs in them. The imprints of what experts say is a human hand were found in the clay hearth lining. The dates at this point are in the range of 35,000 years before present for the hearth materials and 25,000 for the bone point. This is the evidence that the cave's chief scientist, archaeologist Richard MacNeish, says will finish off the skeptics. So far, the skeptics seem not to have accepted their fate.

Latin America appears to be generating more interest in the field of early finds than North America. A number of claims run to around 16,000 years before the present for chipped stone objects found with mammoth bones in Mexico and somewhat earlier for the same associations in Venezuela. In the dry and broken country of northeastern Brazil, along cliffs the colors of sunset, are a number of overhangs. At the base of many of them are setbacks that obviously sheltered people at some time in the far past. The people's paintings of animals and of themselves are on the walls. Their tools lie about. There isn't much objection to dating their presence back to 8,000 years ago, even the sacred 12,000. But the French archaeologist Niède Guidon, who has spent years working these sites, among them a cave in a rock face, has come across charcoal and broken rock that she believes may also be of human origin. The charcoal, some found within circles of burned rocks, has been dated from 14,300 years before the present in shallow layers to an incredible 47,000 years in the deeper ones.

Obviously, the oldest claims are not going to produce much more than head shaking until the evidence has been checked and rechecked. Questions beg to be answered. Why are there no bones in the deeper layers? Has soil acidity eaten them away, or were they never there? Those rocks that appear to have been worked — couldn't they just as well have broken as they fell from the cliffs above? Digging continues at new sites in the area, and believers and nonbelievers wait.

In the lake country of southern Chile, an American archaeologist, Tom Dillehay, and his assistants dug through a bed of peat to uncover what appeared to be a village 13,000 years old. Peat preserves what it covers in near-perfect anoxia. The diggers found mastodon meat; a large number of plants, including wild potato and species used now, and presumably then, to treat intestinal and other ailments; tools, and — a great surprise — remains of a row of huts.

The dating of the village, Monte Verde, goes down fairly well among many archaeologists, but there is more to the story. Digging deeper in a spot near the village, Dillehay encountered stones that looked to him like tools and that dated to 33,000 years ago. Dillehay himself is not saying that he has evidence for settlement that early. The stones may somehow have worked their way down in the soil, though the strata look undisturbed. But there they are, yet more counters in the dating game. With Monte Verde, it is a bit easier now to question the consensus, to ask, if by 13,000 years ago people were not only living but, judging from the remains of food and shelter, living fairly well that far down the long meridional reach of the southern continent, then how many millennia earlier did their ancestors cross from Siberia? And if those stone objects in the deeper layers do turn out to be artifacts dating beyond the thirtieth millennium, what then? What will that do to the overarching theory of Beringian entry?

Stereotypes of bold hunters loping down from the north like the wolf on the American fold have lost some of their strength in these questioning times. There appears to be more room for inquiries into colonization of this continent by trial and error. People could have arrived, looked around, and left. They could have stayed and failed; some prehistorians believe that if you look hard enough, with a sufficiently open mind, in the right places, you might find some Roanokes among the Monte Verdes.

Even the methods of migration are subject to a bit more debate. A few bold archaeologists are reconsidering old notions and advancing new ones about a coastal route followed by experienced seafarers. The boats they used may have been primitive, small craft of hide stretched over bone or wood frames, but they would have been adequate for short voyages within sight of land to explore and to take sea mammals and other marine food. The going would have been harsh and extremely risky, particularly along the most northerly littorals, wedged as they must have been between inland glaciers and great confusions of sea ice. But once through those hazards, the skilled and the lucky would have had several advantages to exploit. Some of them could have moved up the coastal rivers without having to change their ways of life much. Those who kept heading south could have reached South America without having to face the climate, terrain, and teeming pathogens of the Panamanian isthmus, the other land bridge, which would have severely pruned the ranks of terrestrial explorers. Intriguing though they are, the maritime arguments are all but untestable; the beaches, coves, and headlands along which the first people may have voyaged now lie dozens of feet below the Pacific rollers.

What Lewis Thomas once called the "jubilant descant" of argument floats above what relics we have of these ancient times. It is naive to believe that there could have been pre-Clovis cultures here for millennia, populations large enough to avoid extinction, which nonetheless are archaeologically almost invisible. It is naive to believe that Clovis people by themselves occupied both American continents unless we posit a population growth more rapid than anything in human history.

The resonances and dissonances can drown out a very important point: occupation of the Americas was not an isolated adventure. It was a part, a rather late-blooming part, of human migrations that began hundreds of thousands of years ago.

Africa was all a cradle should be to us. Sun and warm rain swaddled us, and what came to hand from plants and the kills of true predators sustained us. As we evolved, from *Australopithecus* to *Homo erectus* to *Homo sapiens* to modern *Homo sapiens sapiens*, we fashioned tools and material cultures and the vocal means for passing on the gist of how we had lived our lives. We found fire, perhaps as much as a million years ago, and in time used it to improve the taste of scavenged meat. With these skills, we drifted into the temperate belt across southern Europe, the Mideast, and eastern Asia.

The tempo of our inventions surged with the return of ice sheets to Eurasia 100,000 years ago. We learned how to shape flint or chert so that we could strike off many blades and fashion them into all sorts of cutting tools. We learned how to make animal skins supple and how to sew them with sinew into clothing. We tinkered with group hunting strategies until we could take mammoths and other large animals efficiently. We continued to press north, first the Neanderthals and then the modern people who succeeded them.

We colonized new lands as they emerged from the ice. We pushed outward from southeastern Asia across the dry sea bottoms, and we crossed open sea to reach Australia 40,000 years ago. We pushed outward from northeast Asia and down the Americas to Tierra del Fuego. Within the past 4,000 years we peopled the Pacific islands, and when we had finished with that, there was no habitable place of significance left for us to settle.

To be interested in the colonizations of North America is to be interested in the colonizations of Europe. The two shared a number of biogeographical experiences during and since the Pleistocene — not surprisingly, when one thinks that both run north past the Arctic Circle and yet in their central and southerly ranges support temperate forests and prairies and arid steppes. The ice of the last glaciation phase lay thick over Ireland and England, over northern Germany and Scandinavia. The margin at glacial maximum (about 20,000 years ago, roughly the same as ours) ran east well past the Urals and then bent sharply north, leaving much of Siberia, except along the Pacific coast, cold and dry and therefore ice-free.

Warming began around 16,000 years ago, and 3,000 years

later the ice had begun to melt back from southern Scandinavia. Seas had regained some of the three hundred feet of depth they had lost to the ice, but western Europe was still high and dry. You could walk from Denmark to Sweden, from Dover to Calais, from Holyhead on the coast of Wales to Dublin. The English Channel did not begin to refill until roughly 8,000 years ago.

As Europe approached the Holocene, temperatures continued to rise, and vegetation expanded into the barrens left by the ice. The patterns were familiar: sedges and rough grasses at first, then dwarf shrubs, then a kind of open birch woodland in the west. The spruce boreal woodlands so common in postglacial North America ranged a good deal farther east in Europe than they do today.

Around 11,000 years ago, the climate reversed itself. Perhaps it was all that meltwater suddenly pouring into the North Atlantic as the St. Lawrence came free of the Laurentide ice sheet. Its volume may have been sufficient to alter oceanic circulation and reduce heat transport from the tropics to northern areas. Whatever the cause, midsummer temperatures in western Europe dove from 18° to 10°C (from the low 60s to 50°F). Birch disappeared in the north and tundra expanded. Blizzards alternated with dust storms in what is now the Netherlands. In the south, grasslands in the process of becoming oak woodlands went back to grass within a few centuries.

The climatic trough lasted for a thousand years, and then warming resumed, erratic as usual, but climbing, as it did in this country, toward temperatures that between about 8,000 and 4,000 years ago reached a couple of degrees Celsius over current July readings. Winters also may have been a bit warmer than current ones, and the climate was on the moist side, unlike early Holocene precipitation patterns in so much of the American interior. Vegetation responded as you would expect, in the direction of the deciduous. The kind times that followed the blowing snow and loess saw northern Europe going back to birch forest and then on to birch and pine with an admixture of elm and ash. Then pine and hazel. Then dense oak forests with a good amount of lime (linden) and elm.

The open country of the earlier millennia supported large and peripatetic animals — woolly mammoth, woolly rhinoceros, herds of horse and reindeer (cousins to the caribou). As the climate warmed, both hirsute herbivores went extinct, while reindeer and other mammals wandered north. Newcomers or the newly dominant appeared, animals of more modest range, animals that did well in and around forests, like the red deer (much like but smaller than our elk), roe deer, the aurochs or wild ox, the European bison, elk (our moose), and wild pig.

The story I am used to hearing about the rise of anatomically modern humans is that they obliterated the older forms of their species as they entered Europe and other lands new to them. I thought I was reading tales of genocide. Later I came to understand that the European moderns may have simply outcompeted the ancient ones. Their tool kit was more diverse, more advanced, and with it and their newfangled ways, they were able to take over the bottomlands and other places of comparatively easy living. Their success meant that the Neanderthals had to make do with what they could find on poor ground, and that meant a very slowly declining Neanderthal population, a protracted case of the dwindles that produced extinction in a thousand years or so. Neanderthals, this line of thinking goes, were about on a par with us in most important ways. Their main problem, I gather, was that they had adapted so well to glacial conditions that their heavy bodies and specialized respiratory systems seemed out of place when those conditions changed. Natural selection worked increasingly against those traits, with the helping hand of intermarriage, if marriage there was, between archaic humans and modern. Today, I have special respect for the uncommonly burly stranger passing me in the crowd. He or she just might carry traces of the lineage that once hunted mammoth, horse, and reindeer within sight of the ice fronts and enshrined the cave bear. We may need those genes again.

Homo sapiens sapiens filtered into Europe about 35,000 years ago and, after some millennia of familiarization with their surroundings, turned to discovering themselves. They created cave paintings of great beauty and made beads and figurines that over broad regions retained a similar style. Beginning around 26,000 years ago, people on the Russian plain were building what appear to have been fairly permanent settlements of dwellings, many incorporating mammoth bones in their structure. That way of life evidently lasted until around 12,000 years ago, when it gave way to a more nomadic one. Its practitioners developed storage pits and trade networks extending five hundred miles or more. Clearly, they and others in early Europe were expressing an interest in rearranging their world.

Twenty-two thousand years ago, the Solutrean culture in Spain was developing projectile points somewhat like those knapped by the Clovis people eleven millennia later — plus microblades that some think came to be mounted on arrowheads to give them greater slicing power. Add thrusting spears, darts propelled by spear throwers, and eventually harpoons, and the result was a tool kit that gave them greater efficiency at hunting. These are the tools that came to be used in some combination by hunters from Europe to Japan. They gave us the earth.

It makes sense to say, as many do, that the migrations up into northeast Siberia and across Beringia were a result of increased demographic pressure on people requiring very low population densities — as low as thirty persons or less per hundred square miles — to be at their best. But I like to believe that some migrants, like the American mountain men early in the last century, kept moving just for curiosity or just to stay ahead of everyone else, in fresh country. And there is always what the archaeologist Robson Bonnichsen calls the "dragon dynamic": global climate change. Bonnichsen, now at the University of Washington but working at the University of Maine when I talked with him, had a map a Russian scientist had made of what was then Soviet Asia, at full glaciation. It showed ice sheets and freshwater seas fully as impressive as those I'd been studying in North America. As these controlling topographic features waned and drained, central Asia began to dry up.

Bonnichsen has a hunch that the desiccation might have affected people living in parts of central Asia. Some scholars think that this region may have been home at one point or another to the ancestors not only of the Clovis folk but of the Na-Dene, who migrated into northwest Canada about 10,000 years ago (and some of whom moved much later to our Southwest to become Navajos and Apaches), and of the Eskimos, who came over to the North American Arctic some 5,000 years ago. Lack of moisture, Bonnichsen thinks, turned some of these people into Okies. "They were driven," he says, "they and their prey." Driven in many directions, including north and eventually east across the land bridge.

When it comes to the colonization of the lands on this side of the bridge, the easiest — which is to say the least controversial — starting point is still the fluted point, the stone weapon with the characteristic flute or channel from the butt up a ways on each face. We know these colonizers by their stone, their knowledge of it, how they would acquire the finest-grained, most beautiful stone for their hunting from hundreds of miles away. When they weren't making or remaking projectile points, they were striking flakes off their flint cores to be chipped into edged instruments for butchering, scraping, scribing. We know from a few examples that they shaped bone into needles and other tools. The rest of their technology — wooden shafts, clubs, perhaps even fiber nets — has long since gone to dust. As have they. There are claims of antiquity for a skull here, a bone there, for Midland Man and Minnesota Man. There was one for a tooth from Nebraska Man, but that turned out to belong to an extinct peccary.

Experts have been looking at other teeth, those of modern native Americans, and comparing them with those of Asian populations. Dentally, they think, and probably genetically, the first people to skirt the northern Pacific and colonize the Americas looked much like those who watched the first Europeans land along the Atlantic coast. They were, in other words, lithe, well muscled, with skin that tanned easily. They were dark-eyed, with dark and thick-stranded hair on their heads and not much elsewhere.

Edward O. Wilson, the Harvard biologist, estimates that "for more than 99 percent of human history, people have lived in hunter-gatherer bands totally and intimately involved with other organisms." Maintenance of that involvement was not achieved through physical diffidence. The first such people here were tough, as a population, in ways we no longer understand. We ask: How could those Chacoans have brought in those logs all the way from the mountains? How could those people in Ozette have towed a dead whale miles to their village? How could that Onondaga boy have run down that deer? How could that Mandan or Mohawk woman have foraged that far leading one child and about to bear another? How could she carry home such a heavy load of nuts or berries? We forget. People everywhere were doing things only a while ago that required as much muscle power, as much conditioning, endurance. It was natural to have a body that could be pushed to physical extremes, even if you had to spend time between those extremes resting up, even though eventually the work got into your joints and bowed you, killed you.

The first American pioneers quite possibly had dogs with them, though whether these were descendants of animals domesticated in Asia, Alaska, or the new homelands can't be determined. It is probable that they had their shamans, for the shaman in Asia had long been the medium through which humans could connect with the spirits of animals and other beings that were constantly tinkering with their destinies. Nothing can be known of the belief systems that sustained these people, but I have a feeling that Joseph Campbell was right when he wrote that certain concepts are common to us all, among them "the idea of survival after death . . . so also that of the sacred area (sanctuary); that of the efficacy of ritual, of ceremonial decorations, sacrifice and of magic; that of supernatural agencies; that of a transcendant yet ubiquitously immanent sacred power; that of a relationship between dream and the mythological realm; that of initiation; that of the initiate (shaman, priest, seer etc.)."

It is chancy to compare modern hunter-gatherers with those of antiquity. The former, most of them, live in marginal lands, often close by more powerful pastoral or agricultural societies. The hunters of old lived in all the best places and were dominant in them. Yet ethnography is about the only hands-on approach we have to the past. There are a number of sources to go to, but I find the most intriguing is a slim volume by Peter J. Wilson, of New Zealand, called *The Domestication of the Human Species*. Talking in great and intriguing generalities, Wilson says that hunter-gatherers tend to form societies that are egalitarian, fluid, but stable. They disdain the dependent person and the braggart. They are not strangers to violence but fear it as a threat not only to themselves but to their way of life; it is not wise to stalk an animal while being stalked by an enemy. Groups may go so far as to ambush and kill a member who is constantly flying off the handle. Sharing is essential in a life where luck on the hunt is never ubiquitous or enduring. Apportionment also minimizes accumulations that might otherwise slow down a ranging band.

Elders — and in fluted-point times these might well have

been men and women over thirty-five or forty — exercise some influence over their bands, but in general decisions are made tacitly. Affection keeps couples, families, and groups together. Lack of it results in people leaving to join other bands or form a new one. Abandonment is greatly feared as a punishment, yet the hunter who has broken an ankle, the woman irreparably injured in childbirth, and the arthritic grandfather expect to be abandoned. Again, the need to retain mobility is paramount.

Foraging societies tend to be open societies, Wilson writes, living an ethic of independence, focusing on one another but not bonding. Anxieties and uncertainties stress those lives as they stress ours, but releases are at hand. Friends are there to hear grievances or break up quarrels. Shamans are there to intercede and to extend the powers of trance and vision. And there is always the exit.

Wilson ends his consideration of hunter-gatherers with what is to me a wonderful irony. He thinks it possible that Paleolithic societies may have lived by the same principles of focus and independence that researchers find in modern hunter-gatherer groups. "This contrasts starkly with the principles on which nonhuman primate societies and, by implication, protohuman societies are founded . . . ," he writes. "Primate societies are founded on dominance and subordination, and dominance is the subject of competition. Human society could have begun, therefore, by refuting hierarchy and dominance and in establishing in their place what John Stuart Mill considered the only true form of liberty, liberty from the interference of others."

Unlike many cultures of the terminal Pleistocene, the American makers of the fluted point had a style that is almost instantly distinguishable wherever it comes to light. Such homogeneity translates in many an expert mind to speed of passage through continents where all was frontier. The voyage from the high plains to New England probably was a matter of several centuries. How many depends on the way these first people thought about pioneering. It must have been clear to them after a while that there were no other humans in front of them. But obviously there were hazards, a point so under-played in many interpretations of colonization that one comes away with the vision of placid and tasty animals whiling away their lives on quiet plains or in sun-dappled glades just wait-ing for the spear. I don't think the short-faced bears would think much of that picture. I wonder how much Clovis or pre-Clovis meat they consumed.

Glacial meltwater was down from the volumes produced by the early glacial retreats, but there was plenty around. "It's very easy when attempting a paleoenvironmental reconstruc-tion to draw meltwater channels draining a few million square kilometers with a Number 2 Koh-i-nor pen," wrote one pre-historian. "It is a quite different matter to stand on the shore and contemplate crossing the thing." Again, we have the prob-lem of boats, or rather, the lack of evidence of them. Still, re-membering Australia, I give the explorers something to float on, if only a lash-up of driftwood as they cross the braided Mississippi. They raft, swim, stagger in this great rush of gray-brown water. Or perhaps they wait to cross the ice bridges of winter.

A sprained joint or broken bone could easily have been a more common cause of abandonment than disease. These people were probably at least as healthy as any other hunter-gatherers. Their long trek through the high latitudes would have filtered out most temperate illnesses they might have started with. Their bands were too small to provide a decent habitat for tuberculosis or other diseases of crowding. But they had their full share of intestinal parasites, if the coprolites from a few western caves are any indication. The soil they walked on could have contaminated a wound with organisms that produce gangrene or tetanus. The animals they moved among could have transmitted trichinosis or lung pathogens or other ailments that, if not lethal, would have forced the healthy to slow down and tend the sick, or leave them. Whatever its cause, debilitation must often have caused more difficulty than death.

Finally, there was the hazard of insufficient food or water, a hazard encountered repeatedly in the great migrations. Lack of water, of course, was a direct threat. Humans need more water per unit of body weight than most other species. But eating the flesh of animals stressed by drought or other pressures could also present problems. A certain amount of fat is absolutely necessary in the diet of the active forager. Consumption of lean meat can lead over time to metabolic breakdown and death. The hunter on his own ground knows where the living is apt to be scant. A hunter walking through seasonal extremes, through environments entirely strange to him, is at appreciably higher risk.

In the midst of the unfamiliar, and sometimes at its mercy, colonizers would be faced fairly often with concerns over adjusting their customs to new country. It seems safe to say that they would not have given themselves to large-scale tinkering, for when all around you is new, it is bad for general peace of mind, let alone survival, to depart from old ways that have worked.

Mobility seems to be a given, since you can't stay in one place and focus on a few sources of food without summoning hunger. But how much mobility? What is the proper pace for roaming a continent? That is an unanswerable question at this point, and its being so makes for some fascinating guesses.

There may have been two basic ways of covering ground: that of the transient explorer and that of the estate settler. The transient explorers were the marathoners. The mission they gave themselves was to move far more often than not. They were more curious than careful, and they didn't mind losing contact with their kind for long periods. For that reason, they suffered the physical problems produced by inbreeding. High mobility, the stresses of constant travel, often mean low fecundity. Death was therefore a constant companion, for individuals and for bands.

But what if the general level of confidence just wasn't all that high? What if the conservatism and caution observed in many of the remaining hunting groups today pertained in this first colonization? People would want to stick together more, for mutual support, for interchange of mates. Groups might leapfrog each other, or several groups might act as base camps for a pioneer band. These "estate settler" groups would fission, but not as the explorers did. People would stay around longer. When a young couple or family decided that the country over the ridge looked more promising than the game-depleted valley they and their kin had been living in, they would try out the new land and, if things worked out, eventually settle there, coming back over the mountain to visit. Adoption of this strategy would mean higher fecundity, fewer incidences of group extinction, and thus a population growth that in the most favorable places and periods would be quite rapid. Migration rates, of course, would be lower than those of the marathoners, but still probably high enough to sprinkle people, estate by estate, the length and breadth of the Americas in not much more than a millennium.

Perhaps they stuck to the river valleys as they crossed. They could have come down the many fingers of the Missouri to the Mississippi and up the Ohio and the Tennessee and the others. Food is easier to come by in the valleys. And there is always the river, the continuity of flowing water, to give a sense of comfort to the voyager in alien country.

Some may have preferred to stick close to tundra and ice, at least part of the way across. There are nitrates in ice, in the rock flour the glacier has milled. Melting spreads them on the raw ground and encourages rapid revegetation of a sort that caribou and other herd animals find appetizing. Weather close in to the ice might have been more tolerable than that farther out, on the periglacial lands.

Early or late, by whatever route, people at last settled in

New England. Archaeologists think they might have been held up a while by the Hudson, carrying the last memories of the Laurentide to the sea. But by the turn of the Holocene, perhaps 10,500 years ago, they were here. Probably not along the Deerfield but in lower and more comfortable ground. Perhaps even then some of them felt hemmed in. They could go north, following the caribou as they followed the tundra. They could wander out onto the dry continental shelf, but that was apt to be swampy and buggy. Weather was finer and food even more plentiful to the south, but there were people there.

People meant the beginnings of competition. Who gets that hilltop over there, the one with the outcrop of fine flint and the view down into the valleys where you can spot game moving? Who gets that ford across the stream where you can make your kills with a minimum of effort? Who gets that hollow tucked out of the reach of winter winds?

In the mere asking of these questions, in the competition for advantage, people were getting to know this country at the end of the endless journey. They were trained as few humans have been to look, to take things in, and, at least in these beginnings, to share what they saw and heard and smelled. There seem to have been places for that sort of interchange. The Bull Brook site, near Ipswich, Massachusetts, and the Debert site, in Nova Scotia, may well have been two. Both show signs of having been visited several times. There are "hot spots" where artifacts and other evidence tell of several people, perhaps family groups, sharing ground.

Ability to read the land must have been severely tested in New England. Prairies and periglacial regions and drainage systems all have texts that vary as you go along. But here in my home region, everything is measured in pockets. What grows is determined by what soils are in the pockets, what nutrients, what patterns of sunlight and shade, of drainage, slope. Since a millennium or two after ice-out, those living in this part of the country have lived in a landscape of mosaics.

Some degree of that early topographic literacy remains. Ron LaFrance of the Mohawks once told me, "I have a friend who can't read or write much. But he can travel anywhere in the U.S., because he's talked to somebody who's been there. These people are visual and oral. You show me something, I'll remember. That's a discipline that's been passed on. We have that." I don't, nor does anyone of my culture I know. I remember the almost universal ability to forget that my training company evinced back in the Korean war. We had an exercise of passing a simple message back, mouth to ear to mouth, along the files. The last man received gibberish.

Those rendezvous at Bull Brook and Debert were more, I think, than occasions for transfer of information or for marital arrangements between groups. Naming went on — naming of ponds and hills and sentinel trees and trails, of plants and animals and winds. Naming is essential to a sense of place, and that was what was building around those hearths. This was an intimacy with landscape that I, a modern countryman, have always longed for and have never had. LaFrance said his people "have to know our complete relationship to an environment — spiritual, psychic, material, human. If we have no sense of that, we have no sense of place." He said he would give me a bizarre example — bizarre, that is, for whites: he knows where his umbilicus is buried. Mine was doubtless dumped in a landfill close to the Boston hospital in which I was born. LaFrance knows precisely where his body will go when he dies, where his spirit will go. He has that.

5

Among Animals

I COULDN'T PLACE the coyotes. They were somewhere down the slope, perhaps at the near edge of the basin. They had been in conversation since a bit before dawn, making the only noise. Even the small wind shoved at the juniper branches in silence. It was a time betwixt, the moon stalled over the basin and the sun just below the Sangre de Cristo Mountains. The plain below the camp, caught in a trick of light, was at once dun and radiant.

I had come to this San Luis country, the headwaters of the Rio Grande high in southeastern Colorado, for the bison. A couple of thousand of them were moving somewhere below me in the tricky light. The signs at the cattle guards across the roads said "Zapata Ranch, No Tresspassing. Danger, Bison! Stay in Your Vehicle. Do Not Approach." I had not come for these animals, this future meat. The ones I wanted to see, what was left of them, lay nearby, a couple of feet down in fine dry earth. Their brown bones were being excavated by two archaeologists from the Smithsonian Institution, Pegi Jodry, the field director for the project, and her husband, Dennis Stanford, one of the most experienced students of the earliest hunters in the West and their prey. They called their dig the Stewart Cattle Guard site.

I sat watching the sun line creep east toward me across the

flats. I thought about hunting as it must have been, its function for the belly and the spirit, and found myself once again with a balky imagination. I could see the handful of men all right, crouching behind the sand rise. I could see their weapons as the sun reached them. I could think about the mortal seriousness and excitement of what they were about to do. But I could not feel it.

When I was ten, my older brother taught me to shoot — first a rifle, then a shotgun, muzzle-loader, and bow. In the beginning I hunted woodchuck and squirrel and just about anything else that moved. I carry the shame of that excess in one memory — a kit fox, half his head blown away, whimpering himself to death at my feet.

As a college student, I would drive with friends to an old apple orchard, and we would wait for deer in the ghostly cold before light. A decade later, I bought a house in fine deer country fifty miles from my magazine job in New York. Every weekend during the bow season found me on stand or stalking and afterward spending a couple of hours at the salt-hay archery butts I had put up down by the brook.

When I killed, in those prime days, I usually felt pride in the shot, if it was clean. There was no shame in the taking then, just sadness for the taken. When I dressed game, I would talk to it sometimes, seeking the spirit in it, seeking a kind of benison older than any church. The better I got, the fewer chancy shots I took and the more satisfaction in simply moving quietly through the woods. I came to love the thud of the heart, like a grouse drumming, at the sight of a buck fifty yards off, ambling through his morning. I always drew on the animal, but I rarely released at that distance. I would hold on him, the bodkin point of the arrow right against the bow, feeling my shoulder muscles ache and then jump, holding, moving with the deer. Once, in high sunlight, in a stand of white birch, I deliberately overshot, just to hear the harp of the bowstring, to watch the shaft fly true into a rotten stump, to watch prey dodge and vanish in a breath.

But after several seasons, hunting lost its lightness. It became duty, a rite, perhaps, to connect me with something of more meaning than my gray commuter's life, to let me imagine myself a man apart from my gray fellows. At the end of a Saturday's stalking, I was usually empty and angry, and in revenge I made silly shots. One rattled through the antlers of a buck drinking at a pond long after sunset. Another arced over a field and a doe turned into it, taking the arrow far back on the left side. I heard her crash into a bush, heard her scramble. It was too late in the day to wait for her wound to stiffen and keep her to ground. I found the bush, daubed with blood. I followed the trail for an hour, bent at the last like an old man to see the trail. I lost her.

There was no conscious decision to quit after that. I just never hunted again. Anything. I can't even bring myself to kill the red squirrel who is busily replacing the insulation in our house with walnuts. What has happened, I think, is that I have convinced myself of the immorality of taking what I don't need, what I never needed. I have matured, as the more sensitive members of my culture count maturing. In doing that, I thought as I sat watching the San Luis plain, I lost far more than that doe thirty years ago. I broke the connection, as tenuous as it was, with my beginnings as animal and then as hunter of animals. Perhaps it was for that reason that my fancy shrank from joining those figures from the early Holocene I had conjured up, hiding out there on the sun line. I had hunted. I had never been a hunter.

My apparitions were Folsom people, part of a group of a hundred or so who wandered in this basin and beyond, taking bison and smaller animals and perhaps some grass seeds and tubers and wildfowl. They showed up here in the eleventh millennium, just after a long dry period had ended. Their style of making tools fitted their needs for perhaps six hundred years and then pinched out. You can find their projectile points — small, heavily fluted, and so thin some of them are translucent — from Saskatchewan south to Texas and from the Great Plains east into the prairies.

The town of Folsom, New Mexico, can't be more than a hundred miles east-southeast of the Stewart Cattle Guard site, and Clovis lies less than three hundred miles to the southeast. Bands of Clovis were around a bit before 11,000 years ago, for something like 300 years. Perhaps, I thought, given the sanguinary nature of my adolescent hunting, I might have done better in my conjuring by beginning with Clovis. That is, if their reputation is deserved.

A number of prehistorians believe that the first hunters coming into North America exerted enough pressure on some of the large mammals they found here to cause their extinction. They talk about a blitzkrieg, carried out by people possessed of the sophisticated tool kits developed in Eurasia and improved upon by the addition of a sophisticated fluted point. These people were transients in the extreme, engaged in what some have called the greatest trek in the history of humanity — a reconnaissance of two great continents in something on the order of ten centuries. They knew mammoths and some of the other large animals encountered south of the ice sheets. But, the blitzkrieg argument goes, they were not familiar with such tameness, such naiveté. All prey animals deal in escape distances — the closest point they will allow a predator to approach before taking defensive action. These undoubtedly applied for bear and wolf and cat. But man, the newcomer, was a puzzle. He was neither very big nor very fast, so his prey may have paid him little mind in the early encounters.

Hunting large animals makes some sense, if you know how to do it. You get more steak per stab, more hide, bone, sinew, teeth, horn or ivory — and, importantly, more personal prestige. If the animals are so tame they permit you to get within easy range of spear or dart, so much the better. You and your band may not pause to devour the ton or so of meat that could be taken from a mature mammoth. You might dry some, but with fresh meat so often available, you might not even take that step.

I am constantly tripped up by how exponential numbers work. A few prehistorians think, for example, that the food supply of the first people here was secure enough to permit growth of population that could have approached some of the higher modern rates at times — say, 3 percent a year. That seemingly piddling increment, if it remained constant, would turn 100 people into 10 million in 400 years. Even given the usual range of mishaps and catastrophes, humans in the Americas could have exceeded the 10 million mark in a thousand years. Whether they ever did or not is another matter.

The same play of mathematics can be applied to animal extinctions at the end of the last glaciation. Working from modern hunter-gatherer and elephant studies, one researcher assigns a Clovis person and a mammoth to each square mile of theoretical terrain. He makes one Clovis in four a hunter and gives him a mammoth kill every two months. That doesn't sound like overkill, but if mammoths were anything like modern elephants in their reproductive habits, six mammoths killed per year per four square miles of habitat would mean that the animals would be gone from that particular terrain within a decade and from the continent in a few centuries.

There is more evidence in Europe pointing to early overkill than there is in North America; witness the thousands of horse skeletons lying at the foot of a cliff in France. Clovis points are not found all that often in association with the bones of mammoths, a favored prey, and less so with the remains of horses, camels, mastodons, and other megafauna that pinched out here at the beginning of the Holocene. The blitzkriegers don't seem much put off by that. They say that absence of evidence is not evidence of absence. In a blitzkrieg, hunters would be moving too fast to leave signs that could be distinguished from ongoing predation by large carnivores.

Those who believe in the myth of ancient man as consummate hunter have found a home among the blitzkriegers. So have those who, advertently or not, hold that the early people here were just as profligate and ecologically irresponsible as we are. Attacking that argument, the Sioux writer Vine Deloria, Jr., argues that "the overkill theory, like the shifting ice corridors that move back and forth across the northern parts of the continent in accordance with scholars' requirements, falls apart of its own inadequacies as soon as it is examined. We are asked to believe that Indian hunters waded through massive herds of buffalo, deer, elk, antelope, and other tasty game animals" to drive into extinction those that were apt to be less palatable and far more dangerous.

We have the tendency to eliminate life here and there on the planet, usually when we find ourselves in a relatively new environment. In just the past few thousand years, the Maoris killed off the flightless moa birds on New Zealand. The Polynesians severely reduced the varieties of life on Hawaii and other Pacific islands. Americans in historic times killed enough passenger pigeons and Carolina parakeets to reduce populations below recovery levels and took out whole regional populations of deer, bison, bears, wolves, and other coinhabitants. Around the world, we, the wise, wise ones, now bulldoze aside species as if they were rocks in a road.

No one is saying, therefore, that the first hunters here did not hunt, and on occasion, hunt hard, only that the blitzkrieg model by itelf may not be sufficient explanation for the great American extinctions. Those who advance environmental causes have been developing more testable models lately. The blitzkriegers may have to revise their ideas if the dates for Monte Verde and other sites come to be generally accepted, since their argument calls for the arrival of hunters in North America to coincide with the centuries of die-off clustered around the 11,000-year mark. The two sides are beginning to meld some arguments. It is entirely possible, I hear, that hunters gave the coup de grâce to big animals already weakened by deterioration of habitat. This may have been particularly true of the Southwest, of places like the San Luis basin. Things were warming up and drying up here at the end of the Pleistocene, and game big and small would have been forced to concentrate near remaining waterholes. It would have been easier then to take a mammoth, driving the beast into the mud and surrounding it.

Tens of millions of animals — large mammals mostly, a number of birds and reptiles, but evidently no invertebrates — disappeared as the Holocene arrived. The timber wolf outcompeted the dire wolf; the brown bear replaced the short-faced bear. As the mosaics of the Pleistocene gave way to long stretches of deciduous forests and grasslands, animals that had been all but marginal took over the country. The cervids — deer and elk especially — thrived like weeds in the new cover, and bison populations exploded on the new prairies into what some naturalists believe was probably the largest concentration of animal life ever to occur on the planet. Bison horn spans and body size may have shrunk as the animals moved south from Beringia in the late Pleistocene. *Bison antiquus* and *Bison occidentalis* were taken by both Clovis and Folsom people. It is their smaller successor, *Bison bison*, that we photograph in the pastures of Yellowstone and that troop in carefully kept herds, like those on the Zapata Ranch, for the delectation of our palates.

The bones at the Stewart Cattle Guard site are mostly those of *Bison antiquus*. Their horn span ran to about two and a half feet, as against a foot and a half for modern bison and over six feet for the animals that crossed from Siberia during glaciations more than 300,000 years ago. The first time I saw the site, I thought I was looking at some sort of art class. The handful of people working there were very quiet. Some of them hunched over what could have been taken for sketching tables, until they began to shake them back and forth. These were rocker screens, which filtered out any object over an eighth of an inch long.

As I walked in from the road, I could see young people,

some carbonized by the fierce sun, working with masonry trowels and dustpans in perfectly constructed squares two meters across, each divided into four one-meter units. The floor of each dig unit is dug down ten centimeters at a time, excruciatingly carefully, the geometry controlled by a surveyor's theodolite. The dirt goes in buckets to the screens, there to be checked for signs of life. Ah, here's a flake of chert from up in South Park, seventy miles to the north. And another flake, struck off in the making or remaking of a tool, this one from the Chusca Mountains to the south, the mountains where the Anasazi of Chaco, living nine millennia later, went to quarry and to cut poles for their great houses. And these tiny flecks of light, brittle rind? Enamel from bison teeth. What is that brown bit? Touch it with your tongue. If it sticks, it's probably old bone. If not, it's a stone.

The larger pieces, mostly bison bone flattened and crumbled by time and overburden, lay in the dig like jewelry on pedestals of earth, each marked with a bright plastic toy — a dinosaur, a car — to keep an errant foot from kicking them out of position. Excavation has been going on sporadically over ten summers, and in that time some stories of what happened here have come up out of the ground. Not fully formed, though. As so often happens in archaeology, life of the present has been manipulating the evidence of life past. Wolf spiders live in the sands of the basin, along with digger wasps, crickets, June bugs, gophers, kangaroo rats, and pocket mice. Alone and in combination, they engage in bioturbation, working the soil, gnawing on bits of bone, moving them around with their tunneling and nesting. Objects of archaeological interest can sink far below their natural chronological level in the strata of soils or rise far above it. Eyes get expert at reading the various polishes on bone and stone, the sheen that wind and fine sand can put on surficial objects, the scratches that a gopher's teeth make on a piece of bison femur.

It was odd, hunkering beside the tan geometries of the dig, to look at the bones on their pedestals. Not one was human. That is the story in almost every one of these Paleo-Indian sites. There are some Folsom dental remains at the Smithsonian. And Dennis Stanford says part of a skull was found not far from the Cattle Guard, though probably it will turn out to be from the Archaic period of the early or mid-Holocene. In New England, the dearth of prehistoric skeletons is explained by the acidity of most soils. But in the West, where preservation is apt to be pretty good, where are the ancient graves? Perhaps no one got gored or trampled during the ambushing at the Cattle Guard, and it's not likely that anyone would have died of disease — certainly not of starvation — during the band's short stay here. If someone did die, the likelihood is that the body was removed from the camp and placed on a scaffold like those later inhabitants of the San Luis region used, or in a tree, or left on the plain for the predators. Only the luckiest seekers could find any of those remains.

So the story comes from the bison and the bits of chipped and broken stone. They say that the Stewart site was a sometime thing, a refueling stop for a band of nomads whose wanderings in this part of the Southwest might amount to 100,000 square miles in a hunter's lifetime. Several score of the Folsom people camped here for a couple of weeks to a month. Their hunters had managed to kill thirty bison, slightly more than usual. They had probably come in quietly behind the low wind-waves in the sand and struck suddenly from good ambushes. The rest of the time here was spent in butchering, preparing the meat, eating well, feeding their dogs well, going at the business of repairing weapons and tools and making new ones, and getting ready to move on. Probably the last thing they did was to crack the femurs and other long bones of the bison and extract the marrow. Marrow doesn't stay fresh in the bone very long, but it will last longer if mixed with some pounded, dried meat and perhaps some berries and stored in skin bags. This pemmican was an important source of what nomadic hunters like the Folsom people treasured and we sedentaries have come to fear — fat.

Archaeologists talk about the lithic industries of these paleopeople, and they mean what they say. Stone supported this culture in a far more intense and personal way than steel and plastics do ours. Clovis and Folsom hunters and those who came immediately after them were scholars of flints and cherts and other particularly fine-grained rocks. In the normal course of their wanderings, they stepped on cobbles that could have served them adequately. But as records show, from the San Luis basin to West Athens Hill near the Hudson, adequate was not good enough. They found outcroppings of stone that the best of them could work to perfection. They quarried the rock and reduced it to shapes and weights easy to carry. It is possible that even in these beginnings they traded some of the stone, always looking for the flawless and often the beautiful. This discrimination, Stanford has written, might have sprung from "respect for the prey animals" or "special powers attributed to special stones."

The precise methods of the art did not survive. Members of knapping clubs meet today to debate the old techniques as they work their own magic with multicolored stones, jet stones, even bottle glass. Their efforts produce sounds like Disney's dwarves picking away in their diamond mine. Over the rhythms of hammer stones and horn batons, they talk about nipples and platforms and faults and flutes, examining their next moves as if the game were chess.

Stanford is nothing if not a hands-on archaeologist. He has used stone implements to butcher a zoo elephant named Ginsberg (who died of natural causes) and to crack the ripe marrow bones of modern bison to study telltale fracture patterns. He taught himself knapping, consulted with experts on the finer points, and now considers himself acceptable as an artisan. Not up to Folsom standards, though, he says. Pegi Jodry told me of how he looked when he found a complete, beautifully fluted point on the surface at the Stewart site several years back. A thunderstorm had surprised them, and they huddled in the sand until it passed, talking about their upcoming wedding. When they rose, Stanford glanced down at where his affianced had been sitting, and his face went prayerful. There was the point, masterfully chipped out of a piece of mineralized palm. It is, obviously, the Wedding Point, and when they showed it to me, the afternoon light shone through the flutes and I thought I could see the ancient grain.

A couple of lithic experts at the dig had brought cores of various rock, and Stanford borrowed one to demonstrate the elements of knapping. His hammerstone was a sandstone cobble from the Hudson River, and his baton, used for finer work, was from the boss of a moose antler. For the most delicate operations, pressure flaking, he had the tine of a deer antler, flexible enough to pop off thin flakes without grabbing for more. His stone was obsidian from California, a volcanic glass as black as jet that is easy to work and easy to deform beyond hope of repair. He sat there in the shade of a juniper up at the camp and began to bring the point out of the stone.

The fascinating, tricky, and sometimes painful part of knapping is that often you don't see immediately what you've done. The stone rests in the palm of the off hand. The master hand brings down hammer stone or baton at a precise angle to the edge of the stone. There is a flat *tick*, and there, lying under the stone on (or at times slicing into) the skin of your palm, is a thin scallop of rock with an edge from Gillette. If your angle is wrong, you may produce much more of a flake than you intended — or merely a few particles of dust from the edge. If it is right, you have successfully performed one out of scores of knaps to produce a killing instrument. In between blows, you must dress the developing point, taking off tiny flakes here and there or abrading the edge, all to create the thicknesses or platforms necessary to keep the reduction and shaping process functioning. How you shape and position the platforms and the way you strike them measure your skill.

Stanford abandoned his aspirations toward Folsom as he worked and settled for something more in the Clovis line, thicker, with the flutes running a shorter distance from the butt up the faces of the stone. He managed one flute nicely. Talk died. He asked for odds on the other flute. Fifty-fifty, said the lithic experts. He swung his baton six times, missing the butt. Then, *tick*. I thought he had done it. But as he turned the work in his hand, it fell into two pieces. He passed them to me, and I still have them, glued together; except in full sun, you can't see the break.

Hafting these early projectile points was a matter of dulling the edges near the butt so they wouldn't cut their sinew wrappings. The point was set in a slot or socket, wrapped in place, and the whole base was often covered with pitch, mixed perhaps with a little charcoal to harden the coating. There is evidence both in Eurasia and in North America that the hunters of the early Holocene hafted their projectile points onto foreshafts — short lengths of wood, bone, or ivory fitted to the main shafts. The best of stone points did their job well, particularly if the hunter was skillful and lucky enough to strike a big mammal from behind and a little to one side, so that the point could penetrate lung or heart without striking and breaking on bone. But since breakage was common, a hunter needed to carry several points. And since it was awkward to tote along a half-dozen hafted spears, it made sense to turn to foreshafts.

The thrusting spear was probably widely used by Clovis hunters. At some point early on, javelins gained ground, particularly darts propelled by atlatls, the Aztec name for spear-thrower. The atlatl in basic form is a mechanical extension of the throwing arm, a shaft about a foot and a half long with a nipple or hook at the throwing end. The butt of the dart, a shaft of cane or some other light wood about five feet long, rests against the atlatl hook. The throwing hand grasps the front of the atlatl and the dart above it. The most powerful cast is overhand, the hunter throwing himself forward and down on one knee, releasing the dart at the point of maximum momentum. A good atlatlist can hit his mark fairly regularly out to twenty-five yards or so. The impact is far greater than that of a hand-hurled spear. Test darts have struck with enough force to destroy the sensors mounted behind the targets or to pass right through the body of a large animal. The weapon isn't much good in close cover. But on the open plains, it must have represented a technological advance of tremendous significance.

My last night in the San Luis camp, Stanford, Jodry, and I went out for a fancy dinner and afterward lay around a pool and watched satellites beetling among shooting stars. Margaritas had made us philosophical, and after a while Stanford allowed as how the thing that bugged him about being an archaeologist was that he couldn't "remember" — couldn't truly connect with what the bones and stones under his feet were telling him. All he could do was infer. I listened to him and thought of another man very much like him, a bit taller but just as ursine and field-smart. His name is Bobby Garvin, and when I met him he was the drilling supervisor aboard an oil rig on Georges Bank, off the coast of New England.

Both men have the muscles of spirit and body that allow them to be very much in the minority whenever they choose.

Stanford interprets data to indicate that the Folsoms were archers, when few agree, and that the Clovis culture may have developed in the Southeast and spread north and then west to link up with fellow descendants of the original human stock, who entered the continent several thousand years before conventional archaeology says they did. Garvin was forever pestering his superiors ashore to try a different drilling strategy or use different hardware. I remember him in the middle of a winter hurricane out on Georges, staring at the drill string as it turned bits in rock more than 10,000 feet below his huge rig. "Goddam sumbitch," he shouted to me through the driving slop, "if I could on'y see what's goin' on at the bottom of that goddam hole."

I lay on the warm concrete by the pool and watched the tracers of meteorites arc in the bowl of night. Yes, I thought, goddam, if only Dennis Stanford and those who get carbonized with him in this high desert could see what had been what in the depths of time.

*

Mammoths must have been difficult enough to bring down, judging from the behavior of modern elephants, the only beings around remotely like them. Mammoths were social in behavior, given to looking out for one another. A swinging trunk or scything tusk could easily break bones or kill outright. Clovis hunters undoubtedly spent much of their time studying their prey, studying the terrain, waiting until one animal wandered far enough from the group onto marshy ground or into an arroyo. Then they could surround, trap, and perhaps take it.

Modern bison are perhaps one fifth the animal the mammoth was. As the signs at the Zapata Ranch warn, they can be dangerous; a male, weighing close to a ton, can charge at thirty miles an hour. We know that the bison that Folsom hunters worked were much larger than the modern animal and had more formidable horns. Perhaps they were a bit slower, but they were certainly fast enough to run down a man on foot. (I still have to remind myself that there were no horses in these hunting camps.) Despite this, the animals were taken on the American high plains for at least 11,000 years. The coming of the Holocene had given them the paradise of grasslands. Warming and drying during the early and mid-Holocene may have denied them some pasturage in the rain shadows of the mountains, but the limitation appears to have been marginal given the overall size of their habitat.

Surprise was everything in the bison hunt, and the technologies of surprise grew increasingly complex over the millennia. Folsom hunting parties obviously knew how to use natural cover to surprise a herd. They may have learned to take their cover with them in the form of animal-skin disguises that enabled them to get within atlatl-cast out in the open. They certainly knew about teamwork. Their predecessors, the Clovis people, had worked together to take mammoths and bison, and the art of cooperation developed rapidly thereafter.

There are beds of bones throughout the high West marking sites where animals were trapped and killed. Some were driven into the soft sand of dunes, others into arroyos or other sharp defiles where they could be held long enough to guarantee a good supply of meat. Bison are not easily driven. They get nervous under all but the most shrewdly applied pressure. But in time, hunters became so expert that they took to forcing the lead animals of a driven herd off preselected cliffs and bluffs. Hundreds of animals died in these "jumps," maneuvered to their death by hunters who positioned themselves along drive lines, marked with stones, that could run for several miles. Many lines ended in a sharp turn leading to the lip of the jump. The idea was to keep a herd moving slowly along the lines, well out of sight of the jump, and then, at the turn and thereafter, force the animals into a headlong stampede over the lip.

The failure rate must have been high, but the potential yield was clearly enough to keep hunting bands tinkering with their techniques. In the centuries before Contact, they advanced from crude jumps to ramps leading down to well-made corrals. In some of these, shamans may have perched on poles, the better to invoke the cooperation of spirits in the kill.

Drive lines have been found up in the Rockies, and the presumption is that they were used for mountain sheep and goats. Corrals were used occasionally for antelope, though the animals have such a low reproduction rate that they can't take much hunting pressure. The middens of a number of sites in the high broken country hold the bones of many deer. In areas of the Great Basin, people ate deer, the occasional bear, rabbits, porcupines, prairie dogs, mice, and wood rats. They ate cakes made out of amaranth seeds and insects; their cave floors were matted with wild onions and Mormon crickets. But where the bison thrived, the herds — their moods at dawn and noon, in the hot grounds of summer and the sheltered stream bottoms of winter — molded the lives of those who lived with them and off them for hundreds of generations.

I was brought up to think that these early hunters, these folk so much more aware of what they were about than I, maintained a rough balance between hunting band and hunted herd. But this certainty is a shield I no longer carry. The amount of protein piled up after one of the larger jumps seems far more than the people who staged the jump could use immediately; at some jumps, animals at the bottom of the pile remained unbutchered. Some surplus could have been air-dried or smoked, of course. Stored food would have been essential for anyone attempting to live through a plains winter, and many of the drives appear to have taken place in the fall, the logical time to accumulate storables.

Peter Matthiessen, as sympathetic to the native American experience as any white writer I know about, said in an early book that the prehistoric bison hunters, "contrary to sentimental legend, had been fearfully wasteful of the bison. . . . If their winter store of dried meat was sufficient, they killed for the buffalo tongues alone, leaving whole plateaus of rotting carcasses to the swarming plains wolves and coyotes." Still, Matthiessen goes on, the total number of hunters was small, and it was climate and nonhuman predation that kept the great herds from "overgrazing and destroying the vast pasture of rich grama grass that rolled from Canada to Texas."

Vine Deloria, Jr., in the essay I've quoted from earlier, admits that some of the kill sites give evidence of what he calls "an extravagant hunting episode. . . . But since we have no idea how many guests were at dinner that day, even this evidence cannot be called wasteful without further data."

Lack of data again. What would we do without it? What would happen to our grand arguments, our great shows of the best emotions, if we really knew what we were talking about? But true enough, the study of prehistoric human diets is, like most things prehistoric, excruciatingly difficult. Its physical range is limited mostly to dry litter on the floors of caves or well-preserved garbage middens. Molecular biology and chemical analyses of bone can give clues as to consumption over a lifetime but not the particulars of what foragers ate in what amounts or combinations or in what seasons. Even if they could, we are still at a loss to estimate how many foragers foraged during a given period in a given area.

There is some evidence that before they went extinct, *Bison antiquus* exhibited signs of stress that could have been the result of heavy hunting pressure. It is also true that the jump is not noted for its precision as a killing technique. Neither were other strategies. In the hills, on the plains, along the rivers and forest margins, the idea most often was, take what you can when you can get it. Whatever I may once have thought about the hunter as conserver, I can now imagine myself on an early bison drive, shouting and jumping, caught up completely in the play of death and living, blood and feasting, the prestige of standing at the crux of the thing. I would not be thinking then of conservation.

Lack of the proper concentrations of bison or hunters, or both, must have meant that jumps occurred relatively infrequently. Perhaps there were never enough humans to make much of a difference to the bison. Whatever the explanation, the ways of the plains hunters were never so excessive as to produce during millennia what white Americans produced in four or five decades — a slaughter on such a scale that, as one witness told Matthiessen, you could walk for miles and be "never out of sight of a dead buffalo and never in sight of a live one."

The vegetational changes that accompanied warmer climates of the Holocene in the East were just as basic as those accompanying the spread of the grasslands in the West. But here it was the rise of deciduous forests that shaped new associations of animals. The prime signal of change was in the forests. Oaks and hickories and other trees sent seasonal showers of nuts and other rich foods to lie as mast on the forest floor. Browsers moved in to feed there, led in numbers and adaptability by the deer.

There may have been some relicts around from the days of

the ice. Mastodon remains in New York have been dated to the ninth millennium. But as Dena Dincauze, the New England archaeologist, told me, such megafauna were so rare by then that "if our Paleo-Indians saw one, they didn't eat it; they talked about it for the rest of their lives." That would mean that their descendants would be talking about it too, making stories. There is one ethnographers picked up in the Northeast about a great stiff-legged bear. It doesn't rupture the imagination to think that the source of that myth might have been a mastodon, alone as was its custom, plodding and feeding in one of the last holdouts of the boreal woods.

Caribou were probably being taken by small bands camping on the lowlands of the Canadian Maritimes more than 10,000 years ago. They moved in large herds and were best hunted by teams of hunters in the old communal style. As the tundra range shifted north, so did the herds, leaving smaller gatherings of woodland caribou in most of the northern states from Maine to Washington.

The reformation of eastern forests was slow there, fast here, but never so fast as to be more than barely perceptible in a human lifetime. Stresses on life were common, even among those beings who could adapt to the new look of the woods. In places, white pine shouldered aside spruce and other conifers in stands so dense that not much grew beneath them, and the foragers drifted on, looking for canopies that admitted more sunlight. Fires and windstorms killed the pine, and in many of those clearings leaf-shedding trees took hold and thrived. And in time, oaks and hickories were common all through the East, from central and southern New England down the mid-Atlantic coast and across to the edge of the midwestern prairies.

Deer spread through these forests, and elk fed in the glades and along the edges. Turkeys clucked and ratcheted, and grouse made that eerie drumming that is more felt than heard. They were part of the array of wild animals and wild plants that nurtured a way of life, perhaps the most sustainable that humans have developed so far, generally called the Archaic in North America and the Mesolithic in Eurasia. In the eastern United States, the Archaic ways of living flourished from roughly 10,000 to 3,000 years ago. In the far West, they persisted right up to the arrival of the whites.

Eastern ecosystems were among the most varied on the continent. A hungry woman could collect rabbits or opossums or squirrels or birds in nets or snares, by herself or as part of a group, and collect berries, nuts, tubers, and greens. A hungry man, more often assigned by the culture to go after larger game, could take some bears in their winter dens. He could join with other hunters to locate gatherings of elk by their distinctive smell, if the wind was right. Most of all, he could follow the deer, the whitetail.

Hunters in the southern reaches of the East were more apt to organize drives, using fire or other techniques to force the animals onto killing grounds in land traps or deep water. In the north they did more stalking, alone or in small groups. Young men would run their prey down, particularly when the development of snowshoes made it possible for them to outpace a floundering deer or moose. Northerners did come to use the drive, though. There is historical evidence of long drive lines built of brush and operated by the Iroquois.

The spear and atlatl did most of the killing for thousands of years. At the New York State Museum is a diorama of an upstate woodland about 4,000 years ago. A bull elk drinks from a small stream. His head is up. He crouches, sensing but not seeing a hunter with his throwing arm cocked, his dart aimed just behind the rib cage. I don't think the dart missed.

The big question is the bow. It does seem to have been part of the late Paleolithic tool kits in Europe and Asia, and thus it could easily have come over from Siberia and down into this country. The only evidence of its early arrival would be stone points, specifically points that are small enough to be hafted on arrows. Fragments of bows themselves dating to about 4,500 years ago have been found in the Canadian Arctic. The preponderance of opinion is that archery didn't become well established in this country until less than 2,000 years ago.

Once arrived, bow coexisted with atlatl for varying lengths of time in the East. Arrow and dart were about equal in terms of penetration. But straight cane or withe for an arrow was a lot easier to find and keep straight than wood suitable for the much longer dart. Also, a bowman can shoot from just about any position, even on his back with his feet bracing his weapon, and his rate of fire is higher. He can hunt in thicker cover and carry more projectile points, while the atlatlist can do better in a wet environment, where sinew bowstrings might stretch.

Once taken, the deer, like the bison or any other prey species of central importance, became the provider of immediate satisfaction and future security for the hunting community. Brains went to process hide. Rawhide went to make bindings or glue. Tanned hide became clothing, pouches, containers of all sorts. Antlers were worked into points for weapons, into knapping tools, decorations, fishhooks, needles. Bones became scrapers, musical instruments, gaming pieces. Sinews were worked into bowstrings and bindings and thread. Hooves made rattles and glue. All this after the meat had been cut away, muscle by muscle, and dried, smoked, ground, mixed with fat, berries, or nuts, or eaten boiled, broiled, or raw, sometimes several pounds at a sitting.

Those who try to reconstruct the doings of whitetails in prehistory think that their range north of Mexico eventually exceeded 3 million square miles. Their greatest number, shortly before Contact, may have been close to 30 million, not much less than minimum estimates for bison of the period and twice the present population. Human hunters may have taken 5 million or more of the animals annually in these last fat years, and wolves, lynxes, bobcats, and bears several million more. The whitetail may have been decimated locally or forced to move on, but it abided. So strong was its influence on humans that *their* numbers, in the northern forests, might have been constrained by the number of hides a group could tan and fashion into clothing that, hair side in, would get them through the blue cold. And even those who left the forests to ride down bison on the plains with the descendants of the Spanish horse remembered the deer. It was, to the Sioux, still "the true meat."

Archaeologists excavating a site near the Delaware River in Pennsylvania were surprised by what they found. They were sorting through the debris left by foragers ten and a half millennia ago — bits of hackberry and plum and other fruit and fragments of fish bones. Prehistorians had come to accept that the first people did some gathering on the side, but they weren't prepared to see evidence of fishing that early in the game.

Some fish could have been running in eastern rivers that early. Shad feel their anadromous urge when water temperatures reach only 40°F, and striped bass wait for only a couple more degrees of warming. Sturgeon, some of them the length of a small canoe, swam in large numbers prehistorically, both offshore and in lakes and rivers. They start nosing around at a frigid 36°.

All of these fish could have been taken in rivers and streams when people were hungriest, when winter stores were scanty or gone, animals were scarce, and spring greens had yet to show. They and their freshwater relatives could have been especially important, to take one example, when pine forests closed in around the lower Hudson in the early Holocene. So were shellfish, to judge from the huge mounds of their remains built up over the centuries in places such as Dogon Point, on the east shore of the Hudson, and, later, Damariscotta, Maine. You don't get fat eating oysters; there are scarcely four hundred calories in a pound of their meat. But you can get to them as soon as the ice goes out in the estuaries, and they will keep you alive.

In fact, the importance of fishing, even in the beginnings of the Archaic cultures, is becoming increasingly clear. Workers at the Milo sites in Maine have evidence that people were eating shad 9,000 years ago and possibly making fishing nets of fiber not long after. For 8,000 years, people went to falls on the Merrimack River in New Hampshire to take fish running in from the sea. Nothing of their catch was preserved, but the soil where they made their camps has been found to contain mercury, a fairly reliable indication that the remains of fish were buried there.

There is even evidence that Archaic foragers regularly went to sea themselves. The Red Paint people of the Northeast, named for the abundance of red ocher found in their burials, left bones and totems behind showing that by the fifth millennium they had developed the technologies necessary to take marine mammals. A branch of the culture in Maine may have harpooned swordfish. Whales were being taken from Long Island to Florida in late prehistory, if not before, and whale and halibut fisheries were probably operating several thousand years ago on the Washington coast. Stranded animals were great gifts. A pilot whale on the beach contains more than thirty times as much fat as a good deer, and no pursuit is required to get it.

Inland waters filled with bass and trout and bream and pike and catfish in the warm times of the early Holocene. People speared them as they swam, and in time learned to build weirs to hold them captive. Hooks of ingenious design appeared, and new methods of curing and storing the catch. In many parts of the country, fishing grew more important than hunting in the summer season. No food supply was ever to be counted on too heavily. But when fish were plentiful, they could be harvested more easily than the man-wise deer or elk, and as always, the return on invested energy was what counted.

I have read somewhere in ethnography that "primitive" youths know enough to be self-sufficient in their cultures by the time they are just a bit past puberty. Perhaps that is so. But I can't see how a youngster following the Archaic way of life in this country could amass such experience and such insight that soon. She or he would need to know hundreds of beings of forests and soils and air and waters, their names and natures. When do they present themselves to be taken? How are the primeval covenants maintained between them and human beings, the ancient agreements under which they give of themselves so the people can survive? Where is it best to go in the round of the seasons to fulfill communal needs for food and clothing and shelter? What are the signs that tell when the journey begins and ends?

This wisdom developed over millennia on the plains of Montana and Mesopotamia, the forests of New England and northern Europe. Despite the differences in environments on every scale, people tended to study a certain terrain, chosen because it was rich in resources — or as rich as they could expect to find, given slowly increasing competition for territory from other groups in the region. In general, they followed the same patterns of moving and camping to catch the main chance. They lived off the wild.

Then, during the first half of the Holocene, Eurasians found a different path, or, more accurately, a different pace, and that has made all the difference.

The story of this divergence, one of the most portentous in the entire experience of modern humans, is the story Rudyard Kipling called "The Cat Who Walked by Himself." It has become my favorite of the *Just So* stories, because it so simply gives the basic sense of a process that modern science has found so complex. "Hear and attend and listen," Kipling begins, "for this befell and behappened and became and was, O my Best Beloved, when the Tame animals were wild. The Dog was wild, and the Horse was wild, and the Cow was wild, and the Sheep was wild, and the Pig was wild — as wild as wild could be — and they walked in the Wet Wild Woods by their wild lones. But the wildest of all the wild animals was the Cat, and all places were alike to him."

In the story, Man and Woman settle down in a nice cave and the smells of their food drift out to the wild animals. Dog decides he will go and investigate. He asks the Woman what it is that smells so good. Mutton, she says, and she makes a new covenant with him. He will get meat in return for helping the Man hunt and guard the cave. All the other animals come, all make the same sort of bargain, except the Cat, the one animal who insists on "walking by his wild lone." When he does visit the cave, he tricks the Woman into letting him sit by the fire and drink milk. But his half-bargain, that he will hunt mice and play with the baby, is only with her. When the Man and the Dog return from hunting, they throw things at him and chase him up a tree.

Kipling has the sequence about right. The dog was probably the first animal to connect with humans, and the cat, to the extent it is connected, was one of the last. The whens and wheres of the various journeys from the wild to our camps and settlements provoke the usual verbal volleys. Some argue that domestication produced changes in body shape, domesticates becoming generally smaller and exhibiting more juvenile features than those of their species still living free. But even that argument is not often of much assistance when the only guides are scraps of bones mixed together in a midden.

Nonetheless, enough of the puzzle has been pieced together to indicate that by 12,000 years ago the dog was part of human communities, at or on the way to the point of separation from its lupine relatives in their wild lone. Dogs showed up early in North America, somewhat later in most parts of Eurasia. Domesticated sheep and goats apparently came next. Both appeared in western Asia during the tenth millennium and spread fairly rapidly throughout Asia and Europe. So did pigs and cattle, which were living in human settlements in the Near East a millennium or less after sheep and goats settled in. (Cattle also appear to have been domesticated in Egypt and its environs at about the same time.) Pigs descended, of course, from the wild boars that rooted and roamed through Europe, North Africa, and Asia. Cattle were once wild oxen, like the aurochs, handsome animals that worked the forest edges, the cows red, the bulls black and sometimes six feet high at the shoulder, with long horns pointed forward like a brace of darts. Horses were broken some 5,000 years ago and a thousand years later were changing the way humans lived on the Asian steppes, and later in Europe. And cats came and went as they pleased until the Egyptians found them hunting rats in their granaries and persuaded them to take up residency in their temples.

The imbalance is obvious. Dogs, sheep, goats, cattle, pigs, horses, cats (plus chickens and ducks in the Far East), entered human societies in Eurasia or northern Africa. Here, across the huge landmass of North America, humans made do with the dog, which may have followed them across the Beringian land bridge from Siberia, and the turkey, domesticated in the Southwest only a few thousand years ago. Domestication was only slightly more widespread in South America, where the llama and alpaca were tamed about 6,000 years ago and the tasty guinea pig, about 3,000.

There were sheep in North America, the mountain sheep in the high country of the West, but there were no goats. Our mountain goat is really an antelope, a relative of the European chamois. There were no wild oxen; the bison is a cousin so distant as to be in a different category. There were no wild boars. Horses went extinct here fairly early in the Holocene. There was nothing around that could pass as a house cat. And the camel, which evolved in North America, left the premises for Eurasia, where it entered into a cranky agreement several thousand years ago with those who valued it as a pack animal in dry country. Even our reindeer, the caribou, have not cooperated. All in all, there was not much to draw from here when it came to faunal domesticity.

Species living with other species is nothing new. Blue jays

and oaks inadvertently help each other to survive. Ants and a couple of hundred kinds of plants do the same. Crabs and sea anemones are found in such a symbiotic relationship, and I hold clear in my memory the sight of a sea turtle rising from a Hawaiian reef with a circlet of golden fish feeding about its neck. We share this old farmhouse above the Deerfield River with squadrons of mice and snakes, some rats, and that nefarious squirrel messing with our insulation. Deer and turkeys graze in our fields but have no intention of coming any closer.

It is this penchant in certain species for sharing space that has given domestication such strength. The great herds in northern Europe let hunters come within a surprisingly short distance before making off, and gazelles in the Near East evidently permitted themselves to be moved toward the killing corrals with far less effort than that necessary to jump American bison. It makes sense, then, that in certain places, under certain conditions, hunters moved toward being herders. So much so that though the European reindeer cannot be said to be truly domesticated, it supports Lapp and other human cultures with milk, meat, and transportation.

Some evolutionary biologists have been working on ideas that explain how symbiosis — sharing — can become outright dependency. Periods of extreme climatic and environmental change, they think, can trigger shifts in evolutionary balances so that genetic advantage falls to organisms that exhibit the greatest adaptability. The late Pleistocene, with its melting glaciers and the ensuing disappearance and emergence of entire ecosystems, was surely such a time. There were new, recently deglaciated lands to explore, new niches to fill. Plants and animals that stuck to old and specialized ways tailored to the exploitation of stable ecosystems were pretty much out of the running. But those who followed the pioneering way — those who survived the pioneering — were liable to prosper. Many beings opted to explore, among them some wolves, sheep, oxen, boars, and ourselves.

The traits that best bolster defense of long-time habitats —

a strong sense of territoriality and attendant suspiciousness and aggressiveness — are not those fit for pioneering. To excel at that, a being needs to be accepting of others, even desirous of their company, to put the usual human interpretation on the matter. That way, it can cross boundaries onto alien turf without presenting much of a threat. It is docile, though not out of fear. If it has a fairly high reproductive rate, so much the better: its progeny can fill up the newly discovered habitat (an animal's address, in ecological terminology) or niches (its "occupation" within its habitat) faster than the competition can.

Biologists call these traits juvenile, and like those exhibited by more "adult" stocks, they are genetic and not merely behavioral. They are the products of evolution, of an evolutionary process called neoteny, in which some groups of wolves, say, remain puppyish into their breeding years and pass on this package of playfulness and flexibility to their offspring. Descendants of the ancient Asian mouflon are believed to have become progressively more neotenous as they moved out of their lands of origin, across Beringia, and down into the Rockies to take up their duties as mountain sheep. Smaller sheep became more inclined to follow large ones, and the horns of the rams grew in size so that it was possible at a glance to recognize who the leaders might be. On their own trek across the continents, following well after the sheep, Amerindian males lost body hair and beards. Fewer men went frontally bald or grayed until they were rich in years, and the differences in body shapes between men and women decreased markedly.

An evolutionary biologist named Ray Coppinger says that neotenous species were "eyeing one another" just before forming what he calls the "domestic alliance of the Holocene." Most of us, if pressed, would guess that as part of the eyeing, people went out and brought home wolf pups to raise as family pets. That doesn't seem to be too viable a way to domesticate, though. A young wolf is still a wolf, and if she sees a child running from her in a certain way, her lupine instincts might lead her to run the child down as prey. Historical evidence indicates that native people of North America were forever bringing home baby wolves and bears and raccoons, even moose and bison. But the pets most often ended up in the pot.

Wolf and human lived very similar lives in the late Pleistocene. Both ranked among the most intelligent of terrestrial animals. Both had the social skills to form groups for the hunt and for survival. Indeed, the two were in some form of association more than 100,000 years ago; archaeologists working in southern France found wolf skulls placed at the front of human shelters in a cave complex. But what Coppinger is saying is that the growth of this association, part of the growth of interdependency among people and plants and animals, was basically not our doing but evolution's. The process followed Kipling's path through the wet wild woods: the animals came to us. In Coppinger's metaphor, we didn't write the story of domestication but simply edited the first draft.

We are awfully good at nonverbal communication. That talent would have made it easier on the approaching animals. Neotenates all, they — or at least their young — were disposed to solicit care from us, and we were not only willing to give it under the right conditions but able to communicate our willingness. The conditions seem to have been that the animals would not seriously compete for the resources sustaining us and that they would not cause a serious fuss in our communities.

As we settled down, we would have furnished animals and plants with one of the central driving forces of evolution: new energy sources. Our middens, our lodges, and what passed for our latrines were loaded with nutrients. Even as nomadic hunters we left some of our kill, along with salty urine, beloved of animals such as reindeer, and feces, food for many canids. Very early on, wolves followed us as we followed the herds. Their young would have wandered into camp, whining and begging as they whined and begged in their parents' dens.

The women, the children, would feed them. The male pups would get obstreperous in time and be driven off or killed. The females would hang around and every once in a while produce a litter; one or two of the pups might survive the hunger or temper of their hosts. And so it would go, over millennia, leading on to dogs.

Hoofed beings, the ungulates, would have been drawn to places where by accident or on purpose we had burned over a stretch of ground, opening the way for the advent of seed- and berry-bearing plants in satisfying variety and profusion. They would have fed on wild grain, as we did, and that must have created severe problems, particularly when we began tending those grains. Again, the wandering calf might be left to its devices while older animals were spooked or hunted down. Again, the males would have been more vulnerable to these pursuits, since they were or appeared more threatening. Their bones are more common than those of their sisters in the garbage pits of the ancient camps. Slowly, the wild sheep and goats and cattle and pigs and horses came into some sort of balance with us and our culture, in which they would tolerate our taking some of them for food and clothing in return for our toleration, grudgingly given though it might be, of their presence in our fields and on our middens. Slowly the balance changed to include the use of their muscles on our croplands or our roads, in return for more intensive care on our part. But that came late, as did the breeding that increased the yields of their milk or the power of their haunches.

Domestication is now so extensive, so apparently irreversible, that it conditions life. Yet it began as a process confined to only a few regions, the Near East prime among them. Why, then, did humans in these few centers of the new covenant act as they did? A conventional guess is that human success in finding food in these places led to expanded populations, which led to increased stress on the food supply and the consequent need to augment that supply. We might do well to reconsider Alice at this point. The business of species eyeing each other is another way of saying, as Dena Dincauze did at the beginning of this book, that "all living things must constantly monitor and respond to each other," especially when the responses they choose produce significant change. The Red Queen, seeking to live in the lands of the Tigris and Euphrates as the Holocene came on, would have had to trot a bit faster to do so.

That is to say, humans forced into hard times by the pressure of their numbers or an environmental change had to make new choices in order to survive. In the Near East, wild gazelles would have sustained them in the early and fat times. But the gazelles (which we may have tried and failed to domesticate) dwindled away. In fact, few wild animals remained, in part because humans had come to haze them from their grain fields. Those that did stay close by were increasingly suspicious, bolting at the sight of people. But the tamer animals, the camp followers and crop stealers, did not bolt. They were the best source of meat. They were what one researcher has called "walking larders," fresh food you could take with you instead of storing and hoping it didn't rot. That advantage may have furthered the domestic alliance in some instances. So might other factors, including our ancient and abiding curiosity, our wondrously powerful drive to intervene. Given the script, why not edit?

I daydream these days of elephants in North America. The Indian elephant was domesticated to a degree, the African elephant far less so. I dream that the Clovis people paused in their killing of mammoths and thought about taming them. They were successful enough to pass on a few semi-domesticates to the Folsoms, who tinkered some more. The net result would have been, of course, that when the Pilgrims landed at Plymouth Rock or Ponce de León on the Florida coast, they would have been met by combat commands of screaming proboscidians. Now, *that* would have been a proper Encounter.

Of course, no such thing would have happened. The Clovis culture obviously had no opening for an animal that needed tons of sedges and coarse grasses to keep it happy. Nor was there much in Clovis camps that even the most enterprising mammoth could put to profitable use. And that kind of interspecific detachment continued through the Holocene. The wild sheep of Eurasia may have been attracted to stands of wild and later domesticated grains in the Golden Triangle, but the sheep of North America stayed in the mountains, far from the larger human concentrations. Ducks and geese did visit the camps as they migrated, yet there is no evidence that they were induced to stay in any numbers. It is also possible that some of our rodents could have been persuaded to act the guinea pig, but the record does not indicate that they were.

John Pfeiffer, a student of prehistory, has written that "no one in his right mind would domesticate animals if he could get meat regularly and without large and increasing exertion in the wild." I have no doubt that during some periods of the American Holocene, especially in arid areas or those struck by drought, people had great difficulty in getting meat. When that happened, they moved on or ate other foods for a time or perished. They had no other choice. The complex preconditions that domestication requires did not exist here, and the only way to get meat was to hunt rather than herd, to keep faith with the prey, to seek the benison. In so doing, the first people here escaped the burdens of caring for dependent animals for thousands of years, only to be themselves burdened eventually by a people who did not.

6

Hands in the Leaves

"STANDING ON A WINDSWEPT ridgetop as a thick fog rolls up the wooded valley, it is easy to imagine the place thousands of years ago and to dream of unknowable things."

That is the last sentence of a five-hundred-page dissertation written in 1985 by C. Wesley Cowan, then a graduate student, submitted "in partial fulfillment of the requirements for the degree of Doctor of Philosophy (Anthropology) in the University of Michigan." The dissertation is called, in the armored terminology of upper academe, "From Foraging to Incipient Food Production: Subsistence Change and Continuity on the Cumberland Plateau." But what it really is is a sleuthing job in the mysteries of the prehistoric use of plants. Cowan sets up hypotheses, drawing from as many disciplines as he can. He tests his ideas with archaeological evidence he and others have gathered from the ridgetops, slopes, and sparse floodplains of the Red River basin in eastern Kentucky. And then he does some extrapolation to build a tale of how America east of the Mississippi came to be a cradle of horticulture in its own right, one that left behind a record in carbonized seeds and desiccated leaves so extensive that it may well serve future researchers as a laboratory for the study of agricultural onset around the world.

Since in my youth I accepted the Big Indian, looking out in his Plains feathers across the Deerfield River, as indigenous to New England, it was only natural that I should associate pre-historic agriculture in the East with the West — the Southwest, to be specific. I knew that the Pueblo people out there grew corn, for my older brother had brought back some of their tissue-thin blue cornbread from Arizona. It made sense, I thought. Some of those Hopis had just picked up and moved east. They probably took pity on the Pilgrim Fathers wandering around lost and cooked them up a mess of corn fritters. Fritters were and are my favorite food, and I could not imagine anyone refusing them, even those insanely temperate, self-purging Puritans.

I had gone a bit beyond these pleasant suppositions by the time I visited the University of Michigan a couple of years ago to talk with Richard Ford, who was the chairman of Cowan's doctoral committee and has spent years in the consideration of how man and plant — actually, in most cases, woman and plant — formed their undying alliances. Ford was generous enough to spend the better part of three days with me, talking plants. He showed me specimens of seeds and fruits that over time produced surplus, the cushion for civilization. And he directed me to Cowan and other colleagues and former students working around the country in the vineyards of paleoethnobotany.

Ford and his network got me started on an idea I could not at first accept: plants, among the most sessile of beings, came to us as much as we went to them. And as was true of the neotenate animals that now graze in our pastures, it was the opportunist, the adaptable, the weed that joined us in our early habitats. We cleared the way for the plants that would be our allies. Our fires burned woodlands and prairies, opening canopies to sunlight, creating mosaics and edges where ruderals could flourish. We tore the earth in our camps, wearing away the cover with our feet, digging in it with sticks to make dumps for our wastes. And the weeds came in, drawn by disturbance and the concentrations of nutrients we provided.

Members of the few remaining hunter-gatherer societies tell the scientists who rain questions on them that they really do love meat. Yet the scientists sit with them at their meals and find that they eat an abundance and great variety of plants. It seems reasonable that to differing degrees, the first people here should have followed that pattern. We find wild onion parts in their caves and fruit seeds near their hearths. At the Monte Verde site in Chile, which, you will remember, has yielded apparently reliable dates back to 13,000 years ago, the remains of 42 species of plants have been recovered. Whether all were used in early diets is unclear, but their abundance in the record is for some researchers an indication that the Monte Verdeans might well have eaten more seeds and leaves than meat.

A story has sprung up that has us becoming the agents of dispersal for plants whose seeds were once carried far afield in the guts of mammoths and giant sloths. Gary Nabhan, a botanist-writer who roams the Southwest, came across a theory that the enormous concentrations of fairly tame animals we encountered as we sauntered down the continent would have captured our attention and imagination to the exclusion of all else. But once climatic change and our skills at the chase had dispersed or killed off the game, our eyes went to the ground. Nabhan found that though bison remained and flourished north of the Rio Grande, few herds of big animals remained in Mesoamerica. But plants that had coevolved with those herds were still there for the taking. Were they — the gourds, the fruits of the yucca — taken? Nabhan made a list of almost a hundred plants that had been in league with the big animals of the late Pleistocene and found that half of them had been tended, transplanted, or in other ways encouraged by early human inhabitants of Central America. "Did these Neotropical dwellers take up the gourd, and its seeds," he asks, "to become their agents of dissemination and increase? Did we, as a species, become one more way that seeds reach suitable sites?"

Mesoamerica — which can be roughly defined as Mexico and upper Central America — has long been a shining star for prehistorians in this country. They have looked at the power of its civilizations and professed to see evidence of cultural diffusion northward. Not many years ago, the temple mounds of the Mississippi River were thought to have been the intellectual if not the physical offspring of construction engineers south of the Rio Grande. And when tiny remnants of squash were found in the Midwest in contexts suggesting they were 7,000 years old, you could almost hear the collective "Aha!" Mesoamericans domesticated a squash or cucurbit 8,000 years ago. Clearly, they had passed on their handiwork to the horticultural dunderheads to the north, still gnawing on underdone meats beside their small fires.

That bias has relaxed considerably of late, and with the broadening of scientific focus has come a willingness to accept native botanic wit for what it was. The scientific memory now speaks of the hundreds of wild plants known and used by North American peoples for food, medicine, and ritual. Grasses in the Southwest, agave, mesquite. Tubers on the plains. Fruits and seeds of dozens of weeds, shrubs, and trees in the East. Something like two hundred plants or extracts therefrom ended up at one historic time or another in our national pharmacopoeia. If native Americans of white acquaintance knew about the makings of aspirin, about digitalis and the beginnings of insulin, if they had access to materials that eased rheumatism and congestion and drew the poisons from infected wounds, then surely at least some of their understanding had been received from generations long gone. After all, some of the plants discovered in the ancient strata of Monte Verde are still used in that region today.

To be fair, prehistorians simply did not have the tools to reach back to the beginnings of horticulture in the United States until the past decade or two. Lacking them, archaeologists often used to ignore plant remains, burying them in the backdirt of their digs. Now they run their sediment through fine screens and then apply a water flotation process that allows buoyant bits of plants to float to the surface. Electron microscopy permits easier identification and, in the case of seeds and their casings, a way of judging whether or how much humans have been tending them. Beams of electrons that can count carbon atoms and establish ratios of carbon isotopes can date plant remains that only recently were too small for that kind of work. Even the analysis of the carbon in human bone can yield an idea of what plants an individual ate.

With this suite of procedures and the fieldwork it has helped encourage, a very different opinion is developing. Those early cucurbits in the Midwest and elsewhere were probably not domesticates. They may well have been not Mesoamerican but rather remains of a native cucurbit, which itself may possibly have been a progenitor of the Mesoamerican squash in question. Wild as it seems to have been, the plant was of enormous use to people who had no handy containers except the paunches and hides of animals they had killed. This alone would have focused human attention on cucurbits, making them a candidate for the processes of alliance: first tending or encouragement by removing competitors or aerating the surrounding soil; then cultivation — active tilling, transplanting, and sowing; then domestication and deliberate breeding of increasingly useful and productive varieties. For cucurbits in what is now the United States, that ultimate taming occurred less than 4,000 years ago, and it occurred in the East. The thinking now in some quarters is that from these gardens, over time, came highly edible squashes like acorns, crooknecks, scallops, and a good many ornamental gourds. The cucurbits of Mesoamerica begat pumpkins, marrows, and a few ornamental gourds. Quite a reversal.

Wes Cowan is a reversalist, one who went out and found a place where he could whittle on his ideas. As a student in Kentucky he had taken to hiking the runneled western edges of the Cumberland Plateau country, in particular the spectacular ridges and hollows of the Red River basin. On one trip in 1976 he and a friend headed for a bald sandstone knob they had located on a topographic map. It was called Cloudsplitter Rock and it looked to have a commanding view of the north fork of the Red. It had that, and it had more. At the base of a sheer drop down the western side of the rock, Cowan found a large overhang. There are thousands of such recesses scalloped out along the miles of cliff lines that run from horizon to horizon in those parts. Sometimes two form on opposite sides of a promontory or ridge and meet in a "lighthouse," which becomes, as differential erosion progresses, a natural bridge. There are more natural bridges around the Red than you'll find in areas of the Southwest that are famous for them.

Like most overhangs or shelters, Cloudsplitter had been worked over hard by people after pots or arrowheads or other items of marketable antiquity or people driven by the myth, common in the Southeast, of a silver mine found by one John Swift and then lost. Some of the digging could have been done in Civil War days, when the nitrite-rich sediments of the shelter floors were used to make gunpowder for the Confederate cause.

Cloudsplitter had more drawbacks. It could be reached only by a steep trail snaking through slicks of rhododendron and mountain laurel. But the potential difficulties faded when Cowan started scratching around the rock falls on the floor of the shelter. He found evidence that sediments there were deeply stratified, and strata bring great comfort to a field archaeologist. The strata also contained things archaeologists rarely find in the Cumberland, or, for that matter, anywhere else where soils are moist and acidic: nut fragments, bits of grass, pieces of wood, and other organics, all preserved by Cloudsplitter's arid interior. Here was a chance Cowan had been eager for, to address the puzzle of how humans had lived at Cloudsplitter over the millennia, how they had altered their way of life with the changing times. He would use plants as the paper trail.

Cowan told Richard Ford about Cloudsplitter. Ford knew

firsthand about the problems of interpreting materials excavated at a rock shelter. Pot hunters aside, these places are home to a number of animals that bring all sorts of objects and bury them, thus raising about as much hell with the stratigraphic context as the wolf spiders and rodents do at the Stewart Cattle Guard site in Colorado. Some wild rats even dig pits and line them in a maddeningly human manner. But the richness of Cowan's evidence was strong, and the two men set about writing grant proposals and making scouting trips to Cloudsplitter. Digging started in 1978, and so much was found that a lot of it is still being studied in Ford's lab in Ann Arbor and in Cowan's in Cincinnati.

Radiocarbon dating of relevant organics indicates that Cloudsplitter was occupied intermittently by small groups of people from about 10,000 to about 2,000 years ago. That roughly coincides with the Archaic and part of the ensuing Woodland cultural periods in eastern North America, during which the continent settled down from its climatic convolutions after the ice of the late Pleistocene began its retreat. Archaic peoples moved about less and less as time wore on. The sweet spots, the floodplains along the larger rivers, filled up first, then the tributary valleys and then the uplands. People became more territorial, though their territories remained large for a long time. Buffer zones developed between territories and other places risky to visit, and these became refuges for deer and other hard-pressed animals.

There were reasons other than social competition for sticking closer to home. As the Holocene warmed, new food resources came into play, and people needed time to get to know them intimately and to perfect technologies for harvesting them. The most welcome, in many places, were the nut-bearing trees. Oaks prospered in California. Piñon spread north along the skirts of western mountains, to the delight of nut gatherers there. In New England, nut trees may have provided enough food to offset the loss of resources as the rising Atlantic sent its fingers inland.

In Wes Cowan's Red River country, as elsewhere in the temperate East, the trees of exceptional merit were black walnut in the early Archaic, and by 6,000 years ago the hickories. Hickories grow today on the steep slopes of the basin, and walnuts in smaller numbers on the bits of floodplain.

There is a law of optimal foraging that archaeologists have borrowed from ecologists. Cowan makes use of it in trying to simulate the decisions Cloudsplitter's occupants made in gathering their food and other necessities. He humanizes the law, which, like so many scientific models, abstracts humanity from what is human. Cowan's foragers have minds of their own, shaped by culture, personal health, personal hunger. They are not always or even often simulants of *Homo economicus*, that eternally rational cipher. But they do tend to understand their tasks somewhat as the law assumes they should. They would agree at some level with what Cowan says by way of introduction to his work, and what we have been saying in earlier chapters: "The most successful foraging strategies are those that minimize the amount of energy expended in foraging activities."

In order to minimize their energy and maximize their return, the people at Cloudsplitter, consciously or unconsciously, would be asking themselves certain questions: What kinds of foods yield the greatest advantage to our band or family? What kinds of places should we visit to get those foods, and in what seasons should we go, and how long should we stay? In what numbers should we forage? A late Archaic or early Woodland forager, one living in the Red River basin during the transition from foraging to food production, would be thinking about how fat and how big and how reliable or predictable a given food resource was, how far away and in what terrain, in what densities, how mobile, how risky to go after in terms of both personal injury and coming up empty-handed.

Animals such as elk, pigeons, and migratory waterfowl could be present in large numbers and the birds in magnificent density, but they were too mobile to be regulars on the list of Cowan's optimal forager. Most other animals in the East don't usually wander very far from home ranges that measure only a couple of miles across on average, but they tend to be solitary except for a few weeks out of the year. In the Red River country, deer, turkey, raccoon, fish, and turtle, in that order, were the most likely to be around. Bears taken in late fall or early winter were the fattest, but there were only a few in the basin. Turkeys came next in fat, thanks to the thick "breast sponges" of the big toms, and then deer, coons, and possums.

Plants producing tubers and greens were the most secure year to year. Fruits, berries, chestnuts, butternuts, black walnuts, and hickories were less so, acorns and blueberries least so. I know about that from the pair of English walnuts growing outside the windows of my writing place. They drop a great crop at the beginning of one fall and practically nothing at all the next. Cowan told me that the same thing applies throughout the eastern mast forest. These natural rhythms are often skewed by late spring frosts that can pinch the flowering trees and drastically cut the fall harvests.

But what the nut trees lack in reliability many of them make up for in fat. The hickories fairly drip in oils. Then come butternuts and, in decreasing order of fat content, black walnuts, acorns, and chestnuts (the last two being high in carbohydrates). In the Red River basin, these trees were numerous enough to provide a great deal of food for man and beast in the good years. Since the bad years were staggered among the species, the overall quantity and quality of nuts, despite frosts, unusually destructive fires, and frequent insect infestations, made them by far the most important of fall foods.

The problem, of course, was late winter and spring. Game animals in any season were nowhere near as plentiful under the canopy of the Red's forests as they were in the open bluegrass country to the west, where deer and other game roamed. The deer that did winter near Cloudsplitter could lose a third of their fat. Greens and tubers didn't show up until spring was well along. So this was often the time of starving, of eating hide and bark and needles. It would have been more so if people had not learned to pay close attention in the glad times of autumn to the rain of hard-cased fruit from the canopies above them.

Wes Cowan took me to Cloudsplitter one hot day in the summer of 1991. We parked just off the road that runs along the north fork of the Red and climbed up switchback trails, over deadfalls, and through the jungles of rhododendron. The cover was so thick I couldn't see the cliff line until we were almost beneath it — two hundred feet of tan wall running the length of the headland and on along the next, and presumably the next and the next. Right above us was the Cloudsplitter overhang, perhaps forty feet high by twenty-five deep and fifty wide. Fallen rock littered the floor, and on one or two of the great slabs the old ones had set up their nutting center. They had made small depressions to hold nuts for shelling and one or two deeper ones that might have served as caldrons. Hickory, the nut of choice, is a devil to work with. Its shell is so convoluted that the meat comes out, if it deigns to come out, in pieces too small to satisfy a mouse. But if you smack the nut and throw it into something that will hold water, and you heat the water with hot rocks from the fire, wonderful things happen. The shell bits sink to the bottom. The meats and oils float. Scoop them out, work them to the right consistency, and you have delicious hickory butter.

Cowan took care as he moved around the rock shelter. He put everything in this repeatedly vandalized place back where he found it, reminding me to do the same (I hankered after a piece of worked chert he had picked up from the floor), even choosing with some deliberation where he would fire off an occasional round of tobacco juice. Probably only one family lived here at first, he said, and they didn't stay long — maybe a few weeks. Later the place may have been a temporary home for the equivalent of two families, say, ten or twelve people.

Digging down in the shelter's sediments, Cowan and his

associates had found layers of nut remains, some a couple of feet across and a foot thick. Then they began to notice that in time the place had become more organized. Living quarters were here three or so millennia ago. And over there was a series of large storage pits. They were empty when uncovered, but some looked as if they had been lined with conifer bark, perhaps against insect invasions. One was big enough to have held 30,000 hickory nuts.

"I view those storage pits as a sort of prehistoric insurance policy," Cowan said. "They were dug in a year of superabundance of nuts, filled, and covered over, hidden away, protected with rocks to keep predators and other people from getting in. Because this overhang is so dry, the nuts could stay here, certainly for a year, probably for a couple. The people who put them here would always know they were here. They would come back if their other groves of hickories went bad that year. The fact that we found those pits empty would suggest that they did have to get into their insurance policies." Those nuts must have tasted like the best of love on a sleeting night in late February.

There were the remains of other plants at Cloudsplitter, scattered at first, almost insignificant in the record. The few shards of hard squash rind weren't particularly surprising. Cowan is something of a squash freak and is forever nosing about with the Smithsonian archaeologist Bruce Smith looking for cucurbits and other plants that were manipulated by prehistoric easterners. He told me that squash containers had been found in Salts Cave and other caverns in Kentucky. They had been brought in by people mining gypsum, probably for its white pigment, and mirabilite, probably for its strong emetic properties — purging being good for both body and spirit.

What was more exciting were the seeds and stems of some plants that didn't grow naturally in the Red River area. They were all annuals, Cowan wrote in his dissertation. They were

and are weeds, "able to withstand a variety of habitat conditions ranging from flood-deposited alluviums to sidewalk
cracks in many of our cities. They are a major pest to our agricultural land because of their ability to invade cultivated fields,
and are controlled only by the application of thousands of tons
of commercial herbicides."

Six of these "problem" plants caught Cowan's attention at
Cloudsplitter. They make up the major share of what Cowan
and Smith and others call the eastern agricultural complex,
the weeds that first set foragers in this country on the trails to
farming.

Sunflower began its association with North American humans probably somewhere in the West. The wild plants usually have many small heads whose seeds fall to the ground in
random fashion. Any good forager would want larger heads
whose seeds would stay in place until late in the fall, and by
collecting plants approaching that ideal and then sowing their
seeds the next spring, people made the ideal a reality. Even the
oil-rich seeds (actually achenes, or small, one-seeded fruits)
grew larger. It is difficult to estimate just how important sunflower became in the East, but examinations of the coprolites at Salts Cave indicate that it constituted a quarter of the
weight of these preserved human droppings.

Sumpweed, or marsh elder, loves the churned soils of river-
banks and grows there in stands paralleling the stream. Its
seeds are quite small, but they too are rich in oil and compare
in overall nutritional value to the hickory and walnut. Sumpweed has been around human settlements in the Midwest for
at least 7,000 years, but no one knows where it was domesticated. Tamed it was, though, as evidenced by an increase in
the size of its achenes.

Goosefoot, a chenopod, is a plant whose seeds are high
in carbohydrates. I am partial to the leaves of a related plant,
lamb's quarters, in a spring salad, and I assume earlier foragers
were too. Goosefoot also seems to have been domesticated, as

the seeds at archaeological sites appear to have lost their thick coats.

Maygrass shows no such genetic alteration, but it was cultivated. So was erect knotweed. Both are starchy and similar to starchy goosefoot in nutritional values. Giant ragweed, the king of disturbed ground, is a relative of sumpweed and probably was permitted to hang around so that people could make use of its oily seeds.

Here are plants that — with the exception of the sunflower, which has gone on to oily glory, and the chenopod, some types of which are grown commercially in Mexico — are all but unknown in this country except to farmers trying to eradicate them. And yet in their time, they made human life substantially more livable. Of course, early yields probably weren't that high in the Red River basin, where flat ground is still held in semisacred esteem. But they increased slowly over a millennium or so. Then suddenly — the dates at Cloudsplitter cover the period from 3,100 to 2,940 years ago — the eastern agricultural complex came to visit: plants, seeds, requisite technologies, and all.

People seem to have left the floodplains to give the plants more room and to have moved themselves into shelters like Cloudsplitter. The increased presence of berry bushes and other changes in forest composition indicate that canopies were opening up and ground was being broken, much of it for gardens along the river lands.

A garden of sunflowers, sumpweed, goosefoot, and the rest, a garden that measured about 225 square feet, would yield about 20 percent of the needs of a family of five people for a month. That's really quite good. Several gardens would have yielded enough for instant consumption and some for storage (knotweed and other seeds have been found at Cloudsplitter in storage cysts). And the more seeds the people in the shelter stored, the more they could offset the bad nut years. With the weeds came a small added measure of the true human grail: security.

They were no miracle food. All were deficient in essential components, such as the amino acid lysine. But you can get lysine from animal flesh. Several of them had to be densely broadcast in the gardens to produce sufficient quantities, but broadcasting is no demanding art. Early on, the plants of the eastern agricultural complex were no more than a dietary supplement. But they made a difference. "For a modicum of effort," Cowan wrote, "a family could *produce* [emphasis his] quantities of storable commodities that could be utilized during the winter and early spring when the natural availability of wild foodstuffs is severely limited."

Cloudsplitter, in prehistory and history, has been on the edge of things, isolated in a beautiful and poor land. If the coming of food production could cause impacts there — growing band size and attenuation of landscapes — clearly it would cause more of them on richer soils. In fact, the eastern agricultural complex came to influence life in a large area of the continental interior between 2,250 and 1,00 years ago. By some estimates, its suite of plants was cultivated or domesticated over territory running from the Louisiana-Arkansas border well up into Illinois and from the Appalachians west to the edge of the prairie. And by then, spreading out from river-bottoms in Ohio were cultures that were producing some of the most eerily beautiful artifacts and constructions ever seen in North America — the early mound builders, those who introduced concepts similar to those carried to such heights at Cahokia.

Few would say that these blossomings were based on sunflower or sumpweed. The Adena culture, whose last and perhaps best remains are to be seen near Chillicothe, Ohio, made its early appearance around three millennia ago and supported itself on wild animals and plants and perhaps some tame cucurbits. But the Hopewell culture, which arose sometime around 2,300 years ago, certainly did avail itself of garden- or field-grown crops.

The Adena and Hopewell cultures appear to me exuberant. They were sufficiently well organized to build impressive earthen geometries — walls and conical or angular mounds and at least one long and sinuous serpent that still draws the summer crowds. One or another of them made pottery vessels, in part to boil plants for their oils. They made striking objects of copper and of several stones — mica cutouts of bird effigies, a raptor's claw; gleaming ear spools; long and perfect ceremonial projectile points of blue-gray chert; pipes carved in the shapes of animals so that you could draw gustatory and visual pleasure from your totems in a single act.

These people traded their goods over a huge area. They brought in copper from the deposits near Lake Superior. Their marine shells came from the Gulf of Mexico, some of their exotic flints from North Dakota and Indiana. They imported obsidian from the Yellowstone region in Wyoming, and steatite, a soft stone for making pipes, from the Appalachians. They brought in quartz from Arkansas, freshwater pearls and lustrous ores of lead from the Mississippi Valley, and silver from Canada. Some of these things went to charnel houses where the dead were prepared for their eternities, and from there, with the bodies, bones, or ashes, to the great mounds.

The mounds probably were ceremonial places. The people may have lived in relatively small settlements, following their seasonal rounds. But as production increased in their plots of goosefoot and sumpweed and sunflower and all, they apparently stayed closer to home. Their tools tell a story of some land clearing here and there. So do shifts in the pollen records and the signs of storage pits for seeds and the proliferation of clay cooking pots.

The taproots of what modern Americans accept as agriculture — that massive improbability by which two or three people out of a hundred keep the rest alive — grew first in southwestern Asia. They grew in an arc from the Jordan Valley up into southern Turkey and on down into the Zagros Mountains of Iran, a great sickle laid across the upper reaches of the Tigris and Euphrates rivers. The ground was prepared for them by the adaptations of hundreds of human generations to the climatic changes following the ebbing of the glacial influence in that part of the world.

The Levant of 11,000 years ago was considerably more hospitable, from a plant's point of view, than it is today. Nut trees spread into the area from the Mediterranean, and pistachios and almonds could be had. Stands of wild cereals — barley and emmer, an ancestor of modern wheat, among them — grew denser and more predictable with the coming of the Holocene. Wild gazelles, sheep, and goats came for the cereals and added to the larder. In time people began to concentrate on the foods that satisfied them most in terms of abundance, fat content, predictability, and just plain taste. They foraged and they harvested. They encouraged their favorite plants to the point of dependence, the one on the other. They tended their favorite animals to the same point, moving from careless herding to serious pastoralism. And at some juncture the two inadvertent processes of domestication became one, and that one spread out to transform the lands of Europe and Asia and, after millennia of further concentration, the Western Hemisphere.

Barley was probably the first cereal domesticated in southwest Asia. The telltales of enlarged seeds began showing up around 10,000 years ago. There is evidence at some sites in the great sickle, the Fertile Crescent, that sheep and goats came under domestication before emmer and einkorn, another important precursor of our modern wheats, and barley and rye and legumes such as peas. But at others the two processes seem contemporaneous, and the ambiguities will remain until a lot more data have been acquired and interpreted.

In arid Mediterranean regions, people looked increasingly to domesticated plants for their security. The two engines of modern agriculture linked up around 8,000 years ago in and around the Near East. The pace is remarkably similar to that of horticulture in eastern North America: first some slow and spotty experimentation over a couple of millennia with one or another plant food source, then the sudden coming together of a complex. The so-called Neolithic agricultural package of domesticated plants and animals caught human fancy in only a couple of centuries.

Between roughly 8,000 and 5,000 years ago, this domestic alliance spread from the Near East northwestward to the Hungarian plain and then across the flatlands of northern Europe. Clearly some groups in its path signed on, but much of the impetus came from colonization by practitioners of the new faith. Farmers were building their settlements in the Paris basin as early as 6,500 years ago and in southern Scandinavia a millennium or so later. The components of the alliance changed with the topography: sheep and goats, essentially open country animals, remained mostly in the south at first, and early farmers in the northern forests concentrated on cattle and pigs; rye and barley did better in northern soils than the wheats of the south. But overall and in time, the process of agriculture turned Europe around. When domestication of the horse brought great power to the nomadic people on the steppes to the east, their most tempting target turned out to be the farms in the west. The long stretch of invasion by mounted hordes could be seen as the first general evidence that stockmen don't like (or are envious of) nesters.

I just placed a small plastic jar on my writing desk. It contains about fifty seeds, not one over a fifth of an inch long, each mottled in off-whites and tans and gunmetals. They look a bit like the fossilized teeth of baby sharks, though their edges are smooth. They are as hard as rock. They are the fruit of a plant that many researchers now believe was the ancestor of the most powerful grass in the Western Hemisphere and, together with wheat and rice, in the world. The grass is, of course, corn, or *Zea mays*. What appears to be the ancestral plant is called teosinte, and it grew and grows in the high valleys of Mexico on down through Guatemala. Like the other signatories to the domestic alliance, it was drawn to the ground humans had disturbed and enriched with their waste.

My seeds are a gift from John Doebley, an evolutionary biologist who works in a high tower at the University of Minnesota near the state fairgrounds. Doebley has been studying how teosinte came to be corn, looking at genetic structures. The transformation is something to see. Teosinte has numbers of branches or laterals, well adorned with tassels and what passes for ears. Corn has a few laterals, some set with large ears where they branch off the main stalk. Teosinte's many "cobs," to start with, were like tiny rattlesnake tails, shorter than my little finger, containing perhaps a dozen or so of these baby shark teeth set in two rows and covered with a hard protective sheath, or glume. Today's many kinds of corncobs have at least eight rows and more than a hundred kernels. The wild teosinte ear shattered and spread its seeds over a fairly wide area. The domesticated corn ear remains intact, waiting for the harvester.

Doebley and his colleagues believe that just a handful of genes accounted for most of the metamorphosis. One was able to soften the armor covering the teosinte kernel, something that would have been disastrous for a plant growing among predators but was acceptable for one growing among human tenders. Another replaced the tassels at the bases of the laterals with ears. Another reduced the ear's tendency to shatter; another doubled the rows of kernels to four. "If you took those [genetic loci] from maize and put them into teosinte," Doebley told an interviewer from *Science*, "the thing you'd have in front of you would be called maize."

Small maize, to be sure, but an improvement over teosinte. And teosinte itself was an improvement over many seed foods. Tiny as they were, its seeds were the largest of just about any wild annual grass in prehistoric Mesoamerica. They may have been tough to dig out from under their coverings, but Doebley respects the ability of hunter-gatherers to take food where they could find it.

No one knows how much of the creation of maize was a willful act. People may have learned quite early that the best way to retain a desired characteristic in a food plant is to isolate it from its kind. But whatever the special tricks, the general techniques of dealing with teosinte could simply have been a part of the overall optimal foraging strategy in those places.

Nothing in the way of genetic change would have occurred so long as gatherers were taking the plants and eating the seeds. But when they began to save the seeds and sow them, the transformation into corn could have begun. Women looking for the seeds would naturally pick ears that had not yet shattered, though the season might be advanced. They would pick ears with larger seeds or more of them or with softer glumes. Some of those seeds would go back in the ground the following spring.

That attention to detail could bring about great morphological changes over a couple of thousand years, perhaps more quickly. And combined with the great genetic variety in plants like corn, it could also create — this time with more deliberate purpose on the part of the handlers — a wide range of shapes and colors and other traits. John Doebley puts part of this fanciness down to the fact that in the Americas, the digging stick and hoe and not the sickle were the tools of choice. In the Fertile Crescent, sickles of stone and later of metal cut down emmer and einkorn plants by the hundreds. There was little chance in this harvesting, Doebley told me, to pick out the few individual plants exhibiting interesting natural mutations. But in the high fields of Mexico, a woman worked from plant to plant. In time she and those who followed her could fashion corn twenty-seven inches high or almost twenty-seven feet high, or beans in genius colors, or chilies that would delight the palate or melt the teeth. In Europe, that range is hard to find; perhaps the broccoli clan, with its cabbages, brussels sprouts, cauliflowers, and others, is the best example.

An early form of maize was found in caves near Teotihuacán in Mexico and dated to around 7,000 years ago. That would make early efforts at making corn out of teosinte roughly contemporary with the taming of cereals in southwest Asia. From its natal basins in Mesoamerica, maize traveled south through Central America into South America. The beginnings of that journey would not have been too difficult, since this scion of a tropical grass was spreading through the tropics. But moving north was a different story. Fairly quickly, maize would have encountered lands where days were longer and growing seasons shorter, and that must have given it pause. Whatever the precise reasons, the plant did not take root in our Southwest, generally considered to be its first home here, for a while. Researchers using accelerator mass spectrometry, a method of directly measuring carbon 14 in very small samples, put the date of arrival close to 2,000 years ago.

The original story archaeologists developed was that corn was at first regarded as just another grass seed, though admittedly one with a lot more carbohydrates produced with more predictability than the wild foods could muster. The first ears were probably of the pop variety — twelve rows on a short cob, a type known as chapalote. When increasing aridity became a problem, they were planted at higher elevations, where growing seasons were shorter but where water, essential for growth, was more plentiful. And they were tended, so the conventional story goes, pretty much the way hunter-gatherers treated so many other plants: with an encouraging hand in the leaves and a promise to return.

If I planted my 'Silver Queen' white corn (sweet corn is a latecomer to the breed) and took off across the hills on other

pursuits, I would be one sad harvester upon my return. My present field is hard by the dog pen, and even with the whole pack of us in residence, rodents and the occasional raccoon drop by for a snack. Our extended absence would be an open invitation for deer and just about anybody else in need of a little starch to come and munch. Perhaps such visitors were rare in the Southwest. Perhaps the loss of a good many ears was acceptable to people who were harvesting hundreds of plant species, but I wonder.

A new story is gathering strength, though. It tells of corn being brought to the southwestern highlands by groups of Mesoamerican highlanders who were cryptofarmers, not just foragers with a yen for some handy grain. These cryptofarmers, more sedentary than the average forager of the region, were forced north, probably by drought, to the then moister Colorado plateau around 2,200 years ago. When the plateau itself began to dry out, say around 1,500 years ago or a bit earlier, maize culture shifted south, to areas where the Hohokam culture developed a sophisticated system of irrigation canals (many of which lie under the asphalt and concrete of Phoenix and its environs) or where the Mogollon culture built check dams and used other techniques to husband water and take advantage of the natural moisture in places as superficially forbidding as the bases of sand dunes.

Real and overt interest in corn doesn't show up in the Southwest until about 1,800 to 1,300 years ago. Even then farmers kept an eye on wild plants, using those that crept into their gardens and fields and going after those in the wild when crops failed. But they worked on their maize, developing an eight-row ear that was easier to grow in dry times and easier to grind. Maize and other plant staples changed these peoples' myths and their world-views. The Zunis of northeastern Arizona were reported by one ethnographer to believe that "of the substance of all flesh is the seed of seeds, Corn! . . . Let us therefore love it and cherish it, as we cherish and love our women; and it shall be the giver of milk to the youthful and flesh to the aged."

In most of the places around the world where agriculture took its firmest hold, there were grasses at hand to provide starch and some sort of legume for proteins: the cowpea in Africa, the mung bean in the Far East, peas and lentils in the Middle East. In Mesoamerica the wild version of the common bean grew together with wild teosinte and — a source of oily seeds and later of edible meat — wild cucurbits. A thousand years ago, only five hundred years before the Encounter, the plants were growing in northeastern fields. The Iroquois and other regional groups called them the Three Sisters. Maize needs nitrogen, and the beans provided some. Squash and beans together provided groundcover that kept heavy weed infestation to a minimum and increased the soil's ability to retain water. And the three together provided a remarkably balanced diet — not perfect, but far better than any of the Sisters by itself.

The appearance of maize in the East is even more of a mystery than its introduction to the Southwest. Some say it was concurrent with that introduction. If that argument turns out to be true, it becomes very difficult to explain how this seed of seeds could have come across the prairies, with their thick sods, and the arid lands of the South at such speed. Perhaps it came along the rivers, downstream to the Mississippi and then upstream into the eastern woodlands.

For about 600 years, from roughly 1,800 to 1,200 years ago, maize was one of many food plants. But then it began to rise toward dominance among the sumpweeds and sunflowers of the eastern gardeners. Plant part analysis shows that, and so does analysis of human bone; corn eaters have more of the isotope carbon 13 in their bones than eaters of hickories or most other plant foods. Between 1,100 and 900 years ago, maize became a true staple in many areas, though the use of wild foods of all sorts continued to be very important. Its use appears to have been greatest in places like Cahokia and Fort Ancient, in Ohio, and the lands of the Iroquois in New York.

By eight hundred years ago, the Corn Mothers were watching over most people east of the Mississippi and two centuries later had extended their oversight along the riverbottoms to the Rockies. By Contact, hundreds of maize strains grew in every imaginable terrain except salt desert and rock peak. Hopis on their mesas grew corn segregated field from field, each strain with its holy color. (And they grew the fiber and ate the fatty seeds of another culture-shaping plant, cotton, brought in from the south, possibly by the *pochtecas*, traders moving out from the centers of high Mesoamerican culture.) Onondaga planted the grain among the bodies of girdled trees. Hurons let their grain ferment into a black mass and ate it. Other peoples ate some of their corn green and parched the rest, or popped it or roasted it. They stored it underground and, in the Southeast, in cribs. They cleared fields or prepared fallow ones by burning, and the ashes sweetened and enriched the soil for a while. They buried few fish in their corn hills, even in coastal New England: the people had no way of transporting the number of fish that would have been necessary to do any good. If Squanto did indeed teach the pale newcomers to manure their fields with herring, he was probably teaching them a trick he had heard about during his time in Europe.

If the chronologies of eastern corn use are correct, someone will eventually come up with a convincing idea that explains why the grain hung around on the fringes of horticulture for so long. Perhaps a lot of the corn was consumed immediately in its green state and not stored for future sowing. Perhaps it was a food reserved at first for the elite or for ceremonial purposes. Perhaps the amount of effort required for its intensive cultivation — especially field clearance and maintenance — was more than gardeners of the time wished to expend. One argument does seem firm: corn did not become important in northern areas until eastern eight-row, a type that could produce well even in southern Canada, became available. But that doesn't explain the lag of maize development in the Southeast, where temperatures and day lengths were well within the range of the early strains.

I remember hearing an archaeologist in Maine, David Sanger, talking about why agriculture wasn't accepted in so much of his region. There were enough frost-free days along the coasts to grow corn, but little was grown north of the Saco River. It turns out that even in southern New England, corn agriculture didn't produce the concentrations of population expected of serious cereal cultivation until after the whites provided a market. Why not? Sanger thinks the answer may have had something to do with the price tag on an ear of maize: "If you grow me, you're going to be stuck here. No more shuffling around. And while you're here, there is going to be a political organization that will control you."

That's a hard bargain for someone who likes the freedom of wandering, even if it's wandering from seasonal camp to seasonal camp. Not that anyone actually paused to read the fine print on the price tag; our sensory equipment is not always up to estimating such long-term consequences of our actions. But word may have drifted through the forest clearings of life in the big villages, where corn was queen, where status was culturally ascribed and not achieved in the hunt or on the warpath, where the elite used grain surplus to increase their power.

Thousands of small choices over sweeps of time eventually became one choice of tremendous importance: to rely on the domestic alliance for survival. Surely a good many alternatives were tried beforehand. People could have fought hunger for a while by moving, shifting their diets, trading for food. But eventually, for many there must have come a time when *not* to grow food would mean shrinking numbers, vulnerability, and either absorption or extinction.

Hierarchical societies sprang up long before the first fully domesticated grains did, in southwest Asia and here. Their chieftains, "big men," and their retinues could have had great influence on the amount and type of foods grown, for whom, and the amounts stored and then distributed or traded. Their priests could have brought a sanctity to the production of food that turned it from choice into cultural destiny. That occurred to a far greater extent in Asia and Europe than it did in North America, but it did happen here.

This process of the world's oldest domesticate domesticating its fellow beings, never inevitable, became in the long course of time irreversible. We began it with choices to spare and ended it with but one choice. It became an enormous engine of production and consumption, one that fed what is probably the most remarkable and certainly the most rapid transformation of human culture in the entire span of our presence. It feeds it still.

You don't go to the Red River in eastern Kentucky to prove that point. Not much prehistoric maize was grown here. A lot more was raised by whites, who cleared fields on the steep slopes and thereby contributed to massive erosion. What does show up here, simply and clearly, is evidence that even small populations grow and that their growth can affect how people live. Wes Cowan knows that nut collecting increased around Cloudsplitter as the Woodland period gathered strength. So did harvests of berries, the fruits that signal disturbance of the landscape by storm, flame, or human hand. To Cowan, these are some of the clues that signify more mouths, more hands in the leaves. A stable population might have been able to deal with periodic failings of nut rain. A larger one would need something else. The need was partially met by plants, many of which were foreign to the Red. To go further than that right now would be to outrun the evidence, to dream of unknowable things.

7

Costs of Living

IT IS LESS than twenty miles from my home above the Deerfield to the hill town of Conway, where I did a lot of my growing up. You drive downstream, past the Big Indian, through Buckland, and then on south. My parents bought property, a ridgetop farm, in Conway in 1927. I remember motoring up there, driving past good grasses bending in the wind, smelling the elixir of cow manure, of open earth. These were the signs for me that I was back in farming country. That made me, a child of summer people, wildly proud. My Conway had farmers. They did the things I dreamed of doing, and they lived in one place year round.

I live in farm country now, though just about every dairyman has sold his herd and what were working fields are now filling up with fake colonial houses. I still want to look on farming as about the most salutary pursuit humans have stumbled upon, a turn toward the light on the road of our existence. But I have heard too much to the contrary to keep a shine on that childhood faith. Prehistorians have told me that agriculture is hazardous to our health. None has said this with a face that stayed straight. It's a hammer stroke, and the point it is intended to drive home is that over much of its short existence, the production of food has also produced stresses on our habitats and on ourselves that have been often high and sometimes intolerable.

Much of the good evidence for this argument is interred with our bones — a femur out of round and marked with strange lines across the end, the eye sockets of a skull so porous they look like grotesque pumice, arrowheads punched through the back of what was once a mouth. Small grains of pollen tell the story, and miles of drowned soils and grassy heaths. Small specks of charcoal tell it, picked from raw mineralized ground where a great pine went over.

The story begins 10,000 years ago, about the time when we who for millennia had been leaving notices in cave paintings and in the boneyards of our animal jumps of our intentions to run the world began to run it. The story carries the sounds of stone axes in the temperate forests and the smell of smoke where the trees thinned to grasses. It carries the memories of endless woodlands turning into mosaics of trees and clearings and, with the coming of the big plows and the ox teams and the machines, returning to homogeneity, the monotony of field after field after field.

As always, parts of the story were around long beforehand. Fire, the early farmer's delight, was ancient when the first of us ran from it on the African savannas (and perhaps returned to prod and then taste the roasted carcass of a rat or antelope). For millennia we had it on loan from lightning strikes and glowing lava. Perhaps 30,000 or 40,000 years ago, we started on the road to becoming a prime source of ignition.

Fires permitted us to head for the northern territories where winters were hard enough to kill us. They teased fats from nuts and flesh and brought stews and mushes to higher levels of palatability. They kept our enemies away or flushed them from dry cover. Used with skill, they could keep woodlands open; the ash fertilized the soil, sunlight brought grasses and tangles of berry bushes to the glades, and deer, moose, elk, bears, and turkeys came after the new foods. We killed the animals and ate the berries and some of the grass seeds. We were the true prometheans, using our flames to make new landscapes, turning woodlands to our advantage, building grasslands where none had existed, building the beginnings of our civilizations.

A lot of skill was involved in all this arson. Sometimes we got careless or forgetful and did our burning when times were not propitious. Then the fires went beyond control and destroyed what they were meant to manipulate. Some think that happened near what is now Boston, to name one name, in late prehistory. But in general we learned what cycles to follow to encourage the particular species composition we favored. We learned that burning too often prevents fuels from accumulating to the point where the flames can perform their assigned tasks, and burning too seldom can result in a conflagration that takes everything. The trick was to have a grasp of the variables — the fuels, the wind and the weather, the season, the life strategies of the forest beings. By and large, we mastered it.

Clovis and Folsom people undoubtedly used fire for hunting and other purposes. Early peoples in California probably used it to keep down insect infestations in their stands of oak. Prairie hunters used it to drive their game herds and to encourage early greening in spring so the buffalo could get a head start on the year. Southeasterners were accomplished burners, especially as their agriculture intensified. So were the inhabitants of the temple towns along the Mississippi and cultures farther east. It is said that the natural philosopher Benjamin Silliman sent out queries from Yale in the early nineteenth century to ascertain why the familiar signs of Indian summer were fading — the red sunsets, smoky air, burning eyes. Oh, said at least one respondent, that's because there are fewer Indians burning the woods in the East. Another wrote, you ought to come out to Wisconsin: we have just the ticket for you when the Indians start touching off the brush for their hunts. Residents of Boston in the 1700s looked up and saw the sky black with smoke from burning forests in Quebec.

Fire historians in this country say that burning by native people changed environments more than any of their other activities did. Yet, to state the obvious once again, their numbers were too low to have much of an effect, except in periods of heavy drought or on the long and heavily fueled fetches of the tall-grass prairies. In the East, you can read their fire histories in the woods around their camps and settlements. They burned a lot in the light soils along the coasts of southern New England. Hempstead Heath, on Long Island, was probably maintained by a burning cycle. But upland woods from the north country down to the Berkshires were usually too moist to burn well and long. They are known in the fire trade as the asbestos forests and contain maple, yellow birch, beech, and hemlock.

"There were far more extensive acreages burning on a regular basis in the past in North America than are burning today," says William Patterson III, a fire ecologist at the University of Massachusetts in Amherst. But he also thinks that "burning forests to get rid of them appears to be more characteristic of early Stone Age people in Europe than it does here." He admits to conjecture but says that "there is no real evidence that Indians converted large areas of forest to open land for agriculture, whereas [people] clearly did, from about 6,000 B.C. on, in Europe."

Of course, they had more practice. Neanderthals were burning European forests 100,000 years ago, and flame and spear traveled together throughout most of the region until well after humans began settling down during the last ice invasion. Thereafter, it was flame and axe and flame and plow — to use the terminology of the fire historian Steven Pyne — that teamed up to produce the open grounds of Europe we see today. Actually, what we see is a good deal more forested than it was a century ago, thanks to advances in farming that have led to the retiring of marginal agricultural land and to the rise of hydrocarbons as the preferred fuel of the Europeans.

There is no such thing as a free lunch. Everything costs. Everything is related to everything else. You can't do only one thing. These are the cautionary canons of our environmental age. Some of us, myself included, no longer question them. But few of us yet understand that they have been true for all life since it began, and especially true for us since we fell in love with our opposable thumbs.

Fire helped us change landscapes so that we could get more of what we needed from them, but over time it also helped turn some of those landscapes into alien terrain. Even the seemingly innocent and advantageous business of settling down eventually tendered its bill. We gradually came in off the trail for any number of reasons. There were too many of us in some regions to permit unrestricted wandering without getting into delicate matters of turf. And the more time we spent in our rendezvous, the more appealing they seemed: feasts and marriages and the telling of tales, the touching. Time in the home camps was easier on the women, for whom pregnancy and childbirth while the band was foraging carried high risks.

A number of researchers who have scratched their heads over these cultural and social developments feel that as home camps were occupied longer, even while we were still leaving them to make our seasonal rounds for this food or that purpose, populations began to increase. Slowly and erratically, yes, as we've seen, but persistently, after the fashion of increments. The idea has been advanced that populations of hunter-gatherers living in Europe just before the beginning of the Holocene were increasing at only 0.01 percent a year. Yet in the millennia just before the arrival of agriculture, Europeans were increasing ten times faster. During these times of slow sedentariness, more children were being born and living longer. The usual forager's birth spacing of about four years,

enforced by regulations on intercourse, by natural abortifa-
cients, by lengthy periods of breast feeding, or by infanticide,
was shrinking perceptibly.

Sedentariness, along with art and other cultural advances,
was once thought to be a product of agriculture, but no
longer. You'll remember that on the eve of the Encounter
there were people in Florida and on the Northwest coast who
had developed fairly complex nonmigratory societies without crops. Even in the cradles of European agriculture, people
stayed pretty much in one place for thousands of years before
they turned from domesticating themselves to taming other
forms of life. In what is now Israel, they were living in permanent stone huts and harvesting wild grains against the winter
when the Beringians were crossing to North America, a feat
that seems somewhat less singular when you consider that
dwellings per se came into use as far back as 400,000 years ago.
And as for art, keep in mind those cave paintings in southern
Europe, done when the glaciers were still standing high in the
north. And keep in mind that several millennia earlier, people
in Europe were making adornments in specific regional designs, and that in central and eastern Europe they seem to
have been storing food on a regular basis.

I have mentioned several reasons that foragers might have
turned to farming — all of them partial, I'm sure. There is
another, more intriguing: seduction. In at least some regions,
domestication of food made life somewhat easier, at first. It
certainly helped during the times when wild foods were scarce.
So much so that fewer died in the hungry months and populations grew faster. Only when the negatives of agriculture grew
high enough to be worth noticing might some fieldworkers
have complained. By then, of course, there were too many
stomachs to fill to risk pulling up stakes. And where could they
go? Their farming had changed their world. Much of the wild
game was dead or had been driven off; many of the wild plants
had been cleared away from their landscapes.

It is easy, once we appreciate the full effects of our curiosity and cleverness, to blame our kind for just about any sort of environmental reshuffling that we don't like. It is also dangerous. Climate, that prime architect of landscapes in the early Holocene, was and is very much with us still. Our goats may have contributed to the extension of deserts and the ruination of Greek hillsides, but it should be remembered that climate shaped the Sahara from 6,000 to 4,000 years ago and created badlands here and there throughout the world as the Holocene evolved. The general rule, often broken, seems to be that climate sculpts on large scales and at higher elevations, while we have preferred to rework the lower lands, bit by bit.

Perhaps the greatest difference between Old World and New lies in their respective pollen records. K. E. Behre, a German palynologist, writes that "in densely inhabited regions, i.e. in large parts of Europe, human activity completely masks the natural factors." In other words, intervention, particularly agricultural intervention, became such a factor over time that it is increasingly difficult to determine what natural vegetation in a given area might have looked like. "This applies to central and northern Europe from the Middle Ages onward," Behre writes, "and to the Mediterranean area since antiquity." By contrast, one survey of vegetational change in eastern North America shows that out of several hundred pollen sampling sites in that region, fewer than a dozen showed definite signs of human intervention in the plant world. Others may show up, but still the difference between manipulation in New World and Old is striking.

It makes sense that the Mediterranean region, especially parts of the Golden Crescent in Mesopotamia, should bear signs of some of the most intense human alterations. Agriculture made one of its earliest and strongest starts there, and it did so on what was delicate land. The look 10,000 years ago was a bit reminiscent of the hills in some parts of southern California — dry but fertile enough to support oaks and pistachios among the herbs and grasses. In fact, the first farming was dry farming, and evidently it was sufficiently successful to produce enough surplus to encourage both population growth and concentration.

The great leap forward occurred in the major river valleys of the Near East as well as in Egypt, China, and India. There, often under skies that gave down niggardly amounts of moisture, people began to dig canals that grew in extent and complexity. Meltwater and rainwater that had once flowed directly to the sea turned in to these elaborate ditches and brought vegetal and cultural life out of aridity.

Clive Ponting, a British historian, has written in some depth about human impacts on the environments of the world. "In its broadest sense," he argues, "human history in the 8,000 years or so since the emergence of settled agricultural societies has been about the acquisition and distribution of surplus food production and the uses to which it has been put. The size of the surplus available to a particular society has determined the number and extent of other functions — religious, military, industrial, administrative and cultural — that the society can support."

Certainly, to the hierarch a surplus of anything valuable is as catnip to the cat. *Someone* has to manage it. And in the process, the managers often manage to organize people in civic brigades which over time can produce first tombs of increasing elegance and in the end cities, which, if the surpluses hold out, offer their citizens such glories as cathedrals and crowds. The bargain has been that the commoners sweat at the monumental stones and the elite, in all their borrowed power, act to allay public fears of disorder and ruination.

Something of this sort happened in Mesopotamia for a while. By 5,000 years ago, dynasties ruled in the region. Writing appeared, much of it evidently devoted to keeping track of the surpluses of grains and fruit and the jewels of trade. In the lands of Sumer, in southern Mesopotamia, a handful of large cities controlled the regional economy and ecology. Irrigation canals were extended farther and farther from the watercourses. Forests were cut for firewood, construction, and manufacturing.

Irrigation can waterlog soils. When soils are hot as well as dry, the sun evaporates the moisture rapidly and salts build up on the surface. Salinization is not always inevitable; the Egyptians along the Nile managed to stave it off. But it happened in Sumer and in many other places throughout history, including areas along the modern Rio Grande. The Sumerians saw their soil whiten. They planted more barley, which tends to resist salinization better than other crops. They fought among themselves and with neighbors for what had become the necessities of their lives. And they lost — to a drier climate perhaps, to superior arms, to the consequences of their own actions.

Middens, not of the pack rat but of a small mammal called a hyrax, tell a similar story about Petra. Abandonment was nothing new in Jordan when Petra got its start. But the city grew into a mercantile center that sparkled right up through Roman and Byzantine times before it disappeared under the sands. What the hyrax gatherings indicate is that by the time the Romans appeared in the city, enough oaks and presumably pistachios and other trees had been cut down to turn the landscape into an anthropogenic steppe.

Shelley's traveler from an antique land saw sights like this before coming across the blasted statue in the sand. It is he who tells us of the ironies of our aspirations, who remembers the words on the pedestal: "My name is Ozymandias, king of kings: / Look on my works, ye Mighty, and despair!"

Plato despaired. He saw what most of us never can bring ourselves to see, the impact of our lives on our world. His was a delicate world, like that of Mesopotamia, not tolerant of our mauling. Humans burned woods in Greece and grazed and farmed. The climate bore down, and the hillsides blanched and went bare. In spots, only the olive could drive roots deep enough to find water. And Plato wrote, "What now remains compared to what then existed is like the skeleton of a sick man, all the fat and soft earth having wasted away, and only the bare framework of the land being left."

Agriculture left fewer scars in northern Europe. It rained there more during the growing season. The soils could take more punishment than those of parched Mesopotamia, and support more vegetation. Smoke from early farms wisped away over forests that often ran from horizon to horizon in the lower lands, relieved here and there by waterways or a reach of grassland.

The first wave of farmers — there were several — came into Europe along the rivers and stayed with them for a long time. Some new work suggests that they were not overly given to swiddens, plots made by the clearing and burning and cropping and moving on usually associated with primitive agriculture. Instead, their settlements were often permanent, islands of humanity on the rich ground of riverine meanders, some of them lasting for several centuries. They lived in longhouses that would have made the proudest Iroquois take notice, some divided to accommodate people, grain harvests, and livestock, others built more grandly, as if to house the elite.

In about a thousand years, say, farming communities in northern France and Germany began moving up the slopes to the edge of plateaus overlooking the valleys. Many were heavily stockaded, indicating a time of raiding and feuding. That in turn would probably mean an intensified competition for resources, owing to population pressure or a harsher climate, or both. Since cattle were coming into popularity at the time, one of the resources in demand might have been grazing land; if so, one reason people were moving out of the valleys was to clear pasturage on the slopes.

In another thousand years, the plateaus themselves came under farming. Nothing could be done with them earlier, since the upland soils were heavy and water lay too far below the surface for the grains to drink. What was needed was a heavy plow that could turn the soil in a furrow and bring the moisture closer to the surface. With such a plow, and the ox teams to pull it, much of Europe opened to agriculture and to the new advantages of agriculture — not just meat but work animals, dairy products, and wool. Resource pressures lessened for a while. Settlers scattered across the uplands, and these new pioneers left fewer signs of want and war in their middens. They didn't stay in one place very long. They may have shifted more to the slash-and-burn tactics of swidden agriculture, a possibility underlined by the rise of the pig, a lover of old fields and new forest edges, among their livestock.

These advances put the forests in retreat. Not all, of course, was our doing. The great elms faded away about 5,000 years ago, as the hemlocks did here a little later, to return in time. Most prehistorians feel that both species succumbed to disease or infestation, though some argue that the gathering of leaves and small branches for winter fodder might have helped elm on its way. (There is also evidence that since the beetle carrying the pathogens of elm blight likes to hang out with insects that like to hang out around dung, animal husbandry might have contributed to the dieback.)

Our use and misuse of Europe's woodlands grew with our numbers. We cut trees to get at the soil beneath them. Over time we cut them for warmth, for housing, for smelting the new metals, especially iron, for building our tall-masted ships. We drove our animals into the ever-expanding marches or margins, where pigs and geese could find mast and cattle and sheep and goats could feed on the grasses in the galleries under oaks. We cut blocks of forest humus for fertilizer, and to the same purpose we dragged out cut limbs and burned them in our fields.

The pollen record shows this. It shows the lime tree declining and declining and the beech, the lover of disturbance, coming in to claim the lime's range. It shows canopy trees shrinking back and small growth covering the ground. It shows woodlands turning to grassland heaths under the jaws of sheep. In northern Europe and in Britain and Ireland, it records the spread of the great blanket bogs. In some areas water tables rose when we cut trees, which had been wicking away millions of gallons of water from the soil through transpiration. Then the ground turned acid and drowned, and the mosses came in, building around and over the trunks of old pines and oaks. I stood once on such a bog in Ireland, looking at the small beauties of its strange flowers. I remember that I jumped hard on the sod and after a short while it responded like a trampoline in a stupor.

I think of the Burren, south of Galway Bay, on the west coast of Ireland. It is the opposite of bog but shaped by the same hands. It is a loaf of limestone, a ridge the color of old steel. It is completely bald, save for the flowers growing in cracks out of the wind. And it carries a geometry of weals, what remains of low walls of stone taken from fields that have vanished. The soils on the Burren were thick enough, just, to support a hazel woodland. They could not support Bronze Age farming.

There is in all of us a ghost of what once moved us at our core. Modern Americans talk of the small family farm, the village, as if these things were still culturally important. Northern Europeans still carry the memory of wildwoods. They, and we of northern European stock here, still read from the Brothers Grimm of the Little People and giants living in the darkling green, and some deep memory nods. The power of those places! I grew up reading the tales of the West Highlands. The one for me was "The Brown Bear of the Green Glen." John, the dim youngest son of the King of Erin, is on a mission. He comes to "a great desert of a wood." He thinks it not canny to continue, with the night upon him. So he climbs up a tree and from there spies a great bear coming to him with a fiery cinder in his mouth. John has found his mentor in the forest, his true intelligence.

John's great desert of a wood has not existed in the West Highlands for centuries. Forest clearance in Britain reached a peak between 3,000 and 2,000 years ago, when bronze was giving way to iron. When Caesar toured his new province just before the birth of Christ, he found it well farmed. The earliest written records of land use in England are in the Domesday Book, an invaluable tallying of wealds and fields compiled in 1086, shortly after the Normans did their conquering. Only about 15 percent of the countryside remained wooded then. The Normans brought the figure down to 10 percent in the first two centuries of their rule.

Feudalism, based on the control by a few of the surpluses produced by the many, found that its forests were in deficit. Peasants, yeomen, one and all, went to the woodlands for survival, hacking away at the greenery and hunting down a rapidly shrinking supply of game. Precisely because of their stringent control, the nobility and the lords of the church were able to rein in these often desperate practices. The numbers of cows and geese allowed into the marches came under regulation, as did the amount of winter fodder allowed out.

It was cruel management to the modern mind: you could lose an eye or an ear for a minor transgression. As any reader of *Robin Hood* remembers, taking one of the king's deer could cost you your life, payable to some high sheriff or other. And despite the cruelty, Sherwood's trees suffered mightily in Robin's time. But feudalism did establish a tradition of resource conservation in some areas, even if those who controlled the conservation were often prone to draw on those resources for their own benefit. Firewood and timber, in increasingly high demand, brought attractive returns to their owners. And the quintessential need for the elite to prove their superiority through elaborate show could take a dreadful toll on forest dwellers. One account has it that in the middle of the thirteenth century, Henry III of England arranged a staggering potlatch, a Christmas feast whose menu called for more than seven hundred deer, over a thousand hares, and enough wild boars to drive what was left of the species on the island into extinction.

North America was simply not in the same league of environmental manipulation. To the south, it is true, there were a few examples of what some take to have been latter-day Sumers. The Mayan civilization, rich with art and science, may have been brought to collapse by unbearable imbalances between population and nutritional necessities. Something similar may have befallen Teotihuacán, and the Aztecs' fondness for bloody ritual and mass sacrifice may have indicated some basic resource stress that would have toppled them even in the absence of Hernán Cortés and his conquistadors.

But then again, all these once strapping cultures might have been weakened far more by executive gridlock, climatic changes, or some other failing than by lack of maize. Mexico is no more an open book than the Mediterranean is. Explaining the demise of Teotihuacán carries as many risks as explaining the fall of Rome or Greece.

If it is true that the Beringians had a strong hand in doing away with the large herd animals they found in what is now the United States, then this country can at least lay some claim to substantial alteration. Driving a beast as big as a mammoth into extinction (if the blitzkrieg theory can prove that point against robust arguments to the contrary) makes human entrance here seem fully as dramatic, as full of impact, as those later expansions that wiped out mere moas on New Zealand or a bunch of bird species in the Hawaiian islands, or that reduced Easter Island to bare grass and an assortment of great stone heads staring out to sea.

Whatever the early pace of manipulation in North America, though, it clearly faded. People here used fire to open forests and increase their productivity. They did not banish forests en masse. The mosaics their gardens and fields created remained mosaics rather than merging into a monotony of croplands.

Certainly, attempts at nucleation produced some scars. I am prepared to believe that overworking the irrigation systems of the Hohokam culture in the Southwest resulted in salinization. The residents of Chaco may have hastened their social demise by stripping away too much forest cover for their great houses and their hearths. And the Cahokians probably removed more trees than sage management would have warranted to build and constantly repair their great stockades. But these degradations are small stuff compared to what was going on in Europe.

Dena Dincauze writes about the contrast in an essay whose title I sorely wish I had thought up: "The Oops Factor" (her subtitle, "Unintended Consequences in Biocultural Evolution," is fine for her academic purposes but wouldn't fit with my less rigorous designs). Dincauze argues that people on this continent might have walked less heavily on their earth because their domestic alliance was far less imposing — and less demanding — than those in Europe. They had no tamed animals requiring large amounts of terrain cleared for pasturage and none to make a real difference in extending natural carrying capacities. The system could support some regional population densities. But North American horticulture, mixed as it usually was with exploitation of wild resources, was too complex and varied to support cultures more than minimally removed from nature. "American farming," Dincauze writes, "was more complementary to the native ecosystem, permitting cyclical recovery and only occasionally swamping it out entirely. . . . It could never have supported populations as large as now exist on the planet. It kept population sizes moderate because the consequences of environmental abuse were only mildly buffered." The connection between getting out of line and going out of business was tighter then in this country.

In evolutionary terms, good health is whatever produces a life long enough to permit the individual to reproduce and care for his or her offspring until they are well on the way to their own reproduction. You can die at thirty and still have created a family far larger than that required merely to replace you and your spouse. It is when large numbers of children begin dying that their society faces shrinkage.

A subsistence society is not necessarily a healthy society as we define the term. Its people may not have enough food to reach maximum stature. They may carry a load of parasites and chronic diseases that would topple a fiber-eating, body-tuning, rosy-cheeked American. But they endure. I remember traveling by horse to a hacienda way to the east of the Peruvian mountain city of Cuzco. The *hacendado* had ordered some of his workers — serfs, really — to carry in luggage and supplies. They kept up with the horses in all but the few flat stretches, and some arrived at the big house well before the guests did. The labor seemed nothing to them, these leathery folk with a hundred different kinds of worms and whatnots in their intestines, with a wad of coca leaves and lime to suck on along the way, talking now and then in a language that is very old and full of the richest poetry.

A central question bothering prehistorians is, what happened to health when people around the world shifted from subsistence based on natural foods to subsistence based on artificially produced foods, the kind produced by the Peruvian porters? In the past two decades or so, paleopathology has developed or improved a suite of techniques with which to test the theories. Fossilized feces are useful in this work, when they can be had; but since few researchers realized the evidentiary value of the common turd until recently, a great many coprolites were thrown away.

Old bones, where they can be found, are the real currency of this endeavor. In the correct combinations, they can indicate sex, approximate age at death, and stature. The roundness of long bones can tell paleopathologists about mineralization. Trace elements can also do that, and a good deal more; high strontium levels in bones indicate a vegetal diet, strontium and zinc a fish diet, ratios of certain carbon isotopes a maize diet. Arrest lines, such as Harris lines, show when a bone began growing again after a period of stasis — a stressful period of malnutrition. Imbalances of vitamins and other substances can cause abnormal development of tooth enamel. Porosity in the skull can be a telltale of anemia. Tuberculosis, yaws, leprosy, and a few other diseases leave characteristic lesions on bone.

Some idea of reproductive habits and childhood survival rates can be gotten from counting pelvic birth scars and comparing them with the number of juvenile skeletons found at a given site. And some idea of regional demographics can be had from simply counting the number of sites dated to successive periods and the number of skulls encountered therein — though much counting remains to be done. More refined estimates are chancy. Yes, you can get a fair idea of the disease history of people whose remains are found in a given tomb or cemetery. But how can you be sure that what you have found is representative of the community the owners of those bones lived in? Younger people were often buried apart from their elders, and elites apart from commoners.

When the clues are retrieved from under the caveats, they do indicate a health change with the coming of settlement and agriculture. For one thing, foragers tended to be somewhat taller than the farmers who succeeded them. The difference appears slight in northern Europe but considerable in Turkey and Greece, where people appear to have shrunk half a foot on average. If the accounts of the first cruisers along the Atlantic coast of this country are to be believed, natives here were appreciably taller than the Europeans peering at them from crow's nests and crossyards.

The foraging lifestyle requires strength and endurance on a periodic basis — when tracking down an animal, carrying its meat to camp, moving over rough ground on the seasonal rounds. Bones are stressed, particularly the hip joints, and the stress shows in wear, arthritic damage. Fractures are more common than among farmers, and there is often evidence of skillful care in their healing. The body is generally more robust, the skeletal anchors for the large muscles more developed. The jaw, conditioned by chewing on tough foods, is apt to be more powerful.

The teeth of hunter-gatherers show distinctive signs of wear, but not of excessive decay. The teeth of grain eaters are subject to caries, the results of carbohydrates being converted into sugars in the mouth. Those same sugars and starches provide considerable energy, enabling the consumer to keep active in the fields. But they do not of themselves provide good, balanced nutrition — the nutrition an eater of wild plant and animal foods is more apt to receive. Grains made into bread in the Near East also may have contained phytate, a salt that inhibits absorption of protein and calcium in the gut.

Weaning is a difficult time under any circumstances, but it seems that in many early agricultural cultures the shift to plant food — grain mushes and the like — was particularly hazardous. A good many toddlers in Europe and America died.

Population pressure on resources cannot always be determined by counting noses. In California, the many hunter-gatherers living under the oaks and along the shores seem to have suffered only minimal levels of stress. Scientists studying their skeletons in the Central Valley have found them "so healthy it is somewhat discouraging to work with them." On the rich floodplains of the lower Mississippi Valley, people took up maize farming apparently without feeling the need evidenced by farmers elsewhere to gather together in large settlements. Maize was a status food at first, rather than a common staple. Heavy population densities and their attendant costs did not appear until long after the first kernels were planted.

The general picture seems to be that where agriculture

mixed with the more diverse and stable subsistence strategies, it offered the benefits of stored foods without exacting the price of malnutrition. But where climate, carrying capacities, or feuding over resources was a problem, decisions to feed on a relatively few crops could and did lead to problems. That was true in dry Mesopotamia and later in dry New Mexico; in both regions reliance on grain farming may have exacerbated the ravages of unpredictable climates.

The process flows through the archaeological records of the Holocene. In the Ohio drainage, the gardens of seed-bearing plants tended by the Adena culture supplemented foraging so that nutritional stress was not a major issue. Adena disappears in the record, for reasons yet to be established (possibly it too exceeded carrying capacities). There is a gap. Then come the Fort Ancient people, about a thousand years ago, and they are in dietary trouble. They are living in growing settlements, raising corn, beans, and squash, supplemented, though not very efficiently, with deer. Almost one fifth of a late Fort Ancient settlement dies during weaning. Infants suffer growth arrests indicating that at birth their mothers were undernourished and unable to nurse well. One out of a hundred individuals lives beyond fifty. Teeth rot. Iron deficiency anemia is widespread, as is an infection produced by treponemata, including the bacterium that causes syphilis when transmitted through sexual contact. (When transmitted by other contact, the same organism causes a milder form of disease called yaws. Syphilis and yaws are indistinguishable in the bone record, but recent finds show that treponemal infections may have existed through much of late prehistory on both sides of the Atlantic and not, as had previously been argued, on this side alone.)

It is when societies enter phases of high-density settled populations and intensive agriculture that health will often turn bad. Signs of physical stress increase along with mortality. Diseases show up increasingly, particularly the diseases of crowding, such as tuberculosis or cholera and — with the advent over the past few thousand years of large urban populations — measles, smallpox, plague, and the like. And another social disease is apt to break out: violence.

Early hunters killed each other; that we know from cave paintings and from stone points driven into bone. But the very fluidity of hunter-gatherer existence — the presence of the exit option for those bored or frustrated by group members — must have tended to work against chronic strife. So did the need to work together in the common business of group survival in a broad and difficult world.

Agriculture has provided much of the impetus for small settlements to grow into great cities. And though hierarchies have functioned well in nonagricultural cultures, they have risen to high and sometimes dangerous heights of power in societies with the talent and muscle to create agricultural surpluses. That power often had roots in the interpersonal aggression arising out of competition for food, for shelter, for simple space. What started out as families and clans spying on each other, accusing each other of thefts and witchcraft in the villages, grew into raids on each other, blood feuds with other villages, then spiraled into strategies of war.

The bow had been bent in Europe since glacial times, though as I have said earlier, it became important here less than 2,000 years ago, by most estimates. The threat of the bow was real. An archer kneeling behind a log could kill a number of enemies quickly. An archer stationed in good cover overlooking a stream could deny the fear-free use of that important avenue of commerce and communication. You would have little trouble dodging a spear arching toward your canoe or dugout, if you had the luck to spot it. An arrow arrives with hissing speed. You wouldn't see it coming. If the person who loosed it was any good, you, or those in the craft who survived you, wouldn't spot him.

Hierarchies could assemble and control large numbers of bowmen and foot soldiers, villagers who submitted to that control in return for the security they felt emanating from the mighty. Bowmen became charioteers, drivers of war machines that swept away armies and cities. Charioteers became cannoneers, machine gunners, missile men. And the violence of the villages became the violence of empires, as deadly as disease or the empty belly. There is to me little difference between the holed skulls found along the Ohio River, the Nubian woman with her mouth full of arrows, an old bone bearing the lesions of tuberculosis, and today's starved child lying face down beneath the noon sun in Somalia.

Until the new techniques of bone analysis were in place, it was possible to think of our species as magnificently adaptable. We were expert at equilibrium, the old argument went, capable of tailoring our numbers and styles of living to whatever climate or resource base we encountered. The new work does not encourage that line of thinking. Though it is next to impossible to tease apart the climatic and the cultural when it comes to changing landscapes, it is clear from the stories told here that we have often overshot the mark. The elm decline in Europe may have been mostly pathogenic, with a helping hand from the farmer, but the Burren seems almost entirely our handiwork.

If mobile groups often adapted themselves to the exigencies of their mobility by keeping families small, sedentary groups often adapted to the needs of their settlements by encouraging larger families. Agriculture must have labor. So must the towns and cities that spring up where harvests are abundant. So must the rulers of those towns, anxious to protect what they have and to lay siege to what they wish to have. Perhaps the idea that there is strength in numbers had its first blooming in the grain fields of the Golden Crescent.

What was true of Sumer has continued to be true in some fashion and in some place through time. Even on the good soils of Europe, not enough food could be produced and distributed to keep body and soul always together among the peasantry. Meat for them often became an intermittent luxury, and even cereals and pulses could be hard to come by. For centuries, animal husbandmen worked in a circle of despair: there were not enough animals to produce enough manure to fertilize pastures to increase the herds and flocks. Only gradually did new fodder crops and fertilizing techniques relieve the situation. It was not until a couple of hundred years ago that agriculture on good land began to approach anything like the "reliability" we know. (The word, so often used, makes light of dust bowls, floods, insect damage, and soil degradation, to which the enterprise is still heir.)

Population during these lean centuries surged and faltered, growing at an average rate that is estimated by some, with no real data to go by, at around a tenth of one percent. That would be one twentieth of world increases today. But it was enough to raise our numbers overall from something like 4 million before the advent of agriculture to 50 million 3,000 years ago and, the rate rising, 200 million by the second century after Christ.

War and social instability kept world population levels fairly steady between 2,000 and 1,000 years ago. According to some estimates, they rose in the next 200 years to roughly 350 million, then stalled as demography overtook food production. There followed a dip in the numbers and a recovery that saw world population still at 350 million by A.D. 1400.

The guesstimates for Europe follow along. Something like 26 million people lived there at the end of the fourth century A.D., 36 by the tenth. A long and intense campaign to "reclaim" land from forest sent the total up to 80 million by 1300. And then death clamped down. Famines became more common. In some, there were true failures of food. In others, food was available, but in the increasingly capitalistic tenor of the period, it was treated as an economic commodity; the poor simply could not buy it and so perished. The famines were terrible. During the worst, in the early 1300s, starvelings ate anything they could find — grass, pig manure, each other.

Three decades later, the rats came — black rats infected

with plague and their complements of infected fleas. They spread out of China along the trade routes — the avenues for so much disease during the late Holocene — and arrived in Europe in 1346. The plague killed within a few days, during which victims howled in pain from swollen lymph glands, vomited, hallucinated. We, the social animals, had become so social, so urbanized, that the plague, and successive waves of the so-called diseases of crowding, rose among us like a flood. The Black Death, in this, its first European engagement, took roughly one out of three inhabitants. The population dropped from 80 to 60 million from beginning to end of the fourteenth century. And yet by 1700, in the middle of the climatic cooling period called the Little Ice Age, when crops were freezing in the higher latitudes, Europeans numbered 120 million mostly miserable, enduring souls.

Whether North Americans would have found themselves eventually on Europe's sad trail to civilization if left to themselves is an impossible question. No one who has seen Tikal in the Mayan jungles can dismiss human capacity for civilization in the Americas. I carry with me the memories of sitting within the walls of Sacsahuaman, above Cuzco, drinking pisco brandy and watching the shadows move among the perfectly fitted stones of the fortress, stones the color of moonlight. Here was high culture, of a sort strange to us. There were no wheels. (Children did play with wheeled toys in the high valley of Mexico.) There were no wheeled vehicles, because there were no animals to pull them. The Incas governed their empire by the grace of trained runners.

People crowded into Cahokia on market days and the days of ceremony, and that great center, while it lived, was a tribute to social cohesion and the human intellect. So were Chaco and Mesa Verde and the other complexes tucked back in the canyons of the Southwest. And, I think, so were the confederacies that developed in the Midwest and Northeast. The Iroquois, one of the most skillful political and military organizations of this country at any time, came out of corn as surely as Parisians and Londoners came out of wheat and barley.

North Americans suffered the same stresses as Europeans; the records of malnutrition, disease, and violence are similar in kind, if not in quantity. And yet the population levels came to be so different. Europe, for all its suffering, was passing 80 million in the period just before the Encounter, a population forty times the number of people living here.

A continent so richly endowed with beings, so lightly burdened with tamable animals and with humans, might have found new roads to follow. The space was here for that. But not the time.

8

The Day Before America

Eves have a way of being eerie. I think of the one before All Saints' Day, when pumpkins laugh their flickering laughter. I think of Henry in the night, walking through his own gloom in the camps of England hours before Agincourt. Owls cry more frequently in those darknesses, and we wrap ourselves as we can against chill anticipation.

The eve of what I, in my ethnocentricity, think of as the most profound encounter in human history was no eve at all. It was a century and more of eves. There was the one at Palos, the now silted port where the Admiral put out into the Western Sea, alone in the dark with his faith and his fears. There was the one near Stink Alley in Leiden, Holland, where an ancestor of mine (and conceivably of upwards of 60,000 others), a printer and bookman named William Brewster, desperately sought a way out of his own religious and social isolation. A separatist, Brewster and a colleague had written to the Virginia Company about starting a colony to the north of the territories claimed by the Admiral's sponsors. "We are well weaned from the delicate milk of our mother's country," the letter said, "and inured to the difficulties of a strange and hard land." Brewster, hounded by the king's men, would sail with his fellow believers from England in 1620, only to return when leaks developed in one of their vessels. They would try again, aboard *Mayflower*. Driven far north of the Virginia Company's chartered lands by storms and the Gulf Stream, they would decide to stick it out where they found themselves. And the printer brooding now in Leiden would go ashore with them in Plymouth, a pilgrim then as never before or after.

I don't mean to say that the day before the Encounter was besieged by owls and auguries. But it was an odd stretch of time, almost feverish. When the Atlantic was still the great divide, lands on both sides were full of comings and goings, risings and fallings away. It would be wise here, I think, to develop what we can of a reality check, to look at ways of life and landscapes on either side of the Atlantic divide as they were just before the two realities became one.

The first Europeans on the Grand Banks — I don't know whether they were Bristolmen or Portuguese or Basques — could not believe what they saw and took. Their ships were "pestered" with fish. In 1602, an Englishman wrote in his journal how his vessel had anchored in fifteen fathoms near a long neck of land. The fish "were very great, some measured five feet long and three foot about," and they schooled so thickly that he thought their backs were the sea bottom. Surely, the fishers thought, that low land on the horizon should be called Cape Cod. Striped bass schooled in that fashion too, and another Englishman new to the country said of them, "The head on one will give a good eater a dinner and for daintiness of diet they excell the merrybones of beef."

Oyster banks ran for miles, and some of the shells were close to a foot long: "This fish without the shell is so big that it must admit of a division before you can well get it into your mouth." Trout up to two feet in length ran in the coastal streams, if you can believe what may well have been a bit of boosterism on the part of the observer. And sturgeon, presumably the sea sturgeon in the inlets, could go to eighteen feet, and summer boaters were advised to steer clear of

them to avoid capsizing. The prince of boosters, Captain John Smith, fair rubbed his hands at these accounts and advised his readers — potential backers of new ventures in this new world — "Let not the Meanness of the word fish distaste you."

Ashore, plant ranges over what would become the contiguous United States were similar to modern ones in the centuries leading up to the Encounter. But abundances obviously were different in the days before plow and saw. The tall-grass prairies are now reduced to strips along railroad rights of way and oases amid the general agriculture. Several species of trees have collapsed since late prehistory, and of these the recent near extinction of the elm and the chestnut have the most direct impact on my New England sensibilities. Some species may have retreated south a bit as the climate entered the Little Ice Age.

Animals were where we would be astounded to find them today. Bison discovered suitable habitats all over the place, from the Plains on east to Florida. There were jaguars and mountain lions in the Southeast, grizzly bears in the Midwest, wolves, elk, and mountain lions in New England. Passenger pigeons flew in their billions, fertilizing forests with their droppings, breaking branches and cornstalks with their collective weight, and Carolina parakeets flashed in bright air before we took them.

One of the most painstakingly assembled estimates of human populations at Contact comes from Douglas Ubelaker, of the Smithsonian Institution. Ubekaler went to the best sources he could find — experts on native tribes who had each prepared demographic information for the Smithsonian's multivolume *Handbook of North American Indians*. He presents a range of figures. These are the ones he favors:

- Arctic: 73,770. Three people per 100 square kilometers.
- Subarctic: 103,400. Two people per 100 sq. km.
- Northwest Coast: 175,330. Fifty-four people per 100 sq. km.
- California: 221,000. Seventy-five people per 100 sq. km.
- Southwest: 454,200. Twenty-eight people per 100 sq. km.

- Great Basin: 37,500. Four people per 100 sq. km.
- Plateau: 77,950. Fifteen people per 100 sq. km.
- Plains: 189,100. Six people per 100 sq. km.
- Northeast: 357,700. Nineteen people per 100 sq. km.
- Southeast: 204,400. Twenty-two people per 100 sq. km.

That comes to 1,894,350 people spread across the land at an average density of eleven people per 100 square kilometers. Averages, of course, mislead. The forefathers of the Makah, those who lived in and around Ozette, lived 340 to each 100 square kilometers, and some close-knit groups in the Southwest undoubtedly reached greater concentrations.

These numbers say nothing about the diversity of human life in North America, the scores of languages spoken, the ways of life running from ancient foraging cultures in places like the Great Basin to the towns of the Mississippi and the Southeast and the developing confederations of the Midwest and Northeast. Then too, numbers are snapshots, whatever their validity. We need to keep in mind the continuum from which they were teased.

The Northwest seems to have been fairly placid just before the Encounter. Populations grew and the taking and preserving of fish, marine mammals, and other foods became more specialized. There was demographic movement in the region, but not much. Perhaps the most significant shift came when a dam of earth formed by a landslide in the middle of the thirteenth century gave way and probably drowned a good many people living in the lower Columbia Valley and parts of the Willamette basin.

Demographic swells flowed across the Southwest all through late prehistory. Chaco and Mesa Verde disappeared early on. The Hohokam culture vanished from the record around the year 1425. Yet the populations of Hopis and Zunis appear to be have been on the rise. And as we have seen, sometime around 1400 Athapaskans from the Mackenzie basin in western Canada began to move in among the empty apartments of the old ones.

We know that Cahokia was long gone by 1492. The Mississippian culture that built it seems to have been under great pressures almost everywhere in its extensive territories. Its northern centers in Wisconsin disappeared around 1300, perhaps because of a more arid climate. By 1400, much of the north-central Mississippi River valley and nearby areas were suffering severe depopulation. The resulting "Vacant Quarter" was quite possibly the most dramatic example of depopulation in the East. Yet again, the pattern was never complete. Among Mississippian societies in the Southeast, groups faded along the central Tennessee River after 1300 and along the lower Savannah a century later, but settlements along the Black Warrior River, in Alabama, seemed unaffected.

Why would people leave the Mississippi and the Illinois but not the Ohio, the Tennessee but not the Black Warrior? In addition to the usual climatic and demographic explanations, there are political ones to consider. The heads of hierarchy were responsible for keeping their communities in balance. Parched fields could lower their standing considerably, a poor showing against rivals even more. Eventually, scarcities of resources caused hungry people to wander into the buffer zones separating chiefdoms. In the Mississippi Valley, these zones were minimal, but in the Appalachians they were apt to be extensive. The more confrontations there were in these zones, the more likely intergroup fighting became. The people of a defeated or disgraced Big Man didn't often stay with him. There is evidence in the Southeast that they drifted off to the simpler ways of life, foraging and gardening in small groups.

The Northeast too was in motion. The Great Lakes no longer seemed a good place to live by 1400, perhaps because of cooler, wetter weather. Here in New England, the old ways of living in watersheds lost their importance. People no longer relied on home drainages to provide identity and the security of buffered boundaries.

The climate had warmed up around A.D. 1000, just for a few centuries, just long enough to encourage people to move north, away from population pressures and related hostilities. The Iroquois pressed up into the St. Lawrence Valley. The Munsees moved down the Hudson and across to the upper Delaware. The Massachusetts drove up the Merrimack, slowed but not stopped by the western Abenakis in front of them. And all through populous southern New England, rivers became secondary to trails.

If you want to see pre-Columbian instabilities, look at the Iroquois. They came to control one of the most strategically important land avenues in the East, the watershed of the Mohawk River, one of the few riverine passages through the Appalachians to the Hudson and the coast. The costs were very high. Iroquois settlements appear to have been increasingly palisaded over time. Their populations grew from a few hundred to well over a thousand — quite a crowd for that sort of social arrangement. The signs of violence are everywhere: heads severed in raids (scalps replaced them eventually, in the interests of convenience on a long carry); skulls opened by clubs; skeletons showing signs of torture, of cannibalism, practices reported by the Jesuits and other early whites in the region. It was this carnage that called to the Peacemaker.

The Iroquois may have been reacting at least in part to pressure from the Mississippians to their west. They grew inordinately large amounts of maize, and some of it may have been sent by canoe into the Cahokian trade complex. When the outlying centers became stronger than the failing temple-mound center, they needed to establish their own food acquisition networks, and hostile competition with the Iroquois was the result. If that can be demonstrated to be the case, then the Iroquois were among the few prehistoric societies here to know what it felt like to be at a disadvantage in a demanding market. All of native America soon would learn the finer points of that circumstance from Elder Brewster and his people.

Fifteenth-century Europe was filled with mourning. The great plague was behind it, though demographic profiles were still skewed by the disease's ferocity and lesser epidemics kept returning. Much of Europe had progressed beyond chiefdoms. Big men had become princes or kings. But their power was almost as evanescent as that of any Mississippian chief, particularly in countries such as Italy, where holdings were apt to be small. In fact, the whole place seems to have lost its head. What had once been raids and feuds grew into wars that went on for years and decades. The new arquebuses and large-bore cannon killed and maimed thousands of people. And when wars did stop, unemployed men at arms wandered about the countryside having their will and pillaging for profit. Vengeance became a public pleasure. People chipped in to buy a condemned brigand and have him burned, drawn, quartered, flayed for their sport. I have read that in Europe, there was at least ten times as much violence in the fifteenth century as in the twelfth, though the method of that measurement was not given. A plague of the spirit seemingly had followed those of the flesh, not for the first time in human history, nor for the last.

The sheer wastefulness of the mayhem finally did set some folk to thinking that perhaps it might be better to organize things a bit. Why not find someone you could get along with — in a manner of speaking — and then join forces in an attack on someone neither one of you liked? Ferdinand of Aragon and Isabella of Castile tried that out with considerable success. Their union made allies of two powerful communities, and together they set about driving out the Muslims who had conquered and civilized much of Iberia. That done, they expelled those who practiced the Jewish faith, something England had attempted two centuries previously.

A certain amount of statecraft grew from all this. On its own ground, Spain went into training for imperialism. It put Muslim centers under siege and, when they fell, colonized them. Not all the new settlers were Spanish. Seville and other cities grew to new wealth with the help of merchants from Genoa. The power of royal armies protected the power of bureaucrats, auditors, and administrators, and Spain developed a sort of civil service that would keep track of things in the glorious future to come.

England developed along different lines. The royal came to share power with the wealthy and the landed, and that tended to give the country a special sense of flexibility and mobility that made of it more of a nation, as we think of nations, than could be found in most other parts of Europe.

Trade had been part of medievalism. But now, with the modern beginning to make inroads on the medieval, investment came onto solid ground — investment in reclaiming land from forests, land from marshes or the sea, land that, worked by populations often transplanted for the purpose, would yield commodities, commodities that would yield profit. In Portugal and in cities of the Mediterranean, markets went to work. In Columbus's time, the Fuggers of Germany were investing returns from wool in commerce and real estate. It was a sign of the times that the son of the founding Fuggers should have been known as Jacob the Rich.

I remember standing in the wind atop the great bluff of Cape St. Vincent a few years ago and looking out east toward Sagres, where another enabling device of Europe's imperialism and commercialism had its headquarters during the day before America. St. Vincent was the landward end of the known world then, a headland from which the Admiral and hundreds of other captains of discovery before and after him took their departure. Sagres is where a remarkable man named Henrique, half English, half Portuguese, is said to have built what would now be called an oceanographic laboratory. In his day, that meant a collection of knowledge about navigation, one of many systems of thought the Christian world was obliged to relearn from the Arab world to bring dawn to the Dark Ages. And learning about navigation meant assembling yarns and looking at logs, anything to advance a primitive understanding of the seas to the west of St. Vincent. From logs and memories and fancies came maps, little more then than indications of the possible.

Henrique, or Henry, called Henry the Navigator, was one of those who made tiny Portugal into an empire that for a while was the greatest in Europe, with holdings in Africa, India, South America, and the Far East. Others were the designers and builders who married the best of early European square-riggers with the fore-and-aft rigs of the Arabs to produce the caravel. She was a novelty at sea, able to sail fairly close to the wind and then turn and run before it. While she was in development, the Portuguese went down the coast of West Africa looking for the queen of commodities, gold, and finding it. They also came across tropical diseases that killed them in great numbers. One estimate is that 80 percent of those who went ashore and stayed for a while did not go home again.

The Iberians began the Encounter, as far as we can tell. They began it out of their experience in fighting the Muslims and in dealing with and to a certain extent accepting the commercial and capitalistic talents of Mediterranean societies. They were seafarers and conquerors. D. W. Meinig, a senior American geographer, notes that those two trades had often been combined before, not least during the Crusades. But, he writes, "Never had such a highly developed set of institutions for the seizure, administration, and resettlement of new territories and their populace, an entire system of conquest, become so fully articulated with such a highly developed set of institutions for the financing, production, shipment, and marketing of goods."

These were essentially and thoroughly predatory traditions, born out of violence. Meinig says that "plunder and conquest were as much a part of the intensely competitive commercial world of the Mediterranean as of the landed world of Iberia, as demonstrated by the Catalans in the Balearics, the Genoese in Corsica, and the Venetians in Crete." They were also traditions firmly based on altering landscapes to fit the demands of markets.

Among the most intellectually courageous of researchers, to me, are those who try to figure out what people of prehistory thought of themselves and of the physical and spiritual terrains in which they lived their lives. Grave goods can help when there is little else to go by. What a person takes with her to the camps of the dead says something about how she lived and what was important to her band. But the foragers of the far past left so little to conjure with. Their lives were not lived on the record. Their history was dreamtime. Their regard for their ancestors was apt to be limited to what could be recounted and passed on, innocent of earth mounds and spired stone.

We know far more about the villagers, if only because they saw to it that we should. Consider the house in the village. It is a remarkable symbol of a change in the way we looked at things. There was, suddenly, permanently, outside and inside. There was thus public and private. Houses set next to each other created neighbors, and ways had to be found to deal with people who were at least as curious about what went on behind your walls as you were about what they did behind theirs. As a forager, you had been subject to chronic but generally mild attention from everyone in the band. As a villager, you were the target of episodic but often intense — and unfriendly — scrutiny on the part of those living close to you.

Villages grew to towns and cities, and for the inhabitants geometry became the ordering force of their lives. In this angled existence, sight became dominant. It is especially important in a town to pay close attention to the rapids and eddies of social intercourse, and vision is the sense that gives itself most easily to that focus. The resident needs to recognize the power each person carries. The resident needs to learn what is expected of him as a small part of the whole, what is to be done, when and how. His learning becomes less and less mimetic, more and more by logical instruction. And in instruction, the diagram, the offshoot of architecture, becomes increasingly the instrument of choice. The diagram needs the eye.

Early foragers located themselves in reference to where their fellows were, where game and water and shelter were. In town, locations were permanent and boundaries everywhere. The townsperson learned a great deal about these boundaries and about himself as a part of the whole geometric construct, the town. He learned rapidly, thanks to diagrams and, later, writing, and he learned rigidly. The implicit, inclusive, flexible life of the wanderer was now alien to him.

What was familiar was division — division by walls, by streets, by districts, by concepts. The house of humanity was itself divided. There was mind, there was body. There was public, there was private. There was male, female, good, evil, mighty, lowly, we, they, thou, it. For the forceful and the fortunate, there was more than enough voltage sparking from these dualities to make the settled life richer in opportunities for achievement than any previous way of living. They made the best of it, at Angkor Wat, Knossos, Versailles, and other examples of what Peter Wilson, the New Zealander scholar, calls the "pinnacles of Neolithic aspiration."

A principal cost seems to have been violence, or, more correctly, violence organized to serve an increasing number of religious, political, and social ends. Wilson goes so far as to argue that "we must reckon this organization of aggression, as well as such other modes as gossip, witchcraft, displays, the evil eye, and so on, as being among the evolved characteristics of civilization or domestic society in the same way as we acknowledge pottery, sculpture, or writing to be among the constituents of civilization."

As the day before America approached, the dichotomies of Western civilization intensified. Whole institutions fell into decay. Corrupt churchmen put a price on anything from indulgences to fake relics, and popes scurried about finding sinecures for their "nephews." Few roads were safe from brigands, and travelers went in groups or prayed a lot. The English mistreated Catholics, Jews, and other Others and engaged in organized decimation of those in Ireland who chose to take a stand against them.

At the broad bottom of society, the peasantry and the urban poor lived lives I read about but cannot imagine. Historians tell me not to apply the mores of my times to those of the past, but I crave exception here. Callousness is callousness in any century, and one of the few pervasive evidences of human nobility I can extract from the fourteenth and fifteenth centuries is the ability of so many people to suffer so much.

I do not forget the high culture of those years — Michelangelo at his sublime ceiling, Dürer in Germany, Bosch in Flanders, Titian, Leonardo. True enough, and Sir Thomas More and Machiavelli and so many other masters of the mind, all touched by the energies of a European civilization gone rampant. The historian Barbara Tuchman took note of all this exaltation of the creative and the settings from which it sprang. "The efflorescence in culture reflected no comparable surge of human behavior," she wrote, "but rather an astonishing debasement."

From these cruel smelters was to come another work of high imagination: man the exalted, man the manipulator of his fate. This was definitely an upper-class concept. Only wealthy, powerful males need apply. God was still very much in evidence, a transcendent male deity. But the best of men were now to be free to make their destinies manifest. Beneath them in this developing bell curve of being were lesser men, all women, animals, and — most alien, most feared — the surviving forests of the land.

Peasants and others living closer to nature could and did retain a more inclusive view of the world. They could dance to bring back the sun and sprinkle fields with cakes and drink.

They went to the woods to get — to poach, when necessary — fuel and fodder and the occasional roebuck. And they returned with fresh respect for the wild men who lived there, the Little People, the bears with fiery cinders in their mouths, all the beings who shared their realities.

The mighty took another course. Some were aware that Plato himself had argued against the value of myth in culture, against the sorcery and spirits that informed the great tales of Homer. Most held to the value of the analytical mind, the supremacy of reason. And that seems reasonable to me. If the beginnings of the analytical mind are to be found far back in the first permanent settlements, then as settlements became city-states, was it not natural to turn to ever more sophisticated mental constructs? How else to impose order on such proliferations of neighbors?

Clocks were spreading through Europe. Time could be measured. Clockwork was like the mind, precise, measuring. The way to progress lay in mechanization, in logic. The new man was apart, using his vision to measure and his mind to analyze. What was seen was an object. The viewer was a subject. Thus separated, things could be properly examined, broken down to components, understood, and manipulated. The concept is exciting still. I remember how powerful I felt when I first encountered the elegant force of logic. It must have been exhilarating to see it sprout amid the chaos of Columbian Europe.

The word *capitalism* wouldn't be common until the nineteenth century, but the forces it describes were stirring amid the high art and low comity of Columbian times. I too fear capitalism's addiction to exuberant excess. Yet it is by its benefits that I sit here, looking over my hayfield, free to contemplate its costs. They are well illumined at this time of year. I write this two days before a Christmas, and even here in the Berkshires it is impossible to disregard the supremacy of capitalism as our motivating force. I buy, therefore I am. The god of the season clearly is Christ the Consumer, Lord of the Mall.

Five centuries ago, the ideas were in place that would legitimize and later help deify this holy child of economics. Certain medieval concepts hung on. There was still talk here and there about the difficulties of the wealthy in entering heaven and the desirability of charging fair prices. Creative usury — using debt and foreclosure to amass one's wealth — was not yet generally accepted. But with the rise of man as the central earthly being and our consequent self-separation from nature and the natural, it was an easy step to regarding nature as essentially inanimate and therefore eminently exploitable.

It would be a century or so before Francis Bacon would declare a "right over Nature which belongs to [us] by divine bequest." But in the meantime, what was once thought of as unified became a collection of useful objects — soils and minerals, trees and streams, animals and the more vulnerable among humans — that with shrewd management and not a little arrogance could be converted to personal, corporate, or national wealth. Each object became a resource, a commodity. And the worth of a slave or a shipment of barley was increasingly measured in terms of the ultimate commodity, money. If the new ironworks devoured thousands of acres of forests each year, if drained wetlands went sour, if cities lived in their own filth, why, that was a sign of great things to come. For hope, rationalism's belief that a better society could be built (with the greatest rewards obviously going to those who took the greatest risks), had taken up residence among the fortunate living in the lands of despair.

This, then, was the gaze Europe turned westward when it realized, finally, what one of its navigators had found at the other side of the alien sea. The mind behind it was creative and predatory, increasingly bedazzled by the power of linear thought and the enticements of progress. It was this worldview that swept west across continents dreaming different dreams.

Ron LaFrance, the Mohawk leader I've talked to, once took time to tell me that even if I learned his language, I could never really understand him. "There is no point of reference in your intellect that can make the same point of reference that I can," he said. "I'm not being insulting." Exclusion is a good debating trick. I didn't know what to make of his statement. LaFrance said of what was in his memory, "Either we've got the biggest imaginations in the world or ninety percent of it is true. I'll vote for the latter." I'm not registered to vote in his nation. Ninety percent seems on the high side, but I wouldn't know where to begin tinkering with his numbers.

The oral tradition is something I know about, having grown up in the house of a poet and a singer. I am happiest when I stand aside and let memory bring an old ballad or round or tale from its clutter and give it air. I have learned that the disciplines of memory require considerable native talent and long training. It is a disgrace to the culture and to oneself to make a mistake in the recitation of a ritual that may take hours and days. Yet despite its rigor, the oral way can be far more flexible than the written. Its followers can and do reinvent themselves, spinning a new past for themselves, as the Sioux did after they moved from their rivers and became the champion cavalry of the plains. We of the written word, in contrast, are apt to be left with texts made for a time far gone. We read words meant for villagers in an arid land and find ourselves struggling to fit them to our urban and well-watered culture. Literates, it seems, must break with their past to change their world-view. Mnemonists simply bend it.

That means, of course, that even the earliest white accounts of native beliefs and views can't be taken as accurate reflections of pre-Contact ways. Acculturation set in not only when Europeans landed but in some measure when their trade goods went before them into the hinterland. Many archaeologists warn against assuming that tribes, the social organizations described by colonists, were representative of social organization before the floating islands dropped anchor. All that can be done is to examine the ancient grave goods yet again, compare their slim stories with what native elders remember now, and interpret as one can.

The story of the earth-divers — animals like the beaver who brought up earth from the bottom of deep water to make a home for creation — can be found in some form from Finland across Asia and into this country. Ron LaFrance knows where his umbilicus is buried, and that calls to mind what peoples in the Southwest say about their origins, that people emerged into this world through a hole in the earth, an umbilicus of great power. The mythologist Mircea Eliade spoke of a time when all men "were less aware of belonging to the human species than of a kind of cosmic-biologic participation in the life of their landscape."

This appears to have remained a universal. A being who lives by the landscape lives in it, is nothing more nor less than one component among many that define that landscape. Only the house and the town and the cultural complexes that go with them have the force to remove us from that life and make of us domesticated creatures that in the deepest sense are homeless.

You cannot live by a landscape on the strength of one sense. You cannot see your way to survival. You must have others to teach you how and when to use your ears, how to hear weather changing, other beings talking among themselves and to you. That caw is a crow telling you that someone is stirring in the marsh. That whistling cough is a buck. There is a hint of wolverine in the still air under the pines. That track looks and feels fresh, and so does the scat near it. Bear has been by this morning. She is old, lame in the left hind foot. This is where she stopped, attracted by something off to her left. This is where she made water.

This is elementary sensing. The best of the foragers could do far better. Some of our most accomplished hunters and trackers can too. But the rest of us have let go. Only occasionally do our senses rouse themselves sufficiently to whisper to us of what sentient living was.

Science has established to its satisfaction that smell is one of memory's most effective triggers. We can, if we would but try, remember as many as 10,000 odors, and our first reaction to each is apt to be emotional. Proust smelled a cookie and that one inhalation produced a flood of memory that took hundreds of pages to absorb. The smells that produce more modest nostalgia are an indication of our age. I, born in the twenties, smell cow manure or newly tedded hay and am immediately back in boyhood. I understand that those born in the sixties and seventies experience the same emotions when there are essences of factory or exhaust emissions or window cleaner or felt-tipped pens in the air.

Pre-Columbian people here took not only memories from the breeze but also a gazette of what was going on at the moment upwind on their home grounds. They did this as a matter of course, as human people living in a world with non-human people. They were what the Iroquois called human-man-beings, keeping up with the doings of deer-man-beings, hickory-man-beings, and lightning-man-beings. Even places could be people, or at least the petrified remains of myths.

George Hamell, of the New York State Museum in Albany, has spent a couple of decades studying what he calls the "mythical reality" of the northern Iroquois. He finds the principles behind these thought patterns quite similar to others found throughout the Americas in that animacy, sentience, and volition are universals. "What the Iroquois do," he told me, "is to extend the qualities of humanness to all these other entities around them. And they extend kinship. Among the Iroquois, the sun is Elder Brother, the moon is Grandmother, the lightning is Grandfather."

Along with the relationships went responsibilities that were both strong and reciprocal, though (in the way of most of our constructs) not necessarily constant. There were many times — we have visited some — when demographics, climate shifts, cultural imperatives, and political strains in various combinations drove humans in America to excessive harvesting among their fellow man-beings. There is no getting around the iron fact that life kills to live. But there seems to me to have been deterrence in mythical reality, cautionary tales to stay the grasping hand when conditions permitted. Gluscap, the teacher/trickster of the Algonquins, captures all the animals in a skin bag and takes them home to his grandmother, Woodchuck. No, she says, let them go. If you don't, you won't have much to eat later on. If you do, you'll grow strong and wise trying to catch the animals, and they will grow strong and wise trying to escape from you. Gluscap opens the bag.

George Hamell says that "the expectation of reciprocity between me as a hunter and the deer-man-being as my prey was such that there was a certain amount of respect there, and the expectation that if I killed more deer than I really needed, I would be punished for it." This wasn't environmentalism, not as we proclaim it. Environmentalism signifies a concern for one's surroundings, and early native Americans seem to have had little sense of being surrounded. They were part, not apart. Neither was this ecology. No one in North America prior to the Encounter talked in terms of dry weights, niches, or habitats. Knowledge came through senses and emotions, not theories. In such a world, subject and object, impersonal observation and analysis, had no place. Nor had individualism, the foundation of my way of thinking and that of hundreds of millions of other citizens of industrialized cultures. The greatest fear I had in wandering back through the Holocene at the beginning of my research was that I would lose my way completely in a landscape where people were far more important than persons. What could I, an individual, possibly make of a society in which group structures were so strong that a gap left by a member's death could be filled by capturing and then adopting a likely candidate from another group?

Nothing seen in these wanderings leads me to believe that people here felt their landscape was sacrosanct. Their faiths were often manipulative toward nature, and their practices often meddlesome. Under their ministrations, true wilderness shrank away in almost every part of the continent. There was some sense of obligation in maintaining balance with other beings. I don't think it is possible to know if they consciously limited their numbers in this regard, but in any event their demands were light. In harvesting, their goal was subsistence with the least effort, not maximization of yields.

In this, their lives differed radically from those of fifteenth-century Europeans. They benefited, according to some accounts, from a sort of ecological lifenet, which improved their health and life expectancy beyond those experienced by many of their European contemporaries. It is easy to say that their use of the land was based essentially on fortuitous abundances, but over the centuries they appear to have lived in a way that only on occasion may have seriously depleted those abundances.

I am reminded of something an environmental historian told a friend and fellow scholar a few years ago. They were comparing the opposing historical notions of Americans as noble pioneers and Americans as rapists of the land. The historian called both concepts true but incomplete. "The real problem," he said, echoing other people in this book, "is that human beings reshape the earth as they live upon it, but as they reshape it the new form of the earth has an influence on how those people can live. The two reshape each other. This is as true of Indians as it is of European settlers."

9

Up Till Now

To ME, the most appropriate crossing point into North American history is a scene one might have happened upon often a couple of decades after whites came ashore in sufficient numbers to start their colonies in New England. Think of a small clearing near the Connecticut River. It is quiet in the clearing. No sound comes from the loaflike dwellings set well away from the edge of the woods. Weather has buckled a rush-and-sapling wall and eaten away at a couple of smoke holes in the roof. Brambles crowd the garden plots, and oak leaves have drifted over the outdoor hearths.

There are bones near one of the hearths, human bones. Animals have been at them, but enough remain to tell a story. No arrowhead in the rib cage, no skull holed by a club or scraped by a scalper's knife. Something more effective than a war party has been here. Its name probably was smallpox or scarlet fever or measles, and it came here in the bodies and on the breath of the Europeans.

These diseases could attack the colonists too, yes, but they had developed considerable immunities over the generations. The native populations, isolated by time and the oceans, were innocent of antibodies. An epidemic hit the eastern part of

Massachusetts in 1616, four years before the landing at Plymouth Rock. No one is sure what it was. Perhaps it started with European fishermen coming ashore to stretch their legs, trade, or dry their catch. Others followed along the New England coast: 1622, 1631, 1633. The Black Death took something like one out of every two Britons in the fourteenth century. Plagues in New England were worse. Western Abenakis all but disappeared. Pocumtucks in the Connecticut Valley lost nine out of ten of their people. The Mohawks and other nations of the Iroquois League over in New York State were cut in half, though true mortalities might be disguised by their practice of adopting members of other groups. The waves of pestilence rolled across the entire country, reaching some Plains communities only around the middle of the last century. A modern American historian looked back in sorrow and wrote, "The American land was more like a widow than a virgin. Europeans did not find a wilderness here; rather, however involuntarily, they made one."

Clearings like the one I imagine went back to woodland. The parklike aspect of coastal forests kept open for centuries by fire faded in shrubbery. Some native groups, like the Iroquois, eventually came back. But they came back to what for them was truly a new world. Even where they retained some of their land, their view of themselves was different from what it had been. The process of acculturation, the metamorphoses that spring from the meeting of cultures strange to each other, assured that. After the plagues had subsided in New England, a survivor, by then an old man, lamented, "A long time ago my ancestors had wise men which in a grave manner taught the people knowledge; but they are dead, and their wisdom is buried with them. And now men live a giddy life, in ignorance, till they are white-headed, and though ripe in years, yet they go without wisdom to their graves."

This, to me, is the real boundary between what is history and what is not — the loss of that wisdom. *Time* magazine mourned the loss in a cover story late in 1991: "Over the ages, indigenous peoples have developed innumerable technologies and arts. . . . If this knowledge had to be duplicated from scratch, it would beggar the scientific resources of the West. Much of this expertise and wisdom has already disappeared, and if neglected, most of the remainder could be gone within the next generation." There was little mention of native North American knowledge in that text, and that is a yet another measure of our continent's tragedy.

More than anything else, the historic reshaping of North America has been a business venture, a corporate venture. Resources (a word coming into vogue in the fifteenth century) have animated the venture, and the drive to extract those resources set the course and speed of our history. Some of the native hunters and farmers in the eastern part of this country at first believed that the beings they saw stepping ashore from their floating islands came from beyond the water at the world's rim. They thought them to be guardians of the bright treasures of the world and bearers of gifts from the Grandfathers. But the Europeans were more in search of wealth than in possession of it. It was the America of the Encounter that gave gifts to the European world, not the other way around. Adam Smith once said that "the colony of a civilized nation which takes possession, either of waste country, or of one so thinly inhabited that the natives easily give place to the new settlers, advances more rapidly to wealth and greatness than any other human society." The natives here did not give place easily. In the main, they struggled to maintain their cultures while adjusting in varying measure to the new ones. But in the end they did give place.

America for the Europeans was release, a deliverance into open spaces that was almost addictive after such close cultural quarters on the mother ground. They often seemed crazy to indigenous eyes, unable to sit still. It took the most aggressive of them a little more than two centuries to get from the green of New England to the dun of the Great Basin, and they were still raring when they got there. They had the Pony Express in operation two years after the first of them arrived and were cutting timber for their mines and smelters in two years more. Perhaps that is what the French historian Fernand Braudel meant when he called this continental sprint and its consequences "the achievement by which Europe most truly revealed her own nature."

The first wave of the Encounter ran up the beaches of Florida. The Spanish moved inland to claim a territory that would include most of the land west of the Mississippi. But they turned out to be occupiers rather than transformers, and in any event their power did not last. Neither did that of the people who had swept into the northlands from the fishing grounds of the Grand Banks to establish their trading posts. The French eventually claimed extensive territories, from the St. Lawrence to the lower Mississippi, but they too did not prevail in continental terms. No, it was the Scots, English, and Irish who turned out to be the masters of transformation. They had plenty of help, some of it involuntary, but it was they who, more than any others, changed the scenery of this land.

Among the first signs of European corporate power were ruined beaver ponds, hundreds of them, the dams breached, vegetation luxuriant in the bottoms. Beaver may have numbered in the tens of millions in the Northeast immediately before the Encounter, but decline set in early and drastically. Many may have perished in outbreaks of tularemia. But the fate of many more was the increasingly common one of transformation from beings to commodities.

Furs for the adornment of the person had been the style in Europe long enough to have reduced its own populations of fur-bearers to negligible proportions. Squirrel and marten furs were coming in from fishing stations along the northern

American coasts. Muskrat, otter, fisher, found a ready market, along with hides of moose and deer. Bison, in time, would join the list. But beaver was the prime metaphor for the market. Hatters in Europe discovered that its fur, glorious in its own right, was well suited to making a superlative felt. French and Dutch traders here in northeastern North America took in 30,000 beaver pelts in 1620 and almost 300,000 in 1690. The slaughter went on, even after shortages took the price of beaver beyond the market's reach. In the early nineteenth century, with the beaver hat craze well in the past, white trappers in the Rockies kept drowning and skinning beaver until even they understood that the return was no longer worth the effort.

Cod from the banks off New England and the Canadian Maritimes was the first solidly successful European venture in North America. The fur trade was its first solidly successful terrestrial undertaking, and it was a joint venture. The partners were the people who watched the Europeans land. Reconciliation of that participation with what we know, or think we know, of pre-Columbian world-views here is both difficult and painful. How could people who conceived of existence in terms of mutual obligation among beings, who told themselves cautionary tales about overhunting, go after fur-bearing animals in this way? How, in particular, could they take such numbers of beaver, muskrat, and other earth-divers, who in mythical reality were the means of creation?

If you could listen to early Dutch traders in their posts on the Mohawk River, you might hear talk about how the Indians thought European goods were vastly superior to their own and would do anything to get them. But if you were to look in on, say, an Onondaga village on its escarpment south of Oneida Lake, you would see that that was not necessarily true. People did prize Dutch loden cloth, warmer than deerskin and easier to work. But they also put European goods to their own purposes, cutting up metal pots to make everything from adornments to arrowheads or reshaping axes into adze-hafted chopping tools.

Peoples caught in the Encounter faced the unintelligible. Undoubtedly, some heeded the myths that excessive trapping would bring revenge from the fur-bearers. It is possible that some thought the animals themselves might be behind the sicknesses that walked with the Europeans and that the shamans were powerless to confront. If the animals had thus broken the old covenants, then was it not just to declare war on them?

To these people, trading was a part of giving gifts. It conveyed individual status and mutual friendship. They did not understand pricing, did not understand why a beaver plew that brought so much powder and ball in exchange one season brought only half as much the next. Perhaps, they said, the trader no longer had love for them. They had never heard of the international enterprise of which he was part. They had never heard of the market forces to which he reacted.

Violence was inevitable, as disease, depopulation, and the influence of distant markets forced a reconstitution of native societies. The Iroquois played politics with the British and the French and raided tribes in New England and farther south. And east of the Connecticut River, a Wampanoag whom the

English called King Philip renounced his friendship with the whites and killed some of them before being driven to ground.

The British appear to have become increasingly self-absorbed about their presence here. With several exceptions, notably the Quakers in Pennsylvania and on Cape Cod, they lost sight of the people who greeted them and helped them through the first winters. They seemed to be pushing them aside, even as they transformed themselves into Americans. Thomas Jefferson, that man of reason, became enraged about native reaction to white intrusion. "This unfortunate race," he thundered, "whom we had been taking so much pains to save and to civilize, have by their unexpected desertion and ferocious barbarities justified extermination and now await our decision on their fate." He would decide, among other things, to urge his compatriots to trade sharp with the Indians, to bring them into debt great enough to facilitate the confiscation of their lands. This would be done, and an enduring landscape would fade into another, in which alteration has become the organizing principle.

The extensive European interventions in Africa and Asia had no such result; colonies there proved temporary, and Africans and Asians retained demographic majorities and claims to their geographies. Here, the British came to stay. Their descendants were the residents of record, and the "unfortunate race," duly reduced in numbers, came to live lives of dispossession.

The domestic alliance of the Europeans changed the land. The offspring of eight pigs brought to Hispaniola on the Admiral's second voyage went feral and rooted in the open forests of the Southeast on their way to becoming razorbacks. Cattle and that great transformer, the horse, came in with the Spanish, along with peaches and other fruit trees from Iberia and tomatoes, chilies, large-cobbed maize, and other garden and field vegetables from conquered Mexico. The Spanish excelled at floral introductions.

The British tried wheat in New England, though the stem

rust eventually got to it. Their pigs roamed the woods. Native grasses weren't nutritious enough for heavy grazing, so farmers imported timothy and other Old World varieties. British weeds, more adapted to open fields than most American varieties, thrived. The natives took to calling plaintain "Englishman's footprint," for it showed up wherever he stepped. They were saddened by the sight of honeybees, for they too were heralds of white presence.

Most of the first whites in New England lived in towns or the buds of cities, walled off from the alien forests. But when they moved into the backlands, the trees told the story. Families, often extended families helped by indentured servants, spent their lives clearing plots of land for their crops. In Petersham, about sixty miles east of our place above the Deerfield, one of the first large buildings built was a sawmill. Wood framed the story of white beginnings all across eastern America. Perhaps 400,000 square miles of forests were cut along the East Coast by 1800, and that was just the start of it.

The forest in Petersham was used to change. Hurricanes, fires, and other forces had created patchy woodland where pine and hemlock mixed with hardwoods. Colonial alteration was on a different scale. The axemen started slow, but by 1840 they had roughly three quarters of the land laid bare for their farms. Wood got scarce, what with local needs and the demands from growing cities to the east. But a combustible new to the region, coal, was beginning to warm urban houses and smudge urban skies. And new lands, with deep soils and few rocks, were opening up to the west. Petersham lost half its population during the nineteenth century, as the great Erie Canal and, a decade or two later, the New York Central and other railroads offered smooth traveling across the Empire State to opportunity that was easier on the back.

What was left went back to woods. Cellar holes gaped along the roads, and stone walls ran more in shade than sun. White pine, in dense stands, took over the fields, and hardwoods —

ash, cherry, maple, chestnut — grew in the understory. Loggers returned to enrich themselves with the pine. When they left, the hardwoods in the clear-cuts took over.

Carolyn Merchant, an environmental historian, writes that the transformation of Europe by two and a half millennia of "social evolution" was recapitulated in New England by an "ecological revolution" lasting only 250 years. In the process, some things have come full circle. Anyone flying over New England today can see a rough caricature of settlement's original landscape: cities, albeit large cities, surrounded by forests of second-growth trees — almost as many trees, runty as some may be, as those that looked down on native trails and gardens before Europe came to America.

By the early 1700s, Europeans were past the Appalachians, cutting and clearing in what were then the western lands. By the early 1800s, Europeans-turned-Americans were opening farms all through the rich country east of the Mississippi. Ohio, once almost all trees, would see its forest cover reduced by 85 percent. This was pacified territory, pacified by treaty, by cession of native lands, by expulsion.

The New England Yankees in the northern midlands were mostly the sons who hadn't inherited the farm or had inherited too many rocks. Traveling in a wide band just south of them were people from the Pennsylvania region, particularly the southeastern part settled mostly by Germans, some of the best farmers to come to America. You could recognize their farms by the neatness of their fields and the spaciousness of their barns. And way south, plantations were going west. The children of those who had built great holdings of rice along the Piedmont and of cotton in Alabama were following the black soils across Mississippi and Louisiana, trying their luck with sugar along the Mississippi levees. The hands that opened the land were most often black, and the work they performed was the labor of coercion.

The East was turning more and more to the market. Farms in New England got smaller, more intensive, more geared to supplying the cities, more damaging to the environment. I have trouble keeping in mind how close industrialization followed on the heels of white settlement on this continent. While trees were falling in Ohio, coal and steam were luring the mills from the eastern streams and into the towns. A truly dynamic economy was forming there, a market whose structures and demands would provide the energy for the midwestern metamorphosis to come.

The square and the rectangle heralded the metamorphosis. This is the only country in which geometry has been of such cadastral importance. Everywhere, with the exception of the thirteen original colonies, annexed Texas, and parts too rough for the surveyor's chain, the right angle became king. The layout was so tight that often no room was left for public roads. What could be more American than imposing an endless assortment of quadrangles on a round earth, than stamping stability on space?

Six hundred and forty acres in a section, divided into farms and towns. This was the result of a federal land ordinance of 1795, a dream of Mr. Jefferson, updated and expanded to give or sell as much land as possible to the veterans of the Revolution or those who, with land, might stay loyal to the Union during the Civil War. Eighty-acre plots were popular in Indiana, and the state's land offices were doing a land-office business. In the 1820s they sold 5 million acres for the modest sum of a little over $22 million. Forty acres were a hot item in Ohio. With luck and some help, a man could clear that much land, working his way out to his boundaries and cleaning up the place, in about eight years.

The speed of the thing! The Midwest went bald in a human lifetime. By 1860 there were no deer left to speak of in Illinois. In just decades, farm goods that once jounced along miserable dirt tracks shifted to flatboats, then steamboats, then railroads. Time remade itself. Trips shrank from several days to several hours.

The government, satisfied with its exercise in geometric geography, deferred to private enterprise in its development. Many of the towns on the prairie were railroad towns, sited by company planners with markets in mind. The railroads leaned on the throttle. They integrated, standard-gauge meeting standard-gauge in a network that covered about 100,000 miles in 1870 and a maximum of 440,000 miles early in the twentieth century. They hauled goods from coast to coast. They hauled immigrants by the millions, Europeans down on their luck or, like the Irish, down to their last potato. They hauled away the old landscapes and returned with the new.

Prairie was prairie to these people. If you could bust sod in Illinois, you could bust sod in the Dakotas. Farmers headed for the high plains, where the grasses grew shorter and rain was a sometime thing. The Yankees settled close to whatever trees they could find in these seas of stems. The Russo-Germans didn't mind the isolation. They knew steppe life, hard life. Their houses, made of rammed earth or manure, leaked and smelled. No matter. Raising grain mattered.

Go West, the boosters said. When you get there, prepare for paradise. The Dakota commissioner of immigration proclaimed that his region was soon to be the "garden spot of the nation." I suggest that we tear down some of the statues honoring the pioneers and replace them with memorials to those who enticed the boomers and their kin to people a continent. They were exceptionally skillful at working a town at the foot of Lake Michigan, the one called Chicago. The Great Lakes were made for trade, they sang. This is the best place for a great city, because the white race that's going to build it builds best here. The climate is temperate, but there are enough blizzards and heat waves to toughen the empire builders.

The place was a village when the 1830s came along. It could barely keep itself dry in the spring wet. It took about half a decade for the village to turn into a chaos of growth. Population increased. Land values rocketed up by a factor of 3,000. The geometric grid surveys made selling land as easy as selling a sheet of brownies. Land, animals, plants, people, were now commodities in the American enterprise centering on Chicago. This great conglomerate, beginning its reaching west to the sierras, east to coastal markets, and south down the Mississippi, would change the continental interior to suit its fancy. Rivers and then railroads would be its arms and the city its brain. Looking at such transformations at the end of the century, a French scholar called America "not so much a democracy as a huge commercial company for the discovery, cultivation, and capitalization of its enormous territory." The company called Chicago oozed mud, stank, and attracted entrepreneurs and workers from all over the world, including a merchant from Glasgow who turned out to be my grandfather.

Wheat was still chancy to grow at first, even on these superb prairie soils, because of its susceptibility to rust and other blights. But corn grew as it had for hundreds of years. The white farmers weren't all that partial to it, but they fed it to their animals. And they shipped it off to market through the Chicago system of elevators and exchanges.

All that activity on the prairie translated into activity north of Chicago. There were carpets of hardwoods close by, and fine stands of white pine farther north, in Michigan and Wisconsin. Some of the trees were six feet through and well over a hundred feet high. And they floated, in rafts and in jams that no Bunyon or Babe could spring loose.

A child of progress cried, "Centuries will hardly exhaust the pineries above us." Just one century was required. The cutovers merged in desolation, and the loggers turned their attention to hardwoods, hauling them out of the woods by rail.

Slash was everywhere, piles of it drying. And after a while, the inevitable happened. Flames drove through the slash faster than a man could run. A fire destroyed the town of Peshtigo, Wisconsin, in 1871 and killed 1,500 people, far more than were killed in the famous Chicago fire of that same year. The conflagrations would continue right into the next century, many of them started by sparks from locomotive stacks and train brakes. Those same locomotives could be the engines of delivery to hundreds of people threatened by fire. Hinckley, Minnesota, went up in flames in 1894, and four hundred townspeople went with it. More would have died if a train hadn't picked up refugees from the town and backed its way through the flames to a small sump outside of town, where they and the train crew sat, scorched and cowering in the water.

The lumber industry moved south to the yellow pine country running from Georgia west to Texas. Lumber towns sprouted and died there as the resources dwindled, and interest shifted to the huge forests of the Northwest. Chicago stayed where it was and added meat to its diet. Live animals, pigs and cattle mostly, began coming in by rail, and dead animals, taken apart with amazing skill and speed, headed out in cooler cars to the customers. Prairie fields and pastures strained to keep up the supply.

Farmers on the mixed-grass and short-grass plains way west of Chicago saw their chance to compete. Wheat could grow well there in wet years, but the droughts were hell on most grains. Meat, some thought, might be more profitable. Bison were meat, yes, and in the years just after the Civil War they must have numbered well up in the tens of millions on the plains. There was some demand for them. Army posts had bison on the menu regularly, and eastern tanners had learned how to tan bison hides and were eager to get them. But in the eyes of the entrepreneurs, these bovids were not the right bovids. Cattle should be here. The market said so.

By 1890 there were fewer than a thousand bison left. They were shot from ambush, from trains filled with sports from cities like Chicago. Their slaughter meant the death of those native cultures on the plains that had survived late-blooming epidemics. That was not entirely coincidental, for the Sioux and the Cheyenne were certainly not wanted in the communities of the new bovids. Many were themselves slaughtered, not a few at a place called Wounded Knee. A year later, in 1891, census takers estimated there were 250,000 native Americans left in the country, 10 percent of what conservative guessers think might have been the pre-Contact population. As Joseph Campbell once said, if you want to know how it feels to lose your environment, ask the Sioux.

And of course the plan worked. Cattle came up from the south to emptied land in Kansas, in Montana, and most of them made the final journey to the killing floors in Chicago and its competitors in the arts of butchery. They were now, for America, the true meat.

William Cronon, who spent years researching the environmental history of Chicago, came across a quotation that I can never forget. He found it in the memoir of a successful northwoods lumberman: "The habitual weakness of the American people is to assume that they have made themselves great, whereas their greatness has been in large measure thrust upon them by a bountiful providence which has given them forests, mines, fertile soil, and a variety of climate to enable them to sustain themselves in plenty."

Cronon wove that into his history of the hog butcher for the world. "To apply for a moment the language of economy to the ecology of the Great West," he wrote, "Chicago's explosive growth was purchased at the expense of prairies and forests. . . . Much of the capital that made the city was nature's own." What made Chicago made the country.

It's odd to think about the trails humans have taken in this land. The first people here did their pioneering eastward and down through the latitudes toward warmth and wet. The sodbusters and ranchers of the high plains went the other way.

Every mile they moved westward meant a shorter supply of rain. They were heading for hardship, and they were determined to turn what they found into the breadbasket of the world.

Odd too that the Euro-American transformation of the plains should have hidden itself so well. There were grazers and grasses here for millennia before the Encounter. There were grazers and grasses after the Americans arrived — longhorns and the newer breeds, and wheat now bred to withstand most of the old pathogens. But beneath the similarities was a great difference, a market, a Chicago dried out and spread thin. John Wesley Powell, the one-armed survivor of Shiloh who came to know the arid West personally and painfully, argued that it should be settled with the greatest care. But prudence has not done well in our history against the passions of our received destiny. Rain, the boosters used to say, follows the plow. That interesting bit of romantic hoopla got lots of people into deep, dry trouble.

The drought of the 1890s was the first big one whites saw on the plains. A lot of farmers gave up, about 300,000 in all. But the first rains brought in a fresh crop of high hearts. New techniques for raising small grains developed early in the twentieth century — dry-farming, farming in strips, one fallow, one seeded. And it seemed to work pretty well. Tractors increased efficiency. Prices were on the rise, and . . .

Here it came again. The thirties were upon us, the Depression, and now this, the Dust Bowl. The clouds on the horizon were the wrong color for rain. They were the land in suspension, and they were moving from the plains east, dropping dust on Pennsylvania, on the swells of the Atlantic. People paid some attention this time. No more square agriculture on a round earth. Farmers plowed by the contour to cut erosion, and they planted trees as if trees could rake water from the air.

But America was soon at war, and the war effort needed wheat. Farmers joined factory workers as national heroes, and prices went up and cautious husbandry went down. The war ended, and the climate got drier, but now the cry was "Feed the world." New hybrids thrived in land doctored with pesticides and fertilizers. Tractors and combines got larger and more expensive. Efficiency was the word. IBM moved into the farmhouse. We *were* feeding the world, and earning a good profit doing it.

What conflagrations do to a forest or a gully to a field is easy to spot. The damage heavy equipment was doing by compacting farm soils below the surface was not. Neither was the damage wrought by changes in the soil brought on by chemicals sprayed on plants above ground. Nor the drop in water tables caused by exponential increases in deep pumping to feed irrigation systems. The colors of modern agriculture in dry America became the green circle on a dun background, the signature of the center-pivot sprayer. The invention has become an important agent in the diminution of the Ogallala aquifer, the water-bearing stratum underlying the plains from Texas up to South Dakota. Wells are going dry, and with drawdowns ranging in many places from six inches to four feet a year, many deeper ones don't have all that much water left to pump.

The plains are one place where our historical mysticism may have got the better of us. We, like any people, have our mythical realities, and one of those is the solitary being who breaks the land, who stands against the elements. The fact that the interactions of our technologies and economies have carried us well beyond the myth seems irrelevant. I hear many more voices than I once heard arguing for a retiring of marginal land, a withdrawal from the tough places, but they still don't have enough volume to keep agriculture and ranching from their appointed rounds. Not when, as one scholar notes, "American farmland policy is still closely connected to the patriotic pieties of frontier individualism and Manifest Destiny." In this crucible of privatism, it can be a blot on one's manhood to advocate anything less than full-bore, fencerow-to-fencerow farming. When the going gets tough, the tough do what they want.

Perhaps the most individualistic individualism to be had, on this continent at least, has its home in the Southwest. I'd like to see what Scottsdale is like. It was comfortably outside Phoenix in 1942. It must be well within the urban maw by now. With the demographic flight to the Sun Belt, Phoenix must today have a population of a million souls. Scottsdale in 1942 was quiet, full of citrus and doves. The groves were, of course, irrigated. You can't have seven inches of rain a year and not water citrus. But today the gem of the desert is out to convince itself that water doesn't matter. Phoenix has declared itself mesic. It has fountains and emerald greens. You could do some fake surfing there, if your thirst for irony was up. Perhaps you still can. I hear you can go to a mall and sit under artificial clouds, though I haven't had the strength to ask why anyone would want to do that.

The city, we know, is built hard by some of the irrigation systems devised by the Hohokam people. Surely, some Phoenicians know that Hohokam means "all used up." Surely, some remember Mesopotamia and the irrigation practices there that literally salted the land. Memories are one thing, mandates another. Desert Americans have their own manifest destiny: make the desert bloom like a rose.

The Mormons were the first whites, and perhaps the best, at working on that covenant. They led canals from the rivers flowing through their assigned place in Utah onto fields and farmed those fields with great efficiency. And when it came time for the federal government to join in the Southwest's blooming business, its projects were often based on Mormon practices and staffed by Mormon experts.

Bureaucrats in wet Washington and rugged individualists in the desert West don't seem like a promising match. They did fight and they still do, but together they have managed to rearrange regional water supplies more thoroughly than a Class A act of God. The Colorado, John Wesley Powell's river, tells the story best for me. There is Lake Powell, backed up a couple of hundred miles above Glen Canyon Dam and covering some of the most beautiful wooded gorges in the country. Then there is Lake Mead and the master of the hundreds of significant dams Americans have spread around their watersheds: Hoover Dam, or, to many my age, Boulder Dam. (They changed the name back to Hoover on me, to my discouragement and confusion.) There is Lake Mojave and Lake Havasu. And then there is Mexico.

It would be a mistake to call the lower Colorado a river. It spends too much of its life in tunnels and concrete canals and spigots here and there. It doesn't flow anymore, it feeds: Phoenix, the cities of southern California. Engineers measured its water during wet years, and so it is called "in deficit" now. As with many overused rivers, its waters become ever more saline as it descends, and the salts collect in the soils it irrigates. The Colorado once hit the Gulf of California like a fist. Now it is a stranger to its own delta. Yet its transformation has been a model for other thirsty societies. Hoover Dam helped convince the Egyptians, whose ancestors, we know, ran a truly sustainable irrigation system out of the Nile, to build a dam of their own. They have it, Aswan, and it is changing the ecological cycles of the Nile Delta in frightening ways; it is trapping the sediments the Nile, like the Colorado, once carried to its floodplains.

We have agriculture from the Colorado and other desert rivers that the Sumerians would have understood — and gasped at. We have electricity. We have fountains, golf courses, palm groves, citrus, artificial surfing. We have salination, water deficits. And we have a human deficit, a cultural overdraft. Perhaps nowhere else do we tend to draw down resources to make a landscape what it is not and then flock to it. In this Americans may be like Anasazi. It may be our hidden intent to catch water in the desert while we can, build grandly on its gifts, and then move on. But where?

*

When it comes to looking at ourselves as meddlers on a national scale, you could focus on sprouting cities or shifting patterns of economic output. But you could do that just about anywhere in the industrializing world. The great Yankee Doodle saga of landscape alteration began in Titusville, Pennsylvania, in 1859 underneath a tall wooden contraption outside town, a derrick being used by a retired railroad conductor named Edwin L. Drake to drill for something that most American drillers up to then considered next to useless. Some sold it as an elixir, a cure-all. But Drake wanted it as a illuminant, something that would light American lanterns.

Rock oil, as they called the stuff in Titusville, isn't an American phenomenon, of course. The Chinese were drilling, presumably for petroleum, nine hundred years ago, and there were a couple of hundred producing wells in Burma when Washington crossed the Delaware. But Drake's successors, in typical Yankee fashion, turned oil into an industry that would account for more personal fortunes and bankruptcies than just about any other venture in this venturesome country.

The story then moves to, say, the Ohio of 1900. Most of the roads there were terrible. The country had arguably the best railroad system in the world at that point and one of the worst road systems — spring ruts and summer dust. The wagon was still the farm vehicle of choice. People themselves had a hankering for the bicycle. There were about 10 million bikes in a population of less then 80 million, and biking associations like the League of American Wheelmen to sing their praises. But in Ohio, if you kept a sharp eye out, you might see a contraption that combined the bike, the buggy, and a rudimentary internal combustion engine. Crude as it was, it would have been doing a fine job of pulling itself through the mud. There were only 4,000 of them in the country in 1900. But their appeal in farm country was evident.

The automobile itself was not an American invention. There was a steam-powered tricycle creeping along French roads almost a decade before Paul Revere went for a gallop. No, the purely American thing about the automobile was what we did with it and what it has done with and to us. The successors to that automated bug have turned out to be the architects of America right through my home century and, I'll bet, far beyond.

The car made us all pioneers, gave us all that spatial freedom that so addicts us. In a book called *The Making of the American Landscape*, John A. Jakle, a geographer at the University of Illinois, looked back to these beginnings and linked our automania to "an American drive for individual fulfillment through freedom of mobility, the love of newness coupled with a naive belief in change as progress, the embracing of privatism fueled by competition rather than communal impulses, the pursuit of the utilitarian that embodies profound disrespect for the environment, and the belief in equality whereby a tyranny of the majority often rules." And he adds, "These social values can be observed in the processes of geographical change for which automobile technology stands symbolic."

The new conveyance got some inadvertent help from the transportation establishment. The railroad barons became so baronial that they started charging the moon for haulage. Some customers saw other ways of moving goods and began demanding more paved roads. Stoplights were sprouting by 1910, and concrete highways. As we got into our first world war, trucks were moving so much materiel east to the ports that they were damaging the nascent road system. That kind of heavy traffic called for licensing and for gas taxes. And for a national song of the road from car manufacturers and automobile associations. Jakle has one highway buff promising that pavement will make of Americans "one highly organized, proficient unit of dynamic, result-getting force electric with zeal."

Within a decade of the first stop signs, some states had more cars registered than most industrialized countries of Europe. Our car companies were buying out and closing down public transit systems in our cities, and no one seemed to mind. Who would, when for only weeks' wages you could buy one of Mr. Ford's jalopies and go anywhere you wanted when you wanted to? Hotcha! It was butt-sprung Fords that carried thousands of Joads west from the floods of dust in Oklahoma to the migrant camps of California. And it was the beginnings of streamlined bodies that took a little sting out of the Depression and gave us dreams. I remember going to the World's Fair in 1939 in Flushing Meadows, outside New York. I was not fazed by trylon or perisphere. But the Futurama had me rooted in the pavement. I stood there, a small blond boy transfixed by automotive malarkey — highways arcing high over parkland to link alabaster skyscrapers. I believed, I believed.

The real power of the automobile showed itself after the Second World War. The railroads that built the country no longer shaped it. Instead, public demands and the influence of oil and automotive corporations drove Congress to put public money on the car. Washington spent almost sixty dollars on highways to every one invested in urban mass transit. Critics pointed out that trains could carry a lot more people in a rush hour than could the long, slim parking lots connecting downtown with out there. But no one wanted to listen.

The landscape began to change as if it were potter's clay. Small business districts hollowed out as citizens opted to drive to larger stores. The American conviction that you could work in Gotham and live in Eden became obsessive. It was the sixties, and I myself was part of the fever. I drove my station wagon to New York and back to upper Westchester County — 104 miles a day every working day. And each year, traffic thickened and clotted while my fellow motorists and I continued to spurn the eight-thirteen to Grand Central and the six-oh-three to the home station.

The expressways have hog-tied us. Boston was once a city that knew about human scale and the value of neighborhoods. Almighty concrete has driven right through the place, tearing

it up, leaving too much of it in the shade of its spans and the stench of its congestions. America is a country drowning in its own motion. Something like 170 million Americans now drive 190 million vehicles of all sizes over 2 trillion miles every year. Distance to an American is now irrelevant. The car and the truck turn suburbs into satellite cities, rural intersections into acres of roofed and heated shopping space, airports into industrial parks.

Almost half of the 250 million human-man-beings who now live in the United States live in the suburbs. Very few of them want to. Most of them say they want to live in small towns. When they act on their dreams, of course, the small towns become large towns that look so much alike you can't tell if you're in Georgia or Oregon. We buy land in pretty hill towns and build second homes in the middle of what were working fields. John Stilgoe of Harvard, who studies such matters, has written that "whatever else the New England rural landscape is, it is for sale." Researchers at the Council for Environmental Quality in Washington figured that the land being converted in this country each year from rural to suburban or urban uses would stretch from coast to coast in a strip more than a mile wide. And that was fifteen years ago. I don't want to think how wide that strip would be now, recent recession or no recent recession.

We are seeking beauty and destroying it. The automobile and its attendant economy have made place as much a commodity as sowbellies. In ninety years, it has us where we evidently want to be. At last we have a truly national culture, one that is flying by so fast we can't keep up with it unless we want to risk getting a ticket.

I wonder at the metabolics of this society, the glory in doing, the impatience. I admire it, I am awed by our transformations. Their limitlessness scares me. I remember a poem my father wrote back in the thirties. It was a "sound track" for a book of Depression photographs called *Land of the Free*, but it fits the nineties. Men fleeing the Dust Bowl are talking, and they say: "We wonder if the liberty was land / We wonder if the liberty was grass / Greening ahead of us: grazed beyond horizons . . ." And later they say, "We wonder whether the dream of American liberty / Was two hundred years of pine and hardwood / And three generations of the grass / And the generations are up: the years over." And all through the long poem, they say, "We don't know" and "We're asking."

They are asking good questions.

10

This One Is Ours

IF MOMENTUM has a mantra, it is "Increase." We hear it in colonial genealogies. There was Increase Mather down in Boston and Increase Arms on the ridge where I grew up. "Increase," stamped on our coins, would be far more resonant, far closer to our nature, than "In God We Trust." It would look just fine stitched into the flag of any nation, city, or sect. But to see it real, in the flesh, all that is necessary is to visit a stadium anywhere in the world, a holiday attraction, a holy river, a bull ring. There we are, in numbers that are astounding to anyone old enough and curious enough to unlimber memory.

I have wandered in a continent unpeopled, in a continent twelve or more millennia later with a few million, in a country whose numbers have grown through 500 years of European occupation to more than 250 million. The entire world, with a few million at the turn into the Holocene, began its demographic bow-bend when the first cities took hold in Mesopotamia about 7,000 years ago, reaching almost half a billion by the time the Pilgrims came ashore in Massachusetts, two billion in 1928, the year of my birth. There are now about five and a half billion of us, and counting. Always counting.

Every one of us is a migrant or descendant of migrants; the only differentiation in that respect is the time and destination of the move or moves. White people were so scarce in colonial America that leaders were begging for warm bodies, British if at all possible, to come and start cutting trees. Which they did. After 1700, the American population began doubling every twenty-five years, something the populations of many poor countries are now doing. White women in America around 1800, native-born or newcomer, had slightly fewer than seven children on average, the family being the principal source of farm labor.

But the hazards of living here declined in time. Life expectancy rose from thirty-five years in colonial times to forty-seven at the beginning of this century. Increases in medical knowledge and practice have kicked the figure up to a bit over seventy-five years in nine decades. Fertility eased off as economic and demographic growth came to supply the nation with enough producers and consumers to keep things humming. Recent fertility rates have bobbed around the replacement rate of slightly over two births per female, but there are now so many potential mothers about that the population will keep expanding for some time.

Demography is full of surprises. A few tenths of a percent here or there can set things skittering. I am not comforted, for example, when told that the population of the United States has quadrupled in the past hundred years, that if we were to grow during the next two centuries at rates recorded over the past two, there would be some *16 billion* of us existing, if that's the proper word, in this country. I have read somewhere that it is mathematically, if not physically, possible for rates of growth sustainable over short periods to produce, if maintained long enough, a mass of human meat and bone exploding outward toward the stars at the speed of light.

Of more practical concern are the patterns of demographic concentration measurable today. We are an exceedingly sociable species, and you cannot keep us down on the farm the way you used to. Urbanization was on the lips of every analyst back in the fifties, when I was a journalist writing about Latin America. Cities there were in flood. They still are. Mexico City had about 4 million inhabitants when I visited it. It has 18 million now. The flood in the United States is best seen on night flights. You can look down on us, slumbering under our city lights: the northeast coast ablaze, and the southern rim of the Great Lakes, and long stretches of southern California along the Pacific, with dimmer but still impressive displays down in Florida. We like coasts. More than half of us live near them already, and the proportion is growing. What gives us our sense of space is mainly the great sweeps of near-empty plains, sparsely populated because their aridity spares them from our fruitfulness.

Americans are really pikers at the game of urbanization. One study compares the growth of our cities to those in mainland Asia. In 1950, North American urbanites numbered 108 million and our Asian counterparts 175 million. Now, the figures are slightly above 207 and 900 million respectively. By 2025, just a third of a century away, we will have 280 million city-dwellers, but the Asians will have *two and a half billion*.

City or country, it is the less fortunate world, as we measure fortune, that stands to grow the most in the coming century or so. Women of childbearing age (fifteen to late forties) are increasing their numbers much faster there than in more affluent societies. And though birthrates are coming down, the momentum of increase is such that during the quarter-century from 2000 to 2025, more than 90 percent of total world population growth is expected to occur among the societies of the less advantaged.

It is that increase more than any other that will double world population to 10 or 12 or more billion in the next century, and epidemiologists believe that not even the devastation of AIDS can do much to reduce that figure. The United States may grow to roughly 400 million around the middle of the century, before, in theory, the factors at play in its population dynamics slow growth and perhaps engineer a decline. The same reversal should begin to show itself at the global scale late in the next century, beginning with the economically developed countries.

At that point, if indeed it is reached, the industrialized world might be expected to sigh in relief. It probably won't. Not only will its cities be crowded to an extent I can only begin to imagine, its urban and rural populations will be aging. So aged, in fact, that an inordinate amount of money and effort will be necessary to care for elderly people, who by then will constitute a large portion of almost every well-to-do society. Without a lot of luck, persistence, and willingness to sacrifice living standards, the costs could beggar the richest nation of the twenty-first century.

I find it fascinating that we Americans would almost always rather pay attention to the fruits of our labor than to the fruits of our loins. The lags of cultural evolution are such that most of us, at some psychic level, are still on the frontier, still begging for more warm bodies. Perhaps we are not yet sufficiently in the present to understand the implications of the numbers we already have. Then too, our economics gets in the way. Henry Ford could not have made over the American landscape without a sufficient number of people earning a sufficient number of dollars to buy his products. Air traffic would still be limited to the daily mail plane without numbers of folk who want to get from one place to another in jig time. No one would be talking about the information age or artificial intelligence if there were not millions of naturally intelligent Americans eager to plug themselves and their new computers into these electronic supergrids. You just can't get very far in our world without the recurrent buying binge. For that, you need crowds to work, the bigger the better.

Whatever the reasons, I do not remember ever hearing a seriously campaigning politician seriously address the issues of American fertility and immigration. Not once have I heard

anyone discuss the feasibility of demographic objectives or limits. Nor do I expect to.

I was thinking these thoughts while driving from Washington to Annapolis on Route 50 east. I had managed to wheel my rental car into an automotive lava flow. A sign at the start of a half-dozen miles of construction said something about "Growing Pains to Get More Lanes." I know about growing pains. I was told I had them when I started to sprout as an adolescent. But this nation is now well past puberty, I thought. Shouldn't a mature country, like a mature person, have the good grace to stop growing?

As I sat listening to the exhaust gases conversing in the tailpipe, I toted up a few reasons why we should do so. We have become so adept in our consumption that we willingly build obsolescence into our products. The whole enterprise is geared to a throwaway rate that makes us the waste kings of the world. In our getting and spending, each of us uses up close to thirty times more energy than, say, a farmer in Africa. We use far more resources in our manufacturing than any other society.

All this makes us, for the time being, the envy of our species, I thought, and remembered a recurrent vision of mine: Uncle Sam is making his way down the steep and muddy trail from the peak of demand when he meets a group of what the euphemists call developing countries toiling up the grade. Don't go up there, he says. You'll be up to your ears in Styrofoam cups and disposable diapers. That's not what you've been telling us, they say. Move aside, old man. You've got yours. We want ours.

Which is another way of saying that though every country wants its own future, most take an occasional if surreptitious look at it through the lens of American history. What will happen if the world a few decades hence is one in which, as one authority puts it, there are "twice as many people who might be seeking three times as much food and fiber, consuming four times as much energy in five times to ten times as much economic activity"? What will happen if China and India, each at present with populations of around one billion, realize their manifest destiny — if China fuels its growth with power and pollution from its enormous coal reserves, if India can create enough jobs to increase purchasing power by orders of magnitude?

Our history and our present offer some clues, though on a modest scale compared with the contemplations above, and they should be of no surprise to you who have traveled these pages. Cost tracks benefit as a hound the coon. The factories and utilities that carried us into the industrial age were until recently emitting enough sulfates and other compounds to bring the acidity of precipitation in the eastern United States to levels approaching that of lemon juice, and it remains to be seen whether the reduction in some of those emissions will be permanent. The automobiles that opened our lives and land-scapes are now numerous and powerful enough to change the chemical composition of air masses, catalytic converters or no. The agriculture that made a metropolis of Chicago and went on to feed the world is operating on thin margins of soil and water in too many regions, and the margins are thinning fur-ther as fields lose their power to nurture, aquifers shrink, and the best loams mount the wind or head downstream. Our greatest cities lie under skies that are often foul, their popula-tions stressed by overcrowding and chronic underfunding of public services, their streets filthy and dangerous. Our coun-tryside, already compromised by the demands of our domestic alliance, now bows before demands for housing, and as it shrinks so do the living spaces that billions of wild beings once occupied. Diseases of crowding — tuberculosis, for one — are with us again, keeping company with cancer, heart ailments, depression, and other handmaidens of our advance.

The National Academy of Science and the Royal Society of London urge us to reduce our populations and our environ-mental impacts to avoid "irreversible damage to earth's capac-ity to sustain life." That is but one of the admonitory broadsides being released by scientific establishments around the world. I collect them, study them. But, perhaps like you, I am better motivated by warnings on a more personal scale. I know we have urban problems because I am terrified to walk after dark in midtown Manhattan, a place where I worked and, after dark, played for years back in the sixties. I know we have problems with biodiversity because I haven't heard the endless questioning of a whippoorwill for years; no one knows why they no longer spend their summers here in the Berkshires, but the theories mention destruction of their wintering grounds and the decline in the populations of their favorite moths. I know we are choking on our waste because they closed my town dump a few years ago, a place with one of the best views of the Deerfield Valley. Now I drive to a refuse station tucked in behind the knoll where the Big Indian stands and toss our paper and bottles into bins. There is no more room here to give garbage a decent burial, and there soon won't be room anywhere near here.

I think I know what global warming might feel like because of the summer of 1988, a sizzler, one of several sizzlers in the past ten years. My wife, Elizabeth, and I took a trip then. My friend Ida, Elizabeth's mother, had just died, and we wanted to make a pilgrimage to the Tetons, the mountains Ida had loved so much. Just before we left, I looked up at a fine old sugar maple near our house and saw that it was as bald as I am. I stood in confusion looking at that wintry sight in the heat of the season. Then I saw another ravaged tree down in the field and, my eye practiced, hundreds of them along the ridge across the brook. The culprits were pear thrips, tiny insects that appear from time to time. The thrips are often drawn, as are other leaf-eaters, to trees that are old or damaged by diseases or climatic extremes or poisons in the air.

We drove west among the smokestacks along the Great Lakes. We drove as part of the great annual automotive migration, and everywhere the radio announcers and the newspaper headlines asked the same question: "When will it end?"

When will the heat end? When will the dead air drift on? When will the rains come? The science columns carried interviews with researchers who thought they saw connections between the great drought — crop yields in the Midwest were down by something like a third that summer — and what could be the beginnings of a long-term warming trend caused in appreciable part by emissions from smokestacks and tailpipes.

The radio told us that in Washington, lawmakers showed considerably more interest in the greenhouse effect than they had in previous, cooler years. I know I did. It was hard to speed through the dry Dakotas in our air-conditioned lozenge, to creep through the palls of burning Yellowstone, and not suspect that we ourselves might be carrying some tiny speck of responsibility.

The idea of the greenhouse effect has been around for almost a century. In 1896, a Swedish chemist proposed that gaseous carbonic acid — carbon dioxide — and other trace compounds in the atmosphere had the capacity to trap some of the sun's energy reradiating from the earth's surface. This was a good thing, said the chemist, whose name was Arhennius, since the dominant atmospheric gases — nitrogen and oxygen — didn't have that capacity. Without carbon dioxide (and, we now know, methane, ozone, and nitrous oxides, and most of all the natural and abundant supplies of water vapor in the air), the earth would be a cold place indeed. With them, it is a proper vessel for life. But, said Arhennius, the vessel might get warmer if people kept burning coal and other matter rich in carbon.

I had never heard of Arhennius until I began doing research for this book. I paid only vague attention to global warming until that blistering summer of 1988. Now I am struggling to put the concept in its proper place. We probably will not be able to establish the presence or absence of the warming until the turn of the millennium, at the earliest. Its effects could be

extremely serious or minimal. But it is one of many consequences of our advancement, and its failure to develop would
relieve us only partially of the need to take or to accelerate a
whole suite of remedial actions.

We will be left with our numbers and their impact on the
earth in so many places. We will be left with the residues of
our technologies: precipitation may still be acidic enough to
weaken life in too many lakes and forests. Our smogs, cooking
in the sun, will produce far too much ozone for the good of
our lungs and our food; even at levels below regulatory maxi-
mums, the stuff can cut yields of corn, soybeans, wheat, and
cotton. And yet strong arguments are made, and strongly con-
tested, that there is not enough ozone where we need it —
in the stratosphere, where it can shield us from excessive dos-
ages of ultraviolet radiation. The international community has
taken steps to cut production of compounds that weaken that
shield of ozone. But the balance on high is a delicate one, and
we do not yet know if more should be done to preserve it. For
each 1 percent of ozone depletion, 2 percent more ultraviolet
radiation reaches the earth. An increase in radiation of only
5 percent might possibly cut the lifetimes of phytoplankton,
the tiny sea plants at the base of the marine food chain, by
half. The chances of that happening in the ocean around Antarctica, one of the most productive, are greater than anywhere
else because of recurring holes in the ozone shield high above
it. Damage to the United States would be less, but probably
still enough to cut crop yields and cause several million additional skin cancers over the next century.

But we focus on global warming, so Damoclean to so
many of us, so much an impending act of God, the supreme
parental punishment. In reality, neither those experts who
predict warming nor those who take issue with their models
and extrapolations can mount a decisive argument. Yet given
its psychic draw, the greenhouse effect has become the lists
for political jousting. On one side are those who believe that

governments can take actions to improve societies and economies and ecologies. On other other are those who do not. The
boosters are there, bless them. Amid all the gloom, it is a relief
to listen to them talk about what individual get-up-and-go can
do to keep America dreaming the American dream. And the
devotees of laissez-faire: not for them any suggestion that the
invisible hand of Adam Smith may be giving us an increasingly
visible finger. Business can find a way out of this, they say, if a
way needs to be found.

Some scientists are trying to balance the probabilities of
global warming against those of cooling, of moving out of
the present interglacial into the long slide toward the next ice
time. Others argue that increased warming will produce more
clouds, which will keep things cooler. Still others argue that
clouds can also trap heat radiating from the earth's surface.

George Woodwell, an ecologist who runs the Woods Hole
Research Center, on Cape Cod, is of the opinion that warming is not only probable but will feed on itself and accelerate
over time. It is a construct, he says, of "a continuous flow
of small decisions by individuals, families, villages, businesses,
industries, and government over decades. . . . Each of the decisions was rational at the time and seems rational now in the
limited context of most human activities, but together they
have brought crisis to the world."

Robert L. Peters, another expert on global change, has good
advice about the specter of the greenhouse, calmly delivered.
"We are in the position of a homeowner who has bought a
house in the Santa Monica mountains of California," he wrote
recently, "only to find that the best guess of fire-control experts is that a continuing buildup of shrubby vegetation will
fuel a large, home-destroying fire during the next thirty years.
I think most homeowners in this situation would sell the house
and move, or they would buy insurance, collectively manage
the vegetation to decrease fire probability, and put a fire-resis-
tant roof on the house. In dealing with the greenhouse effect,

we do not have the option of moving, which leaves us with preventing the warming or mitigating the effects."

The Intergovernmental Panel on Climate Change, which sifts through the findings and speculations of hundreds of researchers around the world, releases annual updates of its major conclusions. You can see its understanding of warming shifting slightly each year: estimates of population growth creep up a bit, and with them estimates of our emissions. Ironies arise. It appears that the loss of stratospheric ozone may result in a beneficial cooling effect as well as damage to plant life and human skin. Sulfur compounds in the atmosphere have deflected enough sunlight in the Northern Hemisphere to cool temperatures appreciably in recent decades — while acidifying precipitation.

The Intergovernmental Panel on Climate Change and many other prognosticators rely increasingly on computerized complexities that seek to carry climatic processes forward in time. The most impressive are the several general circulation models that work on global scales. They run on the laws of physics and on physical parameterizations, or simplifications of such phenomena as cloud cover and the slow pulse of deep-ocean mixing. Building any mathematical model is a bit like writing a short story; the art lies in what you leave out. The power of computers has been soaring, but no machine can take on and process existence in the raw. One model will omit the Great Lakes, say, in the interest of something else. All are forced to a geographic scale too large — grid points for measurement can be three hundred miles apart — to bring even large storms into focus, and this may be one reason that estimating future patterns of precipitation is so difficult for modelers. The essential business of coupling oceanic and atmospheric processes must await the arrival of computers that haven't yet been designed.

The best models are improving their simulations of real climate past and present, and that should mean that they are getting somewhat better at running on into the future. Right now, their output and other data suggest to the IPCC that a doubling of atmospheric heat trapping would result in an increase in the mean surface temperature of 1.5° to 4.5°C (3.7° to 8°F) by the end of the next century. That is a faster clip than the three tenths to six tenths of a degree registered over the past century, an increase that the IPCC hints might have been greater if natural cooling had not set in during the period. It is also a global mean that takes little notice of regional differences. Temperatures in the tropics, for example, are not expected to rise much at all; the added energy of a greenhouse effect would be expended in evaporating more water. But when that warm, moist tropical air is freighted toward the poles by global circulation systems, it should produce a considerably larger temperature change in higher latitudes. The IPCC's best estimate, a 2.5°C rise in the next century, sounds modest. But it hides the strong possibility that temperatures in, say, northern Canada may go up by two or three times that amount.

We have seen that scenery can start changing even under one additional degree of warmth or cooling. Three degrees of warming, the midpoint in the IPCC's current range of predictions, would mean a world warmer than at any time in more than 100,000 years. Four degrees would place us at a level unexceeded, according to some arguments, for 40 *million* years.

Dillon Ripley, who was secretary of the Smithsonian in the seventies, came up with an insightful phrase for the bicentennial: "Look back lest you fail to mark the path ahead." I thought of that while flying out to Minneapolis a couple of years ago to see Margaret Davis. I had talked with her earlier about the impacts on eastern forests of late glacial and early Holocene warmings. Now I was going to get her thoughts on what might await us over the rim of the millennium.

The memory I carried back was of one little kettle hole like hundreds of others set in the lumpy terrain of Upper Michigan, too small to have a name. The half-dozen people who had just packed in a couple of hundred pounds of gear through snow and over deadfalls called it Raven Bog. I heard some eponymous cawing and mewing going on as the birds commented on the scene below. There, beneath a crude scaffold, a middle-aged woman hung in the cold and fitful breeze, her body slowly turning. She sat astride two bars protruding from the barrel of a stainless steel tube, and several young people strained against the rods to keep her revolving.

Nothing macabre there. This was high science, and that was Davis. She sat atop a corer, a tube four inches across and a yard long per section, with teeth at the working end for cutting through mats of seeds, needles, branches, and other plant parts that make up much of the bog sediments. Her purpose at the moment was to add her weight and her encouragement to the effort of forcing the corer down through a thick and sodden chunk of wood.

This was galley labor, and it wore out the strongest of the young bodies present in short order. But the corer eventually plunged through to more passable strata, and in a few minutes a cylinder of peaty earth lay on a special tray, ready for wrapping in plastic and aluminum foil and the long trip back to Davis's lab at the University of Minnesota. There it would be transformed into a vegetational record covering the past several thousand years. Radiocarbon dates would be established for selected points in the sediment column. Then analysis would begin on microscopic grains of pollen and other vegetational markers freed from their matrix by solvents, clues to arboreal comings and goings as new arrivals attempted to establish themselves in the tiny catchment area of Raven Bog.

Eastern hemlock was one of Davis's target species. It had not yet established itself to any degree around the bog. There were seedlings in the area, but the deer kept browsing them back, and that made it harder to figure out what it takes for one kind of tree to invade an established community of other trees successfully. Hemlock is also one of four species that Davis and a colleague, Katherine Zabinski, studied in attempting to figure out what projected warmings in the eastern United States might trigger in terms of range extensions, health, and survival rates. The others are sugar maple, yellow birch, and beech — all familiar inhabitants of woods from the Michigan peninsula to the hills along the upper Deerfield.

Zabinski and Davis used runs from two general circulation models, one somewhat more conservative in its assumptions than the other, to see how the ranges of their four species might shift under conditions approximating those of the doubling of heat-trapping gases that many scientists believe may occur in the next hundred years. Each model had the four ranges trending northward, behaving roughly like climatic zones at the end of the last glaciation. Both models indicated that in about a century, all the ranges would have moved at least three hundred miles to the north. The less conservative one showed that maple would not be able to survive in most of its range except for Maine and parts of eastern Canada. Hemlock and yellow birch would also be forced north, and hemlock, quite sensitive to warm and arid conditions, would abandon its present western boundaries in Minnesota and environs. Beech, the primary casualty, would disappear from a great swath of the United States. Affected mostly by the decreasing precipitation evidenced by both models, it would be limited to smaller ranges, mostly in Ontario and Quebec.

The problem here is not so much the distance to be covered if these and other trees are to preserve themselves, given appreciable warming, but the time available for the journey. Climate change in the late Pleistocene and early Holocene may have advanced in stutters and jumps on occasion, but the general picture I get is one of slow dancing. Beech responded to warmth with an amble covering perhaps twelve miles in a century. Spruce in the West set something of a record, galloping across Canada at about 125 miles per century.

It is possible, of course, that some species caught in that earlier warming could have extended their ranges more rapidly. But an increase in mean surface temperature of two to three degrees Celsius in a century represents what Thompson Webb III, of the Geology Department at Brown University, calls "very rapid rates of change — at least an order of magnitude faster than the past." Some plants and animals may do very well in the speedup. But others may suffer from what Webb calls a "disequilibrium response." They will be outpaced by climate, if the models are telling true stories. They also could be stalled in their migrations by Los Angeles, by the interstate highway system, by the great swath of the corn belt. Beech and other nut-bearers would have no clouds of passenger pigeons to help them out this time. At some point, the laggards and the corralled, most of them, would fail in their efforts to reach canopy height. They would weaken, and their weakness would attract pathogens and insects, like the pear thrips in my maples. Even the healthy would suffer from the wild weather and wildfires that may well attend a great warming.

Recent surveys give a rough idea of what might happen in this country if the kind of warming posited by the Intergovernmental Panel on Climate Change does occur. California warms and dries in the next century. Ponderosa endures, but Douglas fir disappears from coastal lowlands. Precipitation in the Great Basin drops considerably in the increasingly severe continental climate (shades of the late Pleistocene). What snowmelt there is runs off to the sea earlier in the spring, and the season of green contracts. In the Southeast, the tendency in lower latitudes is to go to grass or shrubs. It depends on the severity of the warming. A little would send commercially valuable loblolly pine north to replace the short-leafed variety in Tennessee. A little more would turn eastern Tennessee into savanna. In northern Canada, the tundra's southern edge moves north by as much as four degrees of latitude. The boreal forest moves also. Both biomes shrink in extent, the boreal forest by about a third.

Beings other than trees and plants will be on the move too. Animals, of course, can move over a lot more ground in a year than any tree range. Most stay with the vegetation they or their prey prefer, but that preference has its limits. Trout and salmon can sicken, even succumb to sunstroke, if stream temperatures increase and flows diminish, and they will swim if they can to cooler waters. Grayling appear to be moving north out of Michigan right now, though that may be in response to other factors. Possum have been moving up my way for several decades now, again probably for reasons best known to themselves. But the pattern is intriguing: what once liked to live among the red maples, white pine, and aspen of the southern mixed hardwood forest now seems to be developing a hankering for the sugar maples, hemlock, and birch of the northern woods. In time, microbial life may join the migrations, bringing the usual bag of mixed results. Soil organisms that help plants draw nutrients such as nitrogen and phosphorus from the ground will be needed in the leaner soils of the north. But tropical pathogens may also head that way. That could easily mean that diseases such as malaria will become more common in higher latitudes and elevations. Humans may be able to combat the invasion, but birds, which are also susceptible to the disease, probably will not. The consequent drop in their numbers might easily mean a bloom of insect pests as the cold winters that now keep their populations down turn to warmer winters.

We too may well migrate. It seems likely that hotter summers in some parts of the South will eventually frazzle a number of residents, and it would be surprising if some didn't head for the northern lake country. Water levels there probably will be down somewhat, but not enough to make too much difference. But once there, of course, the newcomers will be competing for space, for habitat, with all the other beings looking for cool. Something will have to give in all this struggling biota. From trees to toads, the experts say, we can expect ex-

tinctions at a much higher rate than we have witnessed —
and, with our interventions, accelerated — during our short
history on this continent. And as in the time of the first human
arrivals here, we will see associations of plants and animals
that are novel to us and to the world. Resilience in nature may
be dimmed, but it will not die.

City-dwellers, which is to say most Americans, can expect
mixed results from a rise of three degrees Celsius by the latter half of the next century. Clevelanders probably will pay
less for snow plowing, salting, and other chores of winter and
more for air conditioning, so net outlays associated with global
warming will remain roughly the same for them. To the south,
air conditioning demand will rise in summer, putting a considerable load on local utilities, enough in some spots to spur construction of new facilities. It follows that utility stacks will
emit more pollutants into the atmosphere, contributing both
to local smogs and to concentrations of radioactive trace gases
higher in the atmosphere.

Higher temperatures will bake urban air more thoroughly.
Ozone concentrations consequently could rise to new levels.
If the San Francisco Bay area were to heat up by four degrees
Celsius, areas where ozone currently exceeds regulatory standards would double, and what the Environmental Protection
Agency calls "people-hours" of exposure might triple. Similar
patterns would develop in spots across the Midwest and the
Southeast. Smog doesn't just smell bad and reduce visibility.
Studies in Los Angeles, which has been fighting air pollution
more intensely than just about any city in the country, show
that smog reduces lung functions of the city's children by up
to 15 percent, and the damage may often be permanent. Attempting to put dollar values on days lost to sickness and lives
shortened in Los Angeles by the effects of ground-level ozone
and fine particulates alone, one group of researchers came up
with a total of $9.4 billion annually.

Some urban water supplies will be exceptionally vulnerable,

especially since it usually takes a decade or more to plan and build systems that can relieve shortages brought on by changes in temperature or precipitation. That infamous summer of 1988 gave us a taste of what heat can do. The Mississippi dwindled so that the city of New Orleans had to invest in a silt dike across the riverbottom to prevent encroachment by a tongue of saltwater that threatened the city's intake system. New York would face increased water demands under global warming, mainly because the evaporation towers that cool its large buildings would be working overtime. At the same time, the heat could evaporate enough water from the reservoirs that feed New York to reduce their supplies by more than 10 percent.

A rise of one degree Celsius can produce enough thermal expansion to raise sea levels around the world by roughly four inches. Then there are glaciers and terrestrial ice sheets to consider. There are no firm estimates as to what will happen if we bring about a superinterglacial. But not much of a rise is necessary to put some of New York's freshwater intakes in danger of saline invasions. Miami is in a more precarious position. It lies low, and its aquifers are porous. Both cities, and dozens of other coastal communities, may suffer as well from an increase in hurricanes and storm surges as the climate changes over the coming decades.

It looks as if our domesticates will follow the wild beings north. Corn, wheat, and soybeans, the great triad of our agriculture, may well need shifting toward cooler and wetter regions if and when higher temperatures in southern regions drop yields enough to make the move worthwhile. It would be expensive for farmers to migrate, particularly the growing numbers of them who rely on some form of irrigation. Putting in a new system of wells, ditches, and pumps can cost several thousand dollars an acre. And it is increasingly difficult for the large-scale, sophisticated agriculture that has made us the envy of the world to thread its way past cities and suburban sprawl to find the land it needs in the quantity it requires. Even if it is successful, the soils it encounters will often be leaner. When you get well into Minnesota or North Dakota, if you mean to maintain your averages, you will have to use a lot of chemical fertilizers, and that may accelerate the nutrient pollution that is already a problem in and around the northern lake country.

Water is of the essence in farming. And in urban expansion. And in livestock expansion. The pressures of multiple water use we have seen in California will increase with global warming. And if the more severe model simulations turn out to be correct, the Great Plains and other arid areas may be forced to install more center-pivot devices, particularly in areas where dry-land farming is now practiced. California may be able to stave off severe problems by shuffling water supplies. But that may not work well enough elsewhere in the Great American Desert. Meantime, economics will see to it that as and if our crop yields drop, the prices for grains and other food crops will rise, and more farmers may be able to afford irrigation, even if many streams and aquifers can't.

Even with adequate water, higher temperatures, particularly if they come in surges like the ones that swept across the country in 1988, can damage crops. Leaf temperatures rise high enough to stunt growth. And if heat wave and blooming coincide, crops such as corn, wheat, soybeans, and sorghum can lose growth momentum and set smaller amounts of seeds. Heat can also affect cattle. Enough of it can cut estrous cycles short, reduce male fertility, and produce a superabundance of pests like the hornfly, which already accounts for significant mortalities among American cattle.

Though crops may be less fruitful if heat bears down on us, there should be enough food for the domestic market. We can probably figure out ways to handle the price increases that warming would bring. But we probably will be forced to cut exports, and that could result in serious international problems. Global warming means what it says. If climate changes here, it will change, in different patterns, almost everywhere. Some countries may gain from increased precipitation or shifts in weather extremes, but many will not. Developing countries under the goad of population pressures will need all the food they can get. And if American farmers are forced to raise prices and focus on markets at home, the social and political results overseas could be explosive and widespread.

Those who model the future have a devil of a time with one variable: human reaction to crisis. Farmers here have made huge mistakes, as those who lived through the Dust Bowl can attest. But they have shown flexibility time after time and will undoubtedly do so if climate shifts beyond their liking. They may decide to practice different forms of tillage, plant varieties of grains that can take the heat and do well in the longer growing seasons that may be our due. They can change their planting and harvesting schedules. In all this, they may get some help here and there from an unlikely source: the very gas whose increase we use as the basic marker of the greenhouse effect.

Carbon dioxide can act as a kind of fertilizer. Laboratory experiments have shown that in elevated concentrations it increases growth in parts of some plants and increases yield in some crops. It does so by making available more carbon, the essence of vegetational tissue. Leaves take in the enriched mixture and pass it on to their chloroplasts, the engines of the photosynthetic process, whereby chemical changes in the presence of sunlight produce carbohydrates that drive growth processes. Normally, photosynthesis involves the loss of a good deal of water through the leaf pores. But with more atmospheric carbon dioxide on hand, transpiration drops off, and with the energy thus saved, photosynthesis rates increase even more.

The problem is that long-term field experiments with enriched carbon dioxide mixtures are few. As usual, when hard data are negligible, opinion has a field day. Those who mistrust the theories of global warming have received news of the invisible helper with a booster's joy. Sure, we'll get a doubling of carbon dioxide, they argue. But we may not get any warming to speak of out of it. Meantime, carbon dioxide will make our day. The more fossil fuels we burn, the greener the earth gets.

Most of those who are involved in carbon dioxide experiments or attempting to model the effects of its atmospheric increases choose to take the middle way. Bert Drake does. His is one of perhaps a half-dozen field programs actually trying to see what high-CO_2 conditions bring about in a natural ecosystem. It was his setup in a salt marsh near Annapolis that I was heading for when I fell afoul of the traffic jam on Route 50.

For six years Drake had been injecting a mixture of air and enough carbon dioxide to represent a doubling of present amounts (to seven hundred parts per million) into clear plastic, open-topped chambers set in almost pure stands of sedges and marsh grass. He reports that plants in the high-gas chambers have grown faster than control plants and that most of the growth has occurred below ground.

Drake is careful not to state that what goes for a Chesapeake marsh will go everywhere. But he does think that if atmospheric carbon dioxide doubles in the next century, it should increase productivity in some forests and fields. The effects would not be uniform. Almost all trees, and crops such as wheat, rice, potatoes, and beans, are what is known as C_3 plants, a reference to the way carbon is organized in vegetal tissue. Their method of dealing with carbon dioxide is such that a doubling of the gas in the atmosphere would tend to increase their rates of photosynthesis markedly. Other plants, such as corn, sorghum, sugarcane, millet, and some grasses, called C_4 organisms, process carbon dioxide in a different way and would benefit less.

Carbon dioxide is no cure-all (nor is increased productivity, for that matter). Increased amounts of the gas can spur growth only where nutrients, water, and other necessities for growth are in proper abundance. Here again, the inequalities of economic development will come into play. Herman Shugart and Thomas Smith, scientists at the University of Virginia, have been running models that look at the implications of global warming for agriculture around the world. They find that the richer nations will be able to pay for the fertilizers and, where sufficient supplies exist, the water systems necessary to take advantage of whatever increases in productivity may accrue from a doubling of carbon dioxide. "The poorer countries," Shugart says, "get hammered."

Drake and many others believe that because elevated carbon dioxide encourages more efficient use of water in plant tissues, some species will be able to extend their ranges into areas now too arid for their survival. Drake is also fairly sure that since the gas induces more growth where temperatures are highest, the stems and root systems of tropical trees should put on mass in coming decades. If they could thus increase the amount of carbon they store, the effect might be to offset to some degree the release of what could become significant amounts of carbon in high northern latitudes. Several researchers have shown that warming in the tundra is causing permafrost to melt and dry out. A continuation of the process could mean that the enormous amount of dead vegetable matter once stored in anoxia in the wet, cold soil will decay and release greenhouse gases to the atmosphere. Many parts of the high north could go from carbon sink to carbon source. It is even possible that a positive feedback could develop, in which warming brought about by climbing levels of atmospheric carbon dioxide and other greenhouse agents would cause the release of even more gases from the ground, further accelerating the warming.

Sinks can have the effect of balancing sources. The ocean is the most important single sink for carbon, receiving carbon dioxide from the air, mixing it with its fluids, and passing it on to populations of phytoplankton, which take it up in photosynthesis and use it as building material in their bodies. Tundra is important, and so are temperate forests, which lock carbon into trunks and limbs for decades or centuries. But Drake and others feel that the tropical forests could perform yeoman service for the world. They could conceivably offset or more than offset what is predicted for the tundra. Temperatures over those canopies are not expected to go up more than a degree or so in the next century. No matter. Things are already hot enough for the fertilization effect of rising carbon dioxide concentrations to produce so much growth that rainforests could become by far the most important carbon reservoir on land.

Whether they do or do not depends on how a number of uncertainties play out. It is not clear, for instance, that nutrients would be present in sufficient quantity to permit rapid growth in tropical forests. Nor is it clear that growth produced by increased levels of carbon dioxide is a long-term event. Some experiments show that the growth curve slacks off, though Drake hasn't yet seen that in his marsh. Others indicate that ecosystems, in all their complexities, may not react to increased carbon dioxide and its way of speeding up carbon and nitrogen cycles in the soil the way individual plants or pure stands of a single species appear to. It seems likely that the effects, like most effects in nature, will be spotty on a continental or global scale. Meantime, we should not disregard further degradation. Tropical forests, we all know by now, are being decimated in many countries. Rising populations should add to that as more people come to demand more land to grow more food or fatten more animals. And once the trees are down, it will be difficult to get replacements to grow. Nutrients in rainforests are stored mostly in the vegetation. When the sun has borne down a bit on cleared land, the soil is apt to turn hard — and dead.

After Drake showed me his experimental plots, he drove me back to his building through old pastures gone to tulip poplars and past a field where one of the largest red oaks in the world soared above the dirt road. Drake said he had done some figuring with the data available and come up with enough sinks to absorb the equivalent of the carbon we now put in the air for about a hundred years more. "After which," he said, "there is no more room for it." He drove awhile and said, "It's not a very hopeful scenario," and, softly, "It doesn't look like the biosphere can really save us from ourselves."

11

A Native Sense

IN RECENT YEARS I have found myself lamenting over how much I have acted in the absence of awareness. I have lived much of my life in places of solitude — in New England, in Andean highlands, on the sea — and I suppose my senses are sharper because of it. I believe that in some stillness of weather, some turning of a season, I have remembered who I am, one creature among a mutuality of creatures. But then I have forgotten memory and returned to live on the surface of my life, pursuing the happinesses of being a fortunate American in what used to be called the American century.

It is not reaching for sackcloth to say that as a result I have lived mostly as a meddler. I accept the idea that intervention is a distinguishing mark of humankind. What unnerves me, now that I have reached the reflective promontory of sixty-five years, is the cumulative effect of my personal meddling. I was a wanton killer rather than a hunter. I reveled in better living through chemistry, regarding DDT and chlordane as gifts from the wizards. I contributed my share of cigarette smoke to the inhalations of all around me. All this was piddling compared to my interventions as a traveler. I estimate that I have made use of engines fueled by petroleum hydrocarbons in some form to travel close to 2 million miles so far — in airplanes, helicopters, boats, ships, tanks, and of course the automobile. Someday I may run into an expert who can tell me what that means in terms of tons of carbon dioxide, nitrous oxides, and other contaminants released to the nurturing air, but I'm in no hurry to find out.

A lot of this malfeasance, particularly the more juvenile offenses, came about through ignorance. What smarts is the realization that for years I have known in some detail about what carbon dioxide, nitrous oxides, and other byproducts of wizardly gifts can do to our surroundings and to ourselves. I drive a pickup truck because, I tell myself, I need it for dump runs and its four-wheel drive. It gets not much more than twenty miles to the gallon. I think nothing of owning a large refrigerator and a freezer and a (small) air conditioner, knowing that upon their demise they will probably release still more chlorofluorocarbons to deplete the supply of high-altitude ozone. I approach the inundations of mail-order catalogues with nothing but recyclement in mind and end up phoning in for things I want but do not need, thus adding to the excesses of consumerism and to the squanderings of forests, fields, and petroleum feedstocks.

After this kind of reflection, I more readily accept the comments on my condition of those whose people lived here before mine. Vine Deloria, as usual, has the target in his sights. "Increasingly," he writes, "American Indians are understanding the European invasion as a failure. That is to say, in spite of severe oppression, almost complete displacement, and substantial loss of religion and culture, Indians have not been completely defeated. Indeed, the hallmark of today's Indian psyche is the realization that the worst has now passed and that it is the white man with his careless attitude toward life and the environment who is actually in danger of extinction." Then Deloria puts his thesis plain: "The old Indian prophecies say that the white man's stay on these western continents will be the shortest of any who have come here. From an Indian point of view, the general theme by which to understand the history of the hemisphere would be the degree to which the whites have responded to the rhythms of the land — the degree to which they have become indigenous. From that perspective the judgment of Europeans is severe." .

Such language can draw from me a grunt of pure liberal guilt. So can Ron LaFrance, talking about the Iroquois' knowing we whites were coming west from the coast, what skills we had, about their determination to work with us to maintain the fine balance of existence as they knew it. "We failed," he once told me with a look of resignation. "We failed to convince you that you were going to eat your own shit, your garbage."

A great deal is in print and on posters these days about the native American view of life. Some of it is pure palimpsest. (I remember the shock of reading that some of Chief Seattle's sonorous prose about his love for the land was really the work of a contemporary white writer.) Much of it can sound as brittle and old as deerskin leggings in a museum. But Deloria, LaFrance, N. Scott Momaday, and many others are alive and vigorous. Their purpose is to resuscitate memory and thus the strength of their cultures, and I take keen interest in what they are doing and saying.

I'm writing in these last pages about a native sense. That does not necessarily mean an Indian sense, though in my view we in this country are blessed to have among us people who to one degree or another remember old ways of being. It does speak directly to what Vine Deloria is complaining about. Americans in general have never become indigenous. *Native* is not a particularly popular word with most of us, partly because of what we have done to natives and partly because our constant movement, like some cultural Cuisinart, stirs us into massive homogeneity. We roam a continent, working in similar jobs, living in similar houses, buying similar things. This flight to uniformity, away from surprise, is what frightens me most about myself and my compatriots. The writer Jamake Highwater, who carries Cherokee and Blackfoot blood, chose these lines from the Mexican poet Octavio Paz to introduce his book *The Primal Mind: Vision and Reality in Indian America:*

> What sets worlds in motion is the interplay of differences, their attractions and repulsions. Life is plurality, death is uniformity. By suppressing differences and peculiarities, by eliminating different civilizations and cultures, progress weakens life and favors death. The idea of a single civilization for everyone, implicit in the cult of progress and technique, impoverishes and mutilates us. Every view of the world that becomes extinct, every culture that disappears, diminishes a possibility of life.

It appears that those humans who have lived lightest and with most respect for the life around them have often been relatively egalitarian foragers, long native to their lands. Colonizers usually have exacted a heavy environmental toll, whether their colonies have been on Easter Island or the East Coast of North America. Frontiersmen at any time have been more interested in the excitement of "new" country than in its preservation. Americans were colonials and frontiersmen only a short time ago, as cultural change is counted. Though we claim sovereignty now and our frontiers are closed, we are still conditioned to think as we thought. It shows in our brand of meddling.

Yet it seems the forager remains within us, dreaming under our dreams of growth and technological wizardry. When economically advanced cultures began moving indoors en masse after the last world war, the forager moved with them. She grew uncomfortable in recycled air, in light that was merely an absence of darkness instead of the mother of existence. She fretted increasingly among the throngs of indoorsmen, their noises, smells, the racing of their minds, and the stagnation of their senses.

Only recently have some researchers come to the conclusion that the forager may be right. Natural light turns out to be essential to good health. The sight of trees outside the patient's window can speed his recovery. The experience of streams and hills may well furnish neural stimuli that our brains need, stimuli no televised nature show can provide. When people are asked — not polled, but asked with concern and understanding — about what they most yearn to see, the answer, from young and old, is often grass. Lots of it, with maybe a few trees and water somewhere. Grass. Rugs may be representations of grass, the mantle of our natal grounds on the savannas. We sit inside, in cells carpeted with plastic nubbins, and the forager within each of us dreams of grass.

Native sense, it seems to me, is carried in this dream, this message from the center reminding us of who we are before we are anything else. It is wisdom not easily reached in the cultures of programmed cleverness. But we can reach it, if we can bring ourselves to see existence as the web it truly is. Americans already have shown wisdom in creating national parks, in passing legislation to offset some of the worst effects of our meddling. Constancy is not one of humanity's most prominent traits, and sour economies and fears of dwindling standards of living have often turned us from our purpose and will continue to do so from time to time. But we can revive our awareness of our native sense if we talk about it to each other, if we listen to our lives in the old ways.

I am impressed by the recent work of two American social scientists who have taken the time to draw out a small number of respondents on their feelings about their surroundings, their environmental values. The study that interests me most involved long conversations with Europeans working in the field of environmental science and policymaking.

The researchers report that American respondents in another set of interviews raised concerns about responsibilities to safeguard the natural world for generations to come. But the Europeans expressed these concerns "in more concrete terms, considered a greater time length, and tied responsibility for the future more to national identity." An Austrian diplomat said, "Everybody here is standing on the shoulders of the previous generation. Next year, it will be a thousand years old, this country. So there is certainly the idea that it should go on, but there are threats to the environment. So we have to take care of the threats to the environment, even if they do not materialize during our lifetime."

Europe has a much longer record of intensive meddling in its past than America does. (The Dutch, having struggled for centuries to reclaim land from saltwater, now find their dikes and drainage systems so damaging to their ecosystems that in some areas they are preparing to let the sea back in.) Yet despite that long experience with intervention and its impacts, it seems that many European policymakers and political leaders still do not speak often about their personal views of nature. Many of those interviewed by the American social scientists had difficulty framing these feelings, and most said they had rarely, if ever, been asked before to do so. Some expressed regret that in their professional work they should consider it prudent to keep value and policy apart. Uniting the two, for me, would be a step toward rebuilding our confidence in our native sense.

A few days before I was to give a lecture about this book at the University of Tennessee, a student reporter there interviewed me by telephone. We were getting along famously when she asked, "Do you think we'll be able to solve these problems?" I mumbled and dodged. After I hung up, the obvious answer appeared to me. I should have said, "No." Emphatically. No, because the stories of this book are not about problems, no matter how often I may have fallen into old habits and referred to them as such. They are about our becomings over millennia upon millennia, the remarkable adaptations we have made and how those adaptations in turn have changed our circumstances. They are about trends.

The trends we've been talking about are for the most part long and laden vessels. They have considerable way on, enough to propel them far into the future without radical change in speed or course. We can turn some of these vessels, if enough of us want to, but probably they will not answer the helm until they have passed into the time of our children or our children's children. That is true of world population expansion, of migration from poor lands to rich, of despoliation of forests, of desertification, of famine, of accelerated extinction of species.

We have moved quickly, as these matters are measured, to halt worldwide production of the substances that appear to be attacking the ozone layer protecting us from ultraviolet radiation. With luck, very little will be produced beyond the millennium. But enough is already in the atmosphere — and in refrigerators and air conditioners like mine — so that substantial restoration of the layer probably won't occur for another three or four decades.

But we still have not recognized another tendency whose consequences may be fully as alarming as the loss of ozone: the increasing dominance of our domestic alliance. At the beginning of the American civil war, humans and their animals accounted for something around 5 percent of global terrestrial life. That figure had doubled by the Second World War, and it has doubled since. By the middle of the next century, the alliance may account for roughly 60 percent of all terrestrial animal life (excluding microorganisms) and 25 percent of all terrestrial plant life. That growth too may be alterable, but certainly not before humans see to their own demographic stability.

The environmental philosopher René Dubos insisted that trend is not destiny. I hang on those words as if they were a life buoy. We can do some things to change some of our worst impacts on the future. But to do them, we need to change the way we have acted in the world, the way that until now has contributed so much to our endurance. We need to stop thinking about tomorrow, recent political theme music to the contrary notwithstanding, and start thinking about life in the seventh generation, the tenth, the twentieth. There is rarely a "Eureka!" to be heard in this kind of work. The more common sound is the grinding of teeth as we try to work out whether to sacrifice now in order to avoid worse pain in the future or to tough it out, take what comes (if it comes), and adapt.

We know that carbon dioxide has been building up in the atmosphere, thanks in largest measure to our activities. The science of the thing indicates what should happen. It also indicates that enough greenhouse gases are already overhead to make it happen to some degree, and that even if we were to cap our emissions tomorrow, the process of warming would continue for decades. But, of course, what we don't know is whether our understanding is sufficient unto the day. What if the sinks for these gases turn out to be more absorbent than the sources are productive? What if we really are running out of the interglacial into a cooling sufficient to neutralize the warming? This is a nightmare, we say. Stop the confusion.

What we forget in all this is that probabilities are mostly what we have to work with in facing ourselves and our futures. The risks of being killed in a car crash, robbed, or flooded out are discernible enough to sustain a huge insurance industry (though damages from recent natural disasters have stressed many underwriters). But some aspects of global change, like many other environmental processes, lie well beyond risk assessment at present. In a decade or so, many of their probabilities may prove less difficult to quantify than those, say, of our eventually encountering a lethal virus now somnolent beneath the litter of a rainforest, but they are nonetheless not yet quantifiable.

I am a worrier, like my father, like his father. I tend to pop awake just before dawn gives an edge to the hills south of the Deerfield; energy suffuses me, gathers me up, focuses my entire being on runaway warming, financial ruin, disease, death, a malfunctioning drain in the kitchen, finishing this book. I lie in the gray-black, staring at disaster. Every environmental and social and personal misfortune my imagination can summon from the future comes to sit on my chest.

Years of experience with these demons have brought me to the notion that worry, personal or collective, is a byproduct of our rage to know the unknowable. Western societies in particular seem to believe that certainty is a human right. We hand over our concerns to people we call experts but believe to be clairvoyants and then are doubly worried when they are unable to come up with sure, simple, and inexpensive ways of dealing with them. The attitude is not ubiquitous — many of us think nothing of investing in stock markets driven by uncertainties — but it is pervasive, particularly when science and technology are involved.

Yet science, the touchstone for our pride in intellect, is itself largely the art of pursuing probabilities, and the pursuit has never been more intense. Quite a number of scientists and technicians these days are deliberately immersing themselves in uncertainties over what may develop well beyond what the lay mind insists is the foreseeable future. We don't know, they say, the chances of eventuality x becoming actuality x. But we know enough about x to set up some interesting scenarios on our computers showing a range of consequences that might ensue. That way, we create a reasonably credible basis for talking about how we might want to react to these uncertainties now. Military people and policy analysts have been among the principal sponsors of this very serious gaming. It is increasingly popular among those who must consider global warming and other environmental indeterminacies.

What I see in their activities is perhaps a way to shed light on what we can only guess at so that it becomes a more

acceptable part of public deliberations over where we are going. The more we admit to uncertainty, it seems to me, the
less of a bugaboo it will be. All of us who wish to can then say,
without risk of embarrassment, It looks as if robots are going
to change how we produce things. If that is so, what might
the benefits be and to whom will they accrue? Who will be
harmed? Biotechnology may revolutionize our lives as has no
other product of our cleverness since the automobile. Since
not one of us "knows," let's see if we can make the most informed guesses we can about what might happen in terms of
increased crop yields or crop failures, higher incomes among
some farmers or the dispossession of others.

When we start to talk together in this way, we might soon
realize how broad the subjects of silence are. The whole question of population size and density is taboo in America and in
many other countries. The taboo is well structured: not only
have we suppressed the topic, we have suppressed the fact that
we have suppressed it. And yet we all know parts of the country that are more thickly settled than they were only a few
years ago. We all know we get stuck in traffic jams more frequently than we used to. I'm pretty sure that if we were to discuss this among ourselves, many would not wish to see the
trend continue.

Discourse, open and as free of hidden purpose as we can
make it, should give discussants the comfort of coming to understand our knowledge, intuition, and ignorance about what
faces us and our descendants. We can listen to arguments
equating the numbers of people present in a society with the
severity of problems, ranging from resource depletion to ef-
fectiveness of government to the quality of life. And to arguments equating the numbers of people present with added
productivity and yet higher sophistication of technology. We
can express our fears about controlling our population, pointing to the astonishingly successful but often brutal programs
in China. We can talk about the advantages of reducing our

numbers as against the threat of lessening our military and economic might or of creating holes in our social canopy that would be filled by immigrants. We can face up to the current rate of immigration and ask ourselves, each of us an immigrant or a descendant of immigrants, what, if anything, we wish to do about the inflow.

We can breach the taboo that keeps us silent about limits and examine how we really feel about economic growth. Can it continue as it has? Will it continue? Will this current slippage in middle incomes in the United States be temporary? Can we keep on consuming almost anything and saving almost nothing and watching our debts rise to levels requiring tax burdens on our children's children that may well be two or three times what we pay? If we continue in our inability to create enough good jobs to go around, and it looks as if we will, would it be wise to encourage ourselves to procreate less and so have more to share? Most important, we can ask, Why have we *not* been talking about these things?

We can look at the prospects for global warming and talk about what we are willing to do or not do to change them. How much real money can we afford to marshal now against half-seen dangers looming above time's horizon? How much should we invest in preserves for species threatened by shifts in climatic ranges? How are we doing on developing seeds that can grow in warmer and wetter or drier weather? What are we truly willing to accept in terms of ways of life that pollute less and conserve more? What are the most critical areas for expanded research? We can listen to the experts argue these points and, instead of turning away in confusion, understand that they are as uncertain as we and join them in trying to find actions that make the most sense to us under the circumstances. We can also address a trend that appears to be strengthening with each item of discouraging news about the effects of our meddling: misanthropy. I hear it in some of my own statements, and I fear it. Hatred of the human race is of course self-hatred, the most disabling animus. We are what we are. We are also what we can be. Misanthropy is not destiny. Neither is the belief in some quarters that the degradations we have visited on our environments, and thus on ourselves, are reversible only through the actions of supreme national or international authority. Nothing in our past indicates that hierarchy can absolve us from our individual shortcomings. Often, it adds to them.

I think of the people at Bull Brook or the first camps in the San Juan basin or around more ancient hearths in Eurasia. They came together to discuss worlds far newer to them than ours is to us. They sat and exchanged information about what was hazardous and what yielded satisfaction. My instincts tell me that those gatherings, of and by themselves, provided more warmth and light than the embers of the night fires. We need to hold such councils.

I would welcome them. Through them we might even make progress in finding a word that describes what *environment* tries with such small success to describe. I don't think there *is* such a thing as environment. The word comes from the verb *environ*, which means to encircle. As I've mentioned before, prehistoric Americans didn't think of themselves as encircled by what they lived in. They considered themselves part of it. We should too, I think. Being surrounded is bad for one's peace of mind. Yet I mouth the word all the time, out of habit, out of the desire to conform, out of lack of any other appropriate noise to define the web of reality. Not man apart, they used to say a couple of decades back, during the organization of the first planetary palaver on "saving the planet." But negatives don't define. Then what does? Nature? Nature is apart, something we visit when we are on vacation. Habitat? A habitat in the public mind is a great tank submerged in the sea or a bubble encapsulating a stretch of desert in which brave or foolish volunteers shut themselves up for inordinate periods of time. Environmentalists have come up with *green*. That is a good try, I think, but seriously flawed. The world comes in many colors. Then too, if concern for green is the measure, then this country's most concerned environmentalists are its captains of industry, its masters of money, the very people the environmentally angry love most to hate.

My one and only suggestion is *Aum*, the Tibetan Buddhist way of approaching creation. It is as lovely as *environment* is ugly, but somehow I don't expect to hear the secretary of the interior or the managers of the Nature Conservancy making use of it anytime soon. And this is sad. How can we heal the rift between ourselves and the rest of existence if we have nothing that properly describes what lies on the other side of the breach — the breach we ourselves made?

A friend of mine, a plant geneticist, and I were pretty well into environmental values and verities one evening after a good dinner when he asked if I spoke to Jesus. No, I said, I speak to bears. I believe he jumped a little. But then he replied, like the good and loving Christian he is, "I guess it comes to the same thing."

I suppose it does. When any of us reaches for connection with creation, it probably doesn't make too much difference which metaphors we use. The bear image I see, shot with silver and gamboling among the stars, happens to work better for me at this point in my life than the great Christian myths I heard as a child, powerful as they still are to me. It does so because it represents that mutuality, that innate relatedness of creatures, that informs native sense as I have come to define it. I do not make any claims for the bear. None are needed. Besides, I cleave to the eleventh commandment, passed on to me by the Quaker skipper of the schooner *Welcome* out on the high Atlantic: "Thou shalt not believe that the Lord thy God is better than anybody else's."

I am grateful to Al Gore, then senator, now vice president, for clarifying the issue of human "dominion" over the world.

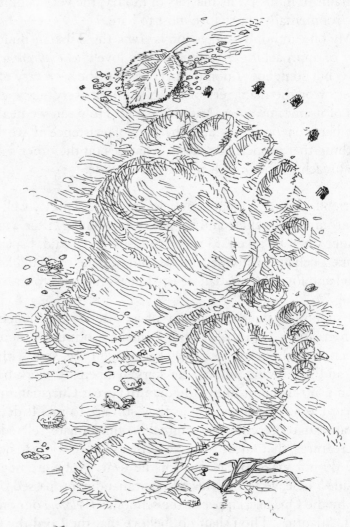

In *Earth in the Balance*, Gore explains that "the biblical passage that grants [followers of the Judeo-Christian tradition] 'dominion' also requires them to 'care for' the earth even as they 'work' it. The requirement of stewardship and its grant of dominion are not in conflict; in recognizing the sacredness of creation, believers are called upon to remember that even as they 'till' the earth they must also 'keep' it." That is an affirmation that many churchgoers in this country are trying to raise up, and I wish them well. For me, though, established religions I have known remain so focused on humankind — and, I might add, on the male of the species — that they appear to skimp on the rest of existence. My hope is that they will pay more attention in future to those who, like Gore, are trying to broaden the focus. James Parks Morton, dean of St. John's Cathedral in New York, comes to mind, and his friend Thomas Berry, the Catholic historian. "We never knew enough," Berry has written. "Nor were we sufficiently intimate with all our cousins in the great family of the earth. Nor could we listen to the creatures of the earth, each telling its own story. The time has now come, however, when we will listen or we will die."

Will we listen? Will we accept what our native sense tells us? The questions stab my mind as I lie in the gray-black. I hear the frightened plea in them: think of something to make it all right. That's about as far as I can get before taking evasive action. This is no time for divination, I say loudly to the dark. We're halfway through the last decade of the last century of a millennium. In no time at all, people will be crowding the hilltops waiting for bangs or whimpers or some other sign of divine displeasure. Belay. Let's think about it after we're safely past the oracles.

When I am awake and aware (two distinct states of being), I say that some of us are listening right now. More will listen when they come to understand that the deaf ear may not be exactly the best instrument to turn to the past. We certainly know a good deal more about our performance as a species than we did even a few years ago, and we will know more as environmental archaeology and paleoecology gain strength. We can see that we are superb at adaptation, that it is a principal agent at once of our advance and of our miseries. We can see that we will always face uncertainty, but we can now do so knowing that we have the responsibility to act in a precautionary fashion. If we say we wish to grow richer, we now have to ask the question that makes ecology so unpopular at the optimists' picnic: "What then?" If we say, as we do, "Let nature take its course," what then? We have much of nature in hobbles. The domestic alliance by now is so pervasive that we, its managing directors, may soon find it impossible to abdicate our responsibility to make choices, terrible and absolutely necessary choices: Which beings will we try to "save" by taming or tending? Which do we wish to leave, at what risks of extinction, in what passes now for the wild?

There is no indication I have come across that all of us will do these things. All of us never have, and some have pinched out along the way as a result. Marvin Harris, the anthropologist, is pessimistic about the outcome of what he calls "nature's experiment with mind and culture." The major developments in that experiment, he says, "do not bear witness to our kind's ability to exert conscious, intelligent control over our species' destiny." I'm sure he is right. But it does seem as if some groups of us, foragers mostly, were able, through what looks in part like deliberate measures, to increase their vagility by holding themselves in rough balance with their surroundings.

Our own culture is full of stories about seeing the light, taking the right turn. I think often of Scrooge. Admittedly, he was frightened into doing so, but there is more than enough fright inherent in social and environmental statistics and uncertainties these days to make Scrooges of us all.

These thoughts may be mostly sixty-five talking, words uttered well down the slope that leads to old age. In this country, the old are thought to suffer from a debilitating nostalgia that clouds their judgment. I admit I no longer keep abreast of some things that were at some point central to my life, and I pay for it with shock over what has happened to them. Hunting bows that were once sweet recurves of wood are now blunt metallic instruments. Lacrosse sticks that once were shaped from steamed hickory are now moldings of plastic. Guitars have been turned into electronic slabs and from them comes sound obviously designed to pester the elders.

Still, age by definition is an accumulation of experience. And being increasingly a stranger in one's own time has its own value. Those who go with the flow get a faster ride in a faster present. But those who from choice or necessity keep to the eddies and the edges have the opportunity of comparing what they see shooting by out in the current with what they *have* seen. And if the result at times is high old passion, a need to cry out against depredations and diminutions, then amen! I could do far worse in my aging than rail against bare maples and dead air, against the spiritual separation of my race from what nurtures it. I could be silent.

Come to think of it, it may be time to change my will. My interest in seeing how things turn out is now so great that I might ask to have my body placed in a cryogenic chamber, there to lie in hoary state until another five hundred years have passed. Who knows? They might be able to animate me. They could tell me what actually happened to global warming. They could tell me if we really are slipping back toward the big ice. By then, humans might have the technology to do that — and a lot more.

But if they do . . .

What then?

NOTES

I. EXISTENCE IN REALITY

Page 1. I describe *Welcome*'s crossing in *The Gulf Stream: Encounters with the Blue God* (Boston: Houghton Mifflin, 1989). According to the historian Samuel Eliot Morison, writing in *Admiral of the Ocean Sea*, Fernando found the passage about Oceanus loosing the chain of things in Seneca's play *Medea*.

Page 2. Dust from the Sahara regularly crosses the Atlantic and is thought to be a source of nutrients in low-latitude forests in the Americas.

Page 6. Jung's concepts of archetypes and the collective unconscious eased my anxieties over travels through prehistory. So did the late Joseph Campbell, who wrote of the "marvelous monotony" of human ritual forms all around the earth.

Page 7. Dincauze made these remarks in a distinguished faculty lecture at the University of Massachusetts in 1989. The lecture was entitled "The Gardeners of Eden."

The Red Queen hypothesis was presented as a "new evolutionary law" for ecological evaluation by Leigh Van Valen, of the Department of Biology of the University of Chicago, in 1973. His arguments appeared in the journal *Evolutionary Theory*.

Page 9. *Man's Role in Changing the Face of the Earth* (Chicago: University of Chicago Press, 1956) was edited by William L. Foster, who developed the symposium and was at the time assistant director of the Wenner-Gren Foundation for Anthropological Research, which funded it. *Man's Role* can be thought of as the midway point in the modern American dialogue over human intervention in the environment. George Perkins Marsh was the pioneer with his work *Man and Nature*, first published in 1864 and subsequently revised and republished, in 1886, as *The Earth as Modified by Human Action*. Marsh was honored by the editors of *Man's Role*, along with the "earliest men who first used tools and fire; and . . . the countless generations between, whose skilful hands and contriving brains have made a whole planet their home and provided our subject for study." In 1987 another group of scholars turned their attention to Marsh's theme under the auspices of Clark University's George Perkins Marsh Institute. The result of those deliberations was *The Earth as Transformed by Human Action* (New York: Cambridge University Press, 1991). The two increasingly emphatic verbs in the title, *modified* and then *transformed*, are telling markers of human progress in a single century.

2. ACROSS THE BORDER

Page 13. Ponce de León and his company may have been influenced by the rumor that natives of Cuba, suffering under the *conquistadores*, had been heard telling one another that if they could reach Florida, they would be young again. They meant young in freedom. The Spanish may have translated that yearning into the vision of a fountain of youth.

My guide in Calusa country was Dr. William Marquardt, of the Institute of Archaeology and Paleoenvironmental Studies at the University of Florida in Gainesville. Marquardt has written extensively on the Calusa and edited a monograph, "Culture and Environment in the Domain of the Calusas," published in 1991. Little remains of the works of the Fierce People. Their mounds and the remains of their canals lie strewn across back lots and pastures or overgrown by mangroves and gumbo-limbo trees in what is left of the coastal woodlands near Fort Myers.

Page 15. Dr. George Milner, of the Department of Anthropology at Pennsylvania State University in University Park, was a helpful source of information about Cahokia. A broad picture of the culture can be found in Chapter 6 of *The Mississippian Emergence*, edited by Bruce D. Smith (Washington: Smithsonian, 1990). The museum at the site is one of the best of its kind I have seen. Its films and dioramas are so compelling that the trails to the mounds themselves are often almost empty; at least, they were so on the lovely spring mornings I walked them.

Page 19. I had the great good luck at Chaco Canyon to fall in with R. Gwinn Vivian, who was guiding a party through the ruins. Vivian practically belongs to Chaco. His father excavated there before him, and he has spent years in the area, studying in particular the techniques by which people in a dry land use water in their subsistence. Among Vivian's publications is *The Chacoan Prehistory of the San Juan Basin* (New York: Academic Press, 1990). One of the most experienced interpreters of the region's environmental changes is Dr. Julio Betancourt, of the University of Arizona at Tucson. He is the author of, among many other papers and books, *Packrat Middens: The Last 40,000 Years of Biotic Change* (Tucson: University of Arizona Press, 1990). George Gumerman, an archaeologist at Southern Illinois University at Carbondale, has also studied the Anasazi and environmental change. Gumerman and a number of other paleohistorians have been pursuing questions of why some early groups of the Southwest built complex cultures only to revert to simpler ways of life. The most comprehensive survey of the region I have come across is *Prehistory of the Southwest*, by Linda S. Cordell (New York: Academic Press, 1984).

Page 22. The descriptions of life at Ozette come in part from conversations with two white archaeologists — Richard Dougherty, recently retired from Washington State University, and Gary Wessen — both of whom have worked closely with the Makah. The bulk of my information comes from a week spent in Neah Bay, Washington, at the Makah Cultural and Research Center. The center houses material recovered from the Ozette site and numbers of other artifacts. It is owned and run by the Makah, and its staffers, native and white, are assisted by elders, some of whom once lived at or near Ozette and who remember its language and customs. Dr. Ann Renker directs the center.

Page 27. Native acquisition and use of the horse have been widely discussed. A classic is *The Horse in Blackfoot Indian Culture*, by John C. Ewers, published and repeatedly reprinted by the Smithsonian Institution. Another is *The Indian and the Horse* (Norman: University of Oklahoma Press, 1955), by Frank Gilbert Roe, an Englishman who came to Canada at the turn of the century and wrote scholarly and lucid works, including *The North American Buffalo*, cited in the notes for Chapter 5.

Page 28. I visited the Great Hill, the escarpment south of Syracuse, with James Bradley, of the Peabody Museum in Andover, Massachusetts. Bradley is the author of *Evolution of the Onondaga Iroquois* (Syracuse: Syracuse University Press, 1987). We went from site to site, many of them lying now beneath cornfields or pastures. You can tell they are there, sometimes, by the greasy feel of soil with a high carbon content, by the color of the ground, or by concentrations of shaped stones in the furrows. The Onondaga nation now owns only about 6,000 acres, but most of its people live in a hamlet near the town of Nedro, toward the head of a broad valley running north and south. They are separated from the sites, and the sites are disappearing under development. For Bradley, that is like "watching a library burn when you know these are the only books left in the world."

Page 29. New findings, reported in the *New York Times* on December 7, 1993, indicate that conventional wisdom about ponderous swings in climate may be flawed. The Little Ice Age, like the Medieval Warm Period, may turn out to have been much shorter-lived and far more regional in impact than once thought.

3. A LAND WITHOUT US

Page 32. Sudden surges of glacial ice might have *lowered* temperatures quite suddenly in parts of the world. Marine geologists and glaciologists are studying the possibility that every so often, the ice domes around Hudson Bay that fed the great Laurentide ice sheet over Canada and the northern United States would get so thick that their weight would create a plastic ice-rock interface at their base. The domes would slide out from under themselves, and whole sections of the Laurentide would go skidding off into the North Atlantic and break up into bergs. The addition of that much ice, according to

Scott Lehman, of the Woods Hole Oceanographic Institution, could have lowered sea temperatures by several degrees in as little as forty years, and the fresh water from that many melting bergs could have altered the oceanic circulatory system, cooling climates in Europe and elsewhere within a few decades. Meantime, the domes, shed of their weight, would stabilize and begin to thicken once more. Another cycle would begin, another short oscillation superimposed on the longer rhythms of climatic change.

The primary source for much of the material in this chapter is a two-volume study published by the University of Minnesota Press in 1983 under the title *Late Quaternary Environments of the United States*. The full Quaternary dates from 2 million years ago to the present. The first volume concentrates on the late Pleistocene, from 25,000 to 10,000 years ago, and the second on the Holocene, from 10,000 or 12,000 years ago up till now. The overall editor is H. E. Wright, Jr., of the Limnological Research Center at Minnesota. Wright, now in his seventies, for years has been recognized as one of the most perceptive students of environmental change in the world. He personally edited the Holocene volume. In his preface he wrote that the Holocene is of scientific interest because of opportunities it affords to study the "changing environments brought about by the basic shift from a glacial to a nonglacial climatic mode" and because it is also "the time of rapid development of human cultures under changing environmental conditions."

Herbert Wright coedited another volume I found useful, this one with W. F. Ruddiman, of the Lamont-Doherty Geological Laboratory. It is called *North America and Adjacent Oceans During the Last Deglaciation* (Boulder, Colo.: Geological Society of America, 1987).

Page 39. Material on Holocene fauna in North America is drawn largely from papers in *Quaternary Extinctions: A Prehistoric Revolution*, edited by Paul S. Martin, of the University of Arizona, and Richard G. Klein, of the University of Chicago (Tucson: University of Arizona Press, 1989). The volume includes papers arguing both for climatic change and for human hunting as a cause of mammalian extinction in North America. It contains "Who's Who in the Pleistocene: A Mammalian Bestiary," by Elaine Anderson, of Boulder, Colorado, an illustrated guide to the animals of a biologically more boisterous time.

Page 41. The quote is from William Least Heat-Moon's *Prairy-Erth* (Boston: Houghton Mifflin, 1991). The elder is a Sioux, Brave Buffalo.

Page 42. Much of the information on climate patterns comes from the work of Thompson Webb III, of Brown University, and John E. Kutzbach, of the University of Wisconsin. A paper by Kutzbach and Webb appears in *Quaternary Landscapes*, a publication put out by the University of Minnesota Press in 1991 to honor Herbert Wright upon his retirement (he was still at work when I saw him in 1992). The paper is entitled "Late Quaternary Climate and Vegetational Change in Eastern North America: Concepts, Models and Data." Webb and two colleagues — George Jacobson, of the University of Maine (quoted on page 33), and Eric Grimm, of the Illinois State Museum in Springfield — put together a series of charts published with *North America and Adjacent Oceans During the Last Deglaciation*, showing how various trees and grasses in the eastern United States shifted their ranges over the past 18,000 years.

Page 46. Victor Baker, a geologist at the University of Arizona, writes in the first volume of *Late Quaternary Environments of the United States* that the floods in the Columbia drainage were "perhaps the most remarkable late-Pleistocene fluvial events on the planet." Baker says a researcher named Bretc, who worked in the Channeled Scabland during the twenties, gave the idea its name.

Page 48. Much of the information here comes from Davis's paper "Climatic Instability, Time Lags, and Community Disequilibrium," in *Community Ecology*, edited by Jared Diamond and Ted J. Case (New York: Harper & Row, 1984).

Daniel Botkin is also the author of *Discordant Harmonies: A New Ecology for the Twenty-first Century* (New York: Oxford University Press, 1990). In it, he points out how much outmoded ideas about nature have interfered with clear thinking about our present ecological crises.

Page 51. Word of the blue jay's interaction with the oak comes from a paper by W. Carter Johnson, a biologist at Virginia Polytechnic Institute, and Thompson Webb III, of Brown.

Page 52. The tally of animal remains is the work of the late John Guilday, a specialist on the Appalachian biota.

Page 53. Some mammoths may have hung on for thousands of

years after their supposed extinction. The fossil teeth of dwarf mammoths dated to 4,000 years ago have been found on Wrangel Island, off the coast of northeast Siberia, along with remains of older, normal-size mammoths. The impact of the find on the blitzkrieg arguments (see Chapter 5) remains to be seen. It is possible that the steppe-tundra vegetation favored by mammoths survived here and there on Wrangel, but that food shortages caused at least the initial phases of the dwarfing.

The "plaids and stripes" phrase is from R. Dale Guthrie, in his paper in *Quaternary Extinctions*.

Page 54. Russell Graham and Ernest Lundelius, from the University of Texas at Austin, are developing FAUNMAP, which does for mammals what the Jacobson-Webb-Grimm maps do for vegetation from full glacial times to the Encounter. FAUNMAP is an electronic database holding data from an estimated 2,500 archaeological and paleontological sites in the contiguous United States and covering 40,000 years. The system can produce a wide range of overlay maps to show distributions of individual species and mammalian compositions over time.

4. CHILDREN OF THE ICE

Page 56. Brian M. Fagan, who teaches anthropology at the University of California, Santa Barbara, has written extensively about North American prehistory. I have two of his books on my shelves. They are *The Great Journey* (1987) and *Ancient North America* (1990), both published by Thames and Hudson.

Page 57. Deloria's quotes, here and in other parts of the book, are from an afterword he wrote for *America in 1492: The World of the Indian Peoples Before the Arrival of Columbus*, edited by Alvin M. Josephy, Jr. (New York: Knopf, 1992).

Page 59. The late Joseph Campbell wrote widely of the spread of myths and beliefs from Eurasia to America. For this chapter, I referred to Campbell's *The Flight of the Wild Gander* (New York: HarperCollins, 1990), and to sections of the first volume ("The Way of the Animal Powers") of his *Historical Atlas of World Mythology* (New York: HarperCollins, 1988).

The first search for evidence supporting human occupation of America during the last ice age began more than a century ago.

Since that time, write two scientists who should know, "The antiquity of the first Americans has been among the most discussed and debated issues in American archaeology, often far out of proportion to the quantity of the evidence at hand." The scientists are David J. Meltzer, of the Department of Anthropology at Southern Methodist University, and Tom D. Dillehay, of the University of Illinois in Champaign-Urbana. They wrote in their capacity as editors of *The First Americans: Search and Research* (Boca Raton, Fla.: CRC Press, 1991). Papers in the volume probe many of the problems involved in entering an unpeopled land, moving through it, and surviving in it.

Page 66. A scientist who argues both for extreme antiquity of human occupation of the Americas and for widespread use of boats to move down the coasts is Ruth Gruhn, of the University of Alberta. She finds great cultural diversity among peoples living at the southern point of South America by 10,500 years ago, an achievement that would have required initial crossings to North America by 50,000 years ago. Other scientists I have talked to dispute the antiquity but are willing to admit to the possibility that boats may have been used at various times during initial entry. Several mentioned that boats had apparently been used in the crossing to Australia 40,000 years ago, a sea journey longer than that required to navigate from the northeastern tip of Siberia to Alaska (coasting along the land bridge, if it were above water at the time, or braving the open Bering Strait).

Page 69. Information on human expansion into Europe comes from *In the Age of Mankind: A Smithsonian Book of Human Evolution*, by Roger Lewin (1988). Karl W. Butzer, at the University of Texas, Austin, applies his knowledge of Old World occupations to the peopling of America in *The First Americans*. Brian Huntley, of the University of Durham in England, discusses climatic and biotic changes in Europe during the Holocene in *Vegetation History*, which he coedited with Thompson Webb III (Norwell, Mass.: Kluwer, 1988).

Page 74. The quote by Wilson is from *The Biophilia Hypothesis*, edited by Stephen R. Kellert and Edward O. Wilson (New York: Shearwater Books, 1993). The book is an examination by several scientists of the concept that human awareness is still very much tied to the natural world.

Page 75. *The Domestication of the Human Species*, by Peter J. Wilson, of the Department of Anthropology at the University of Otago in New Zealand, was published by Yale University Press in 1988.

Page 77. The prehistorian with the Koh-i-nor drawing pen is J. Gordon Ogden III, a biologist at Dalhousie University, in Halifax, Nova Scotia. The quote is from his paper "The Late Quaternary Paleoenvironmental Record of Northeastern North America," in *Amerinds and the Paleoenvironments in Northeastern North America* (New York: New York Academy of Sciences, 1977).

Page 78. The concept of transients and estate dwellers comes from a paper, "Colonizing Continents: Some Problems from Australia and the Americas," in *The First Americans*. The author is John M. Beaton, of the University of California at Davis. Beaton says of his fast-track transient explorers: "The risks they took were very high, or so they might seem to us, but with a generalized tool kit, a naive fauna, an unconstrained social/political environment, and a bit of luck, a lineage might see the Northern Lights, note the transit of the equatorial sun, and feel the chill winds of the southern oceans in the space of ten or fewer generations. This is its own form of success."

In the same publication, T. Douglas Price, of the University of Wisconsin, has a paper entitled "The View from Europe: Concepts and Questions about Terminal Pleistocene Societies." He writes that northern Europe was an "extraordinary laboratory for the investigation of human colonization and adaptation." The area came free of ice at the end of the Pleistocene and shares a number of other similarities with North America, Price says, and "must have offered a number of similar problems at about the same time to new inhabitants we have traditionally called large-game hunters."

5 · AMONG ANIMALS

Page 84. Brian Fagan's *Ancient North America* has good material for the general reader on both Clovis and Folsom cultures.

Page 85. The blitzkrieg and climatic explanations for the extinction of large mammals in North America at the end of the last glaciation are well and abundantly explained in *Quaternary Extinctions*. Paul S. Martin, a coeditor of the volume, is one of the chief proponents of the overkill concept.

Page 86. The ratio of hunters to mammoths is taken from the work of Jared Diamond in *Quaternary Extinctions*. Diamond, a physiologist at UCLA Medical School, is also a student of the rise and fall of species. His book *The Third Chimpanzee* (New York: Harper-Collins, 1992) contains additional ideas on overkill by humans through time.

Page 88. My reference books on mammals that dominated North America in the Holocene include two classics. *The Elk of North America*, by Olaus J. Murie, was published originally in 1951 and reprinted in 1979 by Teton Bookshop of Jackson, Wyoming. Murie was among the finest field naturalists in the country. *The North American Buffalo: A Critical Study of the Species in Its Wild State* (Toronto: University of Toronto Press, 1972) is by Frank Gilbert Roe, mentioned above. *The White-Tailed Deer: Ecology and Management*, edited by Lowell K. Halls (Harrisburg, Pa.: Stackpole Books, 1984), contains some estimates of prehistoric ranges and populations.

The bestiary in *Quaternary Extinctions* contains some illustrations of early bison.

Page 94. I came across a pamphlet on the atlatl called "The Development of the Spearthrower," by William S. Webb (Lexington: Department of Anthropology, University of Kentucky, 1957).

Stories of Bobby Garvin are in my *Oil and Water: The Struggle for Georges Bank* (Boston: Atlantic Monthly Press, 1985).

Page 96. Tourists at Yellowstone and other western parks insist on approaching bison on foot to take pictures, and a few pay the consequences. I saw a man gored once, in the bullring in Lima, Peru, forty years ago. The matador was a noted one, and he was showing off, on his knees facing away from the bull, working the cape behind him. The bull, weighing a little more than half what a bison does, caught him in the buttock, spun him on one horn, and flipped him onto the sand. He arose and, in his trauma, raised his hands triumphantly to the crowd. The gasp from around the ring told him what his numbed body did not. He looked over his shoulder, saw his own blood hosing from him, and collapsed. If I remember correctly, he lived.

The material on hunting bison and other large mammals in the West is drawn largely from *Prehistoric Hunters of the High Plains* (New York: Academic Press, 1991), by George C. Frison, of the University of Wyoming.

Page 98. The Matthiessen quote is from the revised edition of his *Wildlife in America* (New York: Viking/Penguin, 1987).

Page 99. The quote about dead buffalo is also from Matthiessen's *Wildlife in America.*

Page 101. Deer hunting strategies in the East are discussed in *The White-Tailed Deer* and a number of other works. Dean R. Snow covers the subject well in *The Archaeology of New England* (New York: Academic Press, 1980). Snow pays close attention to human-environmental interaction and to the importance of geography — and of river drainage systems in particular — in determining patterns of human occupation and settlement.

The several volumes of *Handbook of North American Indians*, edited by William C. Sturtevant and others and published by the Smithsonian Institution, contain a great deal of information on foraging practices throughout North America.

Page 103. Snow is also a good source of information on the rise of fishing in the East. David Thomas, an archaeologist at the University of Vermont, and James Peterson, at the University of Maine in Farmington, also supplied information on the subject.

Page 104. My books on the domestication of animals include two involving Juliet Clutton-Brock, of the British Museum, a specialist on this vast subject. Clutton-Brock edited *The Walking Larder* (London: Unwin Hyman, 1990) and is the author of *Domesticated Animals from Early Times* (Austin: British Museum/University of Texas, 1981). A popular book on the subject is *The Covenant of the Wild: Why Animals Chose Domestication*, by Stephen Budiansky, a journalist (New York: Morrow, 1992). I talked with Raymond P. Coppinger, the evolutionary biologist mentioned on page 109. Coppinger, who teaches at Hampshire College near Amherst, wrote a paper with Charles Kay Smith of the University of Massachusetts entitled "The Domestication of Evolution," published in *Environmental Conserva-*

tion (Winter 1983). I have also made use of a work by Valerius Geist, *Mountain Sheep and Man in the Northern Wilds* (Ithaca, N.Y.: Cornell University Press, 1975). Geist spent years in the mountains observing the neoteny of mountain sheep.

Page 112. If mammoths had been domesticated, they probably would have shrunk in size in the process. Most animals do. The horse seems to be a rare exception. It grew larger under the hand of humans.

Page 113. The Pfeiffer quote is from his book *The Creative Explosion: An Inquiry into the Origins of Art and Religion* (New York: Cornell, 1987).

6. HANDS IN THE LEAVES

Page 114. Bruce Smith, of the Department of North American Archaeology at the Smithsonian Institution's Museum of Natural History, has devoted a good deal of time to the origins of agriculture in eastern North America. In a paper by that name published in the magazine *Science* (December 22, 1989), he writes that

> the development of agriculture has long been considered a major milestone in human evolution. During the past 10,000 years agricultural economies have also caused significant changes in the earth's ecosystems. This post-Pleistocene transition from foragers to farmers, from a reliance on wild species of plants and animals to food production economies, took place at different rates and times in various regions of the world and involved a rich variety of crop plants. In many regions this developmental transition with its major consequence for human societies and terrestrial ecosystems is far from well documented. As a result of a substantial increase in the amount, quality, and variety of information gained for eastern North America during the past 10 years, this region now provides one of the most detailed records of agricultural origins available.

Smith and Cowan collaborate from time to time in tracking down wild progenitors of eastern domesticated plants.

Page 115. Ford edited a collection of papers, presented in *Prehistoric Food Production in North America* (Ann Arbor: Museum of Anthropology, University of Michigan, 1985). Ford's own contributions are especially valuable in explaining some of the basic whys and wherefores of plant domestication. He argues that migratory people rapidly occupied areas of prime food resources. Those resources might have begun to dwindle because of climatic conditions, disease, or the impact of increasing densities of human populations. They might have been claimed by one group to the exclusion of others. Whatever its causes, resource scarcity necessarily would force people to consider alternatives to conventional foraging, including the alternative of staying put and tending and eventually cultivating food plants in one particular area.

What is "wild" when growing in disturbed soils such as those along a flood-prone river is "weedy" when growing in soils disturbed by humans. Fortunately for us, the progenitors of our crop plants paid no attention to semantics and much to the opportunities that disturbance of almost any sort gave them to move in ahead of the competition.

Page 116. The Nabhan quote is from the first chapter of his book *Enduring Seeds: Native American Agriculture and Wild Plant Conservation* (San Francisco: North Point Press, 1989).

Page 117. Native use of plants for cures, rituals, and plain, ordinary pleasure was almost endless. Alcoholic beverages did not seem to be widespread, but tribes in the Southeast and elsewhere drank copious amounts of an emetic "black drink," which produced ionic imbalances and mild hallucinations, especially when combined with hours of dancing. Tobacco brought in from South America was cultivated in the East when Europeans arrived, and native varieties were collected and probably domesticated in the Far West. Some tobaccos were strong enough to bend the minds of heavy users. Many groups knew that preparations made from willows were effective painkillers (willows contain salicin, a principal ingredient of aspirin). Poplar and aspen, both containing salicin, were used for the same purpose. The Iroquois and other northern groups drank spruce concoctions, high in Vitamin C, and sassafras was widely used for fevers. Sassafras was wildly popular when introduced by the Spanish to Europe. The first Europeans who hove to off Cape Cod were looking not so much for fish as for sassafras, thought by doctors of the time to cure venereal disease and colic.

Page 118. Bruce Smith is the source of these ideas about what developed from cucurbits growing in Mexican and eastern North American gardens. The paper is "The Origins of Agriculture in Eastern North America," cited above. Smith's arguments are collected in *Eastern Origins: Essays on the Origins of Agriculture in Eastern North America* (Washington: Smithsonian, 1992).

Page 128. Brian Fagan describes the Adena and Hopewell cultures in some detail in *Ancient North America*.

Page 129. Some of my readings in the development of agriculture in the Near East and Europe were in *The Holocene: An Environmental History*, by Neil Roberts (New York: Basil Blackwell, 1989). Roberts is lecturer in geography at Loughborough University, in England. Another source is Patty Jo Watson, a professor of anthropology at Washington University in St. Louis, who has spent years in Iran, Turkey, and this country studying early economies and environments. I have made use of her paper, entitled "Origins of Food Production in Western Asia and Eastern North America: A Consideration of Interdisciplinary Research in Anthropology and Archaeology," in *Quaternary Landscapes*, the festschrift honoring Herbert Wright, cited above. I also referred to *A Green History of the World: Nature, Pollution, and the Collapse of Societies* (New York: St. Martin's, 1992). The author, Clive Ponting, is a historian in residence at University College, Swansea, in Wales.

Page 132. Modern geneticists continue to select for this trait or that, to improve yields, resistances to pests and diseases, or simply the storability of this powerful grass. Walton C. Gallinat, professor emeritus at the Eastern Agricultural Station in Waltham, Massachusetts, part of the University of Massachusetts system, took time out from years of serious work with maize to produce a truly "American" ear of corn, one with red, white, and blue kernels.

Page 135. One explorer of evidence that corn may have come later to the Southwest than conventional arguments would have it is Michael S. Berry. Material fom his *Time, Space and Transition in Anasazi Prehistory* (Salt Lake City: University of Utah Press, 1982) was published in Richard Ford's *Prehistoric Food Production in North America* under the title "The Age of Maize in the Greater Southwest: A Critical Review."

The Zuni quote was used by John Doebley as an introduction to one of his papers. It is from *Zuni Creation Myths*, by Frank Cushing, a flamboyant Smithsonian anthropologist. The book was put out in 1896. The full quote is: "Thus, of the substance of all flesh is the seed of seeds, Corn! And suited to all peoples and places; yet we, brothers younger are with ye, favored in the light, in that together we are its priests and keepers. Let us therefore love it and cherish it, as we cherish and love our women; and it shall be the giver of milk to the youthful and flesh to the aged."

Page 136. The classic work on Iroquois use of corn was done early in this century by Arthur C. Parker, an archaeologist at the New York State Museum in Albany who was part Iroquois and spoke the Seneca language. My copy of *Parker on the Iroquois* was published in 1968 by the University of Syracuse Press. It was edited and carried an introduction by William N. Fenton, himself a noted authority on the Iroquois. The book contains three sections: "Iroquois Uses of Maize and Other Food Plants," "The Code of Handsome Lake, the Seneca Prophet," and "The Constitution of the Five Nations."

Page 139. Bruce Smith writes on "Agricultural Chiefdoms of the Eastern Woodlands" in Vol. I, Chap. 5 of *The Cambridge History of the Native Peoples of the Americas, North America*, edited by Bruce Trigger and Wilcomb E. Washburn, to be published by Cambridge University Press.

7. COSTS OF LIVING

Page 141. Steven Pyne, quoted on page 143, is the author of *Fire in America: A Cultural History of Wild Land and Rural Fire* (Princeton, N.J.: Princeton University Press, 1982). He is a historian at Arizona State University in Tempe and a veteran of fire crews working on the north rim of the Grand Canyon. The book has sections on fire and the native American and on white use of fire from colonial times to the present.

Page 142. My information on Benjamin Silliman and Indian summer comes from Eric Grimm at the Illinois State Museum, who worked with Tom Webb and George Jacobson on the maps of vegetational range shifts during the Holocene. Grimm spent a number of years in Minnesota on projects that included the relationship of fire to prairie-forest boundaries.

Page 143. William Patterson works at the University of Massachusetts in Amherst. He and Andrew E. Backman, also of the university's Department of Forestry and Wildlife Management, coauthored a paper for *Vegetation History*, cited in Chapter 4, entitled "Fire and Disease History of Forests." With Kenneth E. Sassaman, an anthropologist at the University of Massachusetts, Patterson wrote "Indian Fires in the Prehistory of New England" for *Holocene Human Ecology in Northeastern North America*, edited by George P. Nicholas (New York: Plenum, 1988).

Page 145. I am borrowing here from the ideas of Clive Ponting and Neil Roberts, cited in Chapter 6.

Page 146. The quote is from Behre's "The Role of Man in European Vegetation History," in *Vegetation History*.

Thompson Webb III told me about the paucity of evidence for human intervention in eastern North American pollen samples. Other surveys may show more significant meddling here, but the difference between the European and North American record should remain evident and enormous.

Page 147. The Ponting quote is from *A Green History of the World*, cited in Chapter 6.

Page 148. The Petra story is from Jared Diamond's *The Third Chimpanzee*, cited in Chapter 5.

Page 149. Plato's quote is from Ponting.

"Early Farming in Northwestern Europe," by John M. Howell, which appeared in the November 1987 issue of *Scientific American*, was the principal source for this section. Howell is at the University of Liverpool in England.

Page 150. The reference to the elm blight beetle and dung is from "The Hunter-Gatherer/Agricultural Transition and the Pollen Record in the British Isles," by Kevin J. Edwards, of the University of Birmingham, published in *The Cultural Landscape: Past, Present and Future*, edited by Birks, Birks, Kaland, and Moe (New York: Cambridge University Press, 1989).

Page 151. "The Brown Bear of the Green Glen" is part of *Popular Tales of the West Highlands* (London: Alexander Gardner, 1890), a remarkable collection of stories told in Gaelic and translated by J. F. Campbell in the middle of the last century.

Page 152. Henry III's feast is reported in Neil Roberts's *The Holocene*, cited in Chapter 6.

Page 154. "The Oops Factor" was written during the preparation of Dincauze's forthcoming *Principles of Environmental Archaeology*, to be published by Cambridge University Press, probably in 1995.

Page 155. One of the most comprehensive treatments of disease in early societies is *Paleopathology at the Origins of Agriculture* (New York: Academic Press, 1984). The editors are Mark N. Cohen, of the State University of New York at Plattsburg, and George J. Armelagos, of Emory University. Papers discuss disease in North America and in Europe. I was drawn especially to a chapter synthesizing the material presented at the conference of which *Paleopathology* is the proceedings: "Population, Health and the Evolution of Subsistence," by Anna C. Roosevelt, of the Museum of the American Indian in New York.

Page 158. Deborah Martin, a physical anthropologist at Hampshire College, talked with me about health problems in New Mexico and surrounding areas. She is a contributor to *The Organization and Evolution of Southwest Society*, edited by George Gumerman and Murray Gell-Mann, to be published by Cambridge University Press.

Page 159. John Blitz, of the CUNY Graduate Center in New York, published a paper in *North American Archaeologist* (Vol. 9, No. 2, 1988) entitled "Adoption of the Bow in Prehistoric North America," and I have adapted some of his material. Archaeologist Stewart J. Fiedel, of Lyndhurst, N.J., supplied me with citations and some puzzles. The bow, he informed me, was used in Amazonia and in Patagonia at the time of Contact. How did it get there? It could have diffused south from North America, but if so, its passage left no imprint in Mesoamerica, where the atlatl remained the weapon of choice. Fiedel also ascribes the lack of stringed instruments in pre-Columbian America, "in contrast to Africa and Eurasia," to "the very late adoption of the bow (from whence would derive the basic principle of the vibrating, taut string")."

The effect of the bow on travel and communication came up in a conversation with Richard Ford. As a former archer who, as a boy, foolishly agreed to join his elder brother in stalking each other with lightly padded arrows, I can attest to the bow's performance.

Page 161. These estimates, taken from Ponting and other sources, are mere indications of demographic trends. I use them to give an idea of growth patterns.

8. THE DAY BEFORE AMERICA

Page 164. The information about Brewster comes from *William Brewster of the Mayflower: Portrait of a Pilgrim*, by Dorothy Brewster (New York: New York University Press, 1970).

Page 165. John C. Pearson did an exhaustive survey of aquatic abundances in his report "The Fish and Fisheries of Colonial North America, Part II, the New England States," written in the 1890s for the U.S. Fish and Wildlife Service.

Page 167. Information on distribution of wildlife came from Adele Conover, a staffer at *Smithsonian* magazine, who collected data on population ranges to accompany my piece "1492 America: The Land Columbus Never Saw," published in November 1991.

I have taken demographic data from Ubelaker's paper "North American Indian Population Size, A.D. 1500–1985," in the *American Journal of Physical Anthropology* 77 (1988): 289–294. Some argue that Ubelaker's estimates are too low. Henry Dobyns, of Chicago's Newberry Library, worked from early colonial references to local native populations. He extrapolated from rough estimates of human carrying capacity, using the Malthusian arguments that human populations increase to the limits of essential foods. He came up with 18 million people living north of Mexico around 1500. His research is presented in *Their Number Become Thinned: Native American Population Dynamics in Eastern North America* (Knoxville: University of Tennessee Press, 1983). It deals not only with pre-Contact populations but with the effects of post-Contact diseases. Prehistorians I have talked to appear to favor Ubelaker's methods of estimation. The issue itself is now highly politicized. Eighteen million people sounds better than two million to those eager to postulate a strong native presence in this country prior to the Encounter — and the most brutal decimation thereafter.

Page 168. Brian Fagan writes of late prehistoric societies of the

Pacific Coast in *Ancient North America*, cited in Chapter 4.

Linda Cordell discusses late pre-Contact events in her *Prehistory of the Southwest*, cited in Chapter 2.

Page 169. Bruce Smith deals with the Mississippi Valley and the Southeast in several of his papers. The most concentrated treatment I have come across is that of David G. Anderson, now at the U.S. Park Service office in Atlanta, in his doctoral thesis "Political Change in Chiefdom Societies," prepared under Richard Ford at the University of Michigan.

Dean Snow deals with events in the Northeast in *The Archaeology of New England*, cited in Chapter 5.

Page 170. Dena Dincauze and a graduate student, Robert J. Hasenstab, presented their argument for Mississippian pressures on the Iroquois in *Centre and Periphery* (London: Unwin Hyman, 1989), edited by Timothy Champion, of the University of Southampton, in England. Their paper is "Explaining the Iroquois: Tribalization on a Prehistoric Periphery."

Page 170. Timothy Foote of *Smithsonian* wrote a description of fifteenth-century Europe in the December 1991 issue of the magazine. It was entitled "Where Columbus Was Coming From." Ponting also comments on the period, as does Roberts.

Page 173. My reference is to the first part of Meinig's work, *The Shaping of America*. Volume I (New Haven: Yale University Press, 1986) is devoted to Atlantic America, 1492–1800. Meinig is at Syracuse University.

Page 175. As indicated, the material here is from Peter Wilson and *The Domestication of the Human Species*.

Page 176. The Tuchman quote is from *The March of Folly: From Troy to Vietnam* (New York: Knopf, 1984).

Page 178. Kirkpatrick Sale, an environmental philosopher, says of emergent capitalism that it was to fashion a "world more mechanistic than organic, more corporeal than numinous, from which intimacy, sacredness and reverence have all but vanished . . . and in which something colder, duller and more lifeless presides instead." The quote is from *The Conquest of Paradise: Christopher Columbus and the Columbian Legacy* (New York: Knopf, 1990).

Page 180. The quote by Mircea Eliade is from *Discovering the*

Vernacular Landscape, by John B. Jackson (New Haven: Yale University Press, 1986).

Page 184. The environmental historian is William Cronon, author of *Changes in the Land: Indians, Colonists, and the Ecology of New England* (New York: Hill and Wang, 1983). The quote ending this chapter is from a conversation Cronon had with his friend and fellow historian Richard White, of the University of Utah (Cronon was at Yale when I met him and is now at the University of Wisconsin). Their comments were published in the August–September 1986 issue of *American Heritage* magazine as "Indians and the Land."

Richard White has written widely on this subject. I found most useful his essay "Native Americans and the Environment," a critical review of literature on this topic, published in *Scholars and the Indian Experience*, edited by W. R. Swagerty (Bloomington: Indiana University Press, 1984). White and Cronon together wrote "Ecological Change and Indian-White Relations," published in Vol. 4 of the *Handbook of North American Indians*, edited by William C. Sturtevant and Wilcomb E. Washburn (Washington: Smithsonian, 1988).

9. UP TILL NOW

Page 185. The epidemics introduced by Europeans into North America are widely described. In *Ecological Imperialism: The Biological Expansion of Europe, 900–1900* (New York: Cambridge University Press, 1987), Alfred Crosby, of the University of Texas, groups the alien pathogens with plants, animals, and other items of the "portmanteau biota." William Cronon treated the epidemics extensively in *Changes in the Land*. Francis Jennings, who directed the Center for the History of the American Indian at the Newberry Library in Chicago, did so in *The Invasion of America: Indians, Colonialism, and the Cant of Conquest* (New York: W. W. Norton, 1976).

Page 186. The historian quoted is Jennings.

The sorrowful elder is quoted in "Early Indian-European Contacts," by T. J. Brasser, in Vol. 15 of *Handbook of North American Indians*.

Page 187. The *Time* cover story appeared on September 23, 1991. Alfred Crosby uses the Smith quote, from *An Inquiry into the*

Nature and Causes of the Wealth of Nations, in *Ecological Imperialism.*

Page 188. Kirkpatrick Sale refers often to Braudel in *The Conquest of Paradise,* from which this quote is taken. Braudel's argument is that fifteenth-century Europe, consuming its own resources at a frightening pace, "needed" the outside world for its own survival.

Sale has some interesting comments about the fur trade. My comments about the uses to which native Americans put European trade goods come from conversation with James Bradley, my principal source on the Onondaga, and with Peter Thomas, of the University of Vermont.

Page 190. The argument that native Americans turned on fur-bearers for breaking covenants is best presented by Calvin Martin, of Rutgers, in *Keepers of the Game: Indian-Animal Relationship and the Fur Trade* (Berkeley: University of California Press, 1978). Martin has his supporters but has been widely criticized for basing his theory on inconclusive evidence. George Cornell, an Ojibwa involved in native American studies at the University of Michigan, claims that "the disintegration of cultural systems provided an appropriate environment in which the [fur] trade could occur. Once the trade cycle began, and Native peoples came to rely on European trade goods, indigenous practices and material culture fell into disuse. This, when coupled with the tremendous effects of disease upon Native populations, tied Native peoples to the trade to sustain themselves."

Page 191. Thomas Jefferson's comments are quoted in Jared Diamond's *The Third Chimpanzee.* The presidential tone does not improve with time. Diamond has dug up this bit of intemperance from Teddy Roosevelt: "The settler and pioneer have at bottom had justice on their side; this great continent could not have been kept as nothing but a game preserve for squalid savages."

See *Ecological Imperialism* for greater detail on introduced species.

Page 192. Landscape as a product of human interference is a relatively new concept to the popular mind in this country. One of the best explications I have come across is *The Making of the American Landscape,* edited by geographer Michael Conzen, at the University of Chicago (London: Unwin Hyman, 1990). In the book, Karl Butzer examines native influences on the landscape. There are chapters on Spanish and French legacies. The bulk of the book focuses on geographical transformations emanating from the Northeast and the transition to national landscape patterns. I was helped most by Hildegard Binder Johnson, writing on the imposition of the Jeffersonian grid system; Michael Williams, on forest clearing; John C. Hudson, on agriculture on the grasslands; James L. Wescoat, Jr., on the desert; David Meyer, on industrialization; Edward K. Muller, on the effects of urbanization; and — a wonderful piece — John A. Jakle, on the automobile as landscape designer.

The environmental historian Donald Worster has written at length about many of the topics covered in this chapter. His most recent work is a collection of essays entitled *The Wealth of Nature: Environmental History and the Ecological Imagination* (New York: Oxford University Press, 1993).

Petersham is home to the Harvard Forest, a research forest that houses a museum containing dioramas of landscape alterations since the arrival of European settlers. The museum offers a booklet, "The Harvard Forest Models," describing the dioramas and the work that went into them.

Page 193. Merchant is an environmental historian at the University of California in Berkeley. The book I refer to is *Ecological Revolutions: Nature, Gender, and Science in New England* (Chapel Hill: University of North Carolina Press, 1989). William Cronon's *Changes in the Land* also provided material for this section.

Page 195. The material on Chicago is drawn largely from Cronon's *Nature's Metropolis: Chicago and the Great West* (New York: W. W. Norton, 1992).

Page 197. The Peshtigo and other fires are described in Pyne's *Fire in America* and in the forest chapter of *The Making of the American Landscape*.

Page 199. Donald Worster won the Bancroft Prize in 1980 with *The Dust Bowl* (New York: Oxford University Press, 1982). Dust storms are also described in the grasslands chapter of *The Making of the American Landscape*.

Page 200. The quote is from J. Opie in *The Law of the Land* (Lincoln: University of Nebraska Press, 1987). I found the quote in "The United States Great Plains," a chapter by William E. Riebsame, of the University of Colorado at Boulder, in *The Earth as Transformed by Human Action*, cited in Chapter 1. Riebsame goes on to warn that individualism and manifest destiny blind true believers to the inevitability of surprises, such as increased competition from Canada and other agricultural producers around the world and the possibility of more severe droughts in the plains as and if the world warms.

Page 203. The material on the discovery and early history of oil comes from my book *The Gulf Stream*. The rise of the auto is based on Jakle's chapter in *The Making of the American Landscape*.

Page 207. *Land of the Free*, by Archibald MacLeish, was first published in 1938 and republished in 1977 by Da Capo Press (New York).

10. THIS ONE IS OURS

Page 208. Some of the information on Euro-American population trends comes from Caroline Merchant's *Ecological Revolutions*.

I went through too many demographic projections to list here. Both Worldwatch Institute and the World Resources Institute put out useful data in their annual reviews. "Crowding Out the Future: World Population Growth, U.S. Immigration, and Pressures on Natural Resources" pulls together figures from the United Nations, the United States Bureau of the Census, and other sources in well-designed graphics. The pamphlet is a publication of the Federation for American Immigration Reform, of Washington. It is produced by Robert W. Fox and Ira H. Mehlman and makes its point with a minimum of rhetoric. The Population Information Program at Johns Hopkins University publishes "Population Reports" that synthesize the findings of scores of demographic publications around the world.

An organization called Negative Population Growth sponsored the publication of *Elephants in the Volkswagen: Facing the Tough Questions about Our Overcrowded Country*, a collection of essays by scholars alarmed by demographic and technological trends in this country (New York: W. H. Freeman, 1992). The book was edited by Lindsay Grant, formerly a State Department official who dealt with environmental and demographic affairs.

Page 213. The quote is from "Synergisms: Joint Effects of Climate Change and Other Forms of Habitat Destruction," by Norman Myers, in *Global Warming* and *Biological Diversity*, edited by

Robert L. Peters and Thomas E. Lovejoy (New Haven: Yale University Press, 1992).

Page 214. The joint statement on population by the Royal Society and the National Academy of Sciences was reported by the *New York Times* on February 27, 1992.

Page 218. Wallace S. Broecker, who works on climate change and ocean circulation at Lamont-Doherty Geological Observatory, wrote a balanced paper about the ambiguities of greenhouse arguments in the April 1992 issue of *Natural History.* The title is "Global Warming on Trial."

Woodwell made this statement in "How Does the World Work? Great Issues of Life and Government Hang on the Answer," his chapter in *Global Warming and Biological Diversity.*

Peters's quote is from his introduction to the same book.

Page 219. The Intergovernmental Panel on Climate Change puts out regular global scientific assessments. I have used its 1992 supplement.

Page 222. Davis and Zabinski's findings appear in the Peters/Lovejoy book as "Changes in Geographical Range Resulting from Greenhouse Warming: Effects on Biodiversity in Forests."

Another source on vegetational shifts past and future is *Quaternary Ecology: A Paleological Perspective,* by Hazel R. and Paul A. Delcourt (London: Chapman and Hall, 1991).

Page 223. Passenger pigeons may be gone, but another form of transport is still available to plants seeking to relocate: ourselves. Our intentional introductions of flora are fairly obvious by now, but our inadvertent ones deserve further research. Muddy trucks and cars carry seeds hundreds of miles from home ground. Our clothing and the fur and feathers of our pets can pick up and retain spores and plant parts. Herbert Wright, the quaternarian cited so many times above, told me that back in the days when pants had cuffs, one researcher would hang around airports and ask to examine the contents thereof. Sure enough, he found seeds — in among the cigarette ash.

The surveys mentioned are *Global Warming and Biological Diversity* and *The Potential Effects of Global Climate Change on the United States,* edited by Joel B. Smith and Dennis A. Tirpak, of the Environmental Protection Agency (Bristol, Pa.: Hemisphere, 1990).

Page 225. Officials of the South Coast Air Quality Management District, based in Los Angeles, told me about the health cost studies.

Page 229. Among papers related to Drake's Chesapeake marsh experiment is one by H. A. Mooney, Drake, R. J. Luxmoore, W. C. Oechel, and L. F. Pitelka entitled "Predicting Ecosystem Responses to Elevated CO_2 Concentrations" (*BioScience* 41, no. 2).

Page 230. Smith and Shugart have written extensively on their modeling work. A representative paper, written with G. B. Bonan and J. B. Smith, is "Modeling the Potential Response of Vegetation to Global Climate Change," in *Advances in Ecological Research*, Vol. 22 (New York: Academic Press, 1992).

Page 230. George Woodwell addresses the probable consequences of the positive feedback described here in "How Does the World Work?" a chapter of *Global Warming and Biological Diversity*. He writes that

> the warming of the earth that has occurred over the past century has probably stimulated the decay of organic matter in plants and soils of the middle and high latitudes and may be contributing an additional increment of carbon as carbon dioxide and methane to the atmosphere. . . . Biotic influences on the composition of the atmosphere are . . . large enough to change the amount of carbon dioxide in the atmosphere by several percent within a few weeks. . . . The safest assumption is that the warming will proceed rapidly over the next decades. Rapid change is the enemy of life. If uncontrolled and allowed to follow the current course the climatic changes will . . . be continuous and accelerating. The earth is simply not moving to another climatic equilibrium. It is moving from a period of slowly changing climates to one in which the warming will accelerate and be continuous.

Page 231. Fahkri Bazzaz of Harvard has been conducting experiments with elevated levels of carbon dioxide in his greenhouse. He finds that the growth binge produced by high gas levels tapers off in time.

11. A NATIVE SENSE

Page 237. The processes of knowing where we are are attracting serious attention these days. A serious and readable look at them can be found in *The Experience of Place: A Completely New Way of Looking at and Dealing with Our Radically Changing Cities and Countryside* (New York: Knopf, 1990). The author is Tony Hiss, who has been writing about place for more than a decade.

Hiss quotes Dr. John Falk, an ecologist formerly at the Smithsonian Institution, on his research on the human preference for grass. Falk told Hiss that it gives us "a built-in reading of our optimal level of environmental stimulation, which is to say, of the kind of complexity we need — in things to look at, listen to, sniff, and otherwise interact with — in order to be at our best."

Psychotherapists are paying increasing attention to the connection between the psyche and the natural world. A story in the *New York Times* of August 30, 1993, quotes a "theorist of ecopsychology," D. James Hillman, of Thompson, Connecticut: "Our fantasies about the environment are a sign that we're reconnecting to the natural world, waking up to it. . . . Our usual relationship to what in classical times was called the *anima mundi*, or soul of the world, has been numbed, anesthetized."

Mott T. Greene, of the University of Puget Sound, has put the essence of what moving indoors has cost us into one paragraph. It occurs in the introduction to *Natural Knowledge in Preclassical Antiquity* (Baltimore: Johns Hopkins University Press, 1991). He calls his book "a series of meditations on the relationships between mythology and natural knowledge both in antiquity and in the present." He then writes,

> The "ancients," as we generally refer to everyone from the time of Plato back to *Homo erectus*, lived and worked outdoors, and did most of their thinking there as well. Because we have come indoors in the last hundred years, much that was obvious to earlier generations of scholars about ancient mythology is no longer obvious to us. That myths are to a large extent stories about nature has passed in the last few generations from something that "goes without saying" to something that "cannot be said." When Darwin wrote *The Origin of Species* in 1859, he introduced the volume with a long disquisition on the breeding of domestic animals, as a way of leading his audience to the difficult terrain of natural selection through a familiar backyard (and barnyard) path. Today, this material is as foreign to most readers as the subject it was meant to illustrate — and this is because we have, in the intervening century, come indoors.

Greene also takes a cool look at our proclivity to skew the past in order to put ourselves in the best light. He writes, "The entire complex of evolutionary sequences, of ages and epochs, however sophisticated, serves in every period of the intellectual history of the modern world to maintain a fixed vision of the ascent from savagery to barbarism to civilization in measurable steps. It is not a mean-spirited vision, but its purpose is to maintain the myth that we are somehow special and different or even new, in some significant sense."

The American researchers on environmental values are Willett Kempton and Paul P. Craig. Kempton is senior policy scientist at the Center for Environmental Policy at the University of Delaware in Newark. Craig is in the Department of Applied Sciences at the University of California in Davis. I first saw their work in the April 1993 issue of *Environment* magazine.

Page 239. The expansion of the domestic alliance is described by Arthur H. Westing in *Maintenance of the Biosphere: Proceedings of the Third International Conference on Environmental Future* (Edinburgh: Edinburgh University Press, 1990). His contribution is entitled "Our Place in Nature: Reflections on the Global Carrying-Capacity for Humans." Westing is, among other things, a senior research fellow at the International Peace Research Institute in Oslo, and a contributing editor to *Environment*.

Page 241. I'm talking here about an approach to analysis involving the precautionary principle, a way of examining what present actions seem most prudent in the light of what we think may happen in the future. Robert Costanza, director of the Maryland International Institute of Ecological Economics, and Laura Costanza, a research associate at the institute, discuss a version of the principle in the November 1992 issue of *Environment*.

Page 243. The current inability to create decent jobs in decent numbers is not limited to the United States. In the September 1993 issue of *Harper's*, Richard Barnet, of the Institute for Policy Studies in Washington, writes that

> the problem is starkly simple: An astonishingly large and increasing number of human beings are not needed or wanted to make the goods or to provide the services that the paying customers of the world can afford. Since most people in the world depend on having a job just to eat, the unemployed, the unemployable, the

underemployed and the "sub-employed" — a term used to describe those who work part-time but need to work full-time, or who earn wages that are too low to support a minimum standard of living — have neither the money nor the state of mind to keep the global mass consumption system humming. Their ranks are growing so fast that the worldwide job crisis threatens not only global economic growth but the capitalist system itself.

Misanthropy was on the mind of Donnella Meadows, a member of a team of researchers that for many years has been investigating limits to global economic growth, when she wrote her contribution to *The Earth in Transition*, edited by George Woodwell (New York: Cambridge University Press, 1991). "Environmentalists have gotten a reputation for being unnecessarily gloomy, and for liking birds and bunnies more than people," she wrote. "To some extent we deserve that reputation. Some of us deliver dire warnings with undisguised relish. Many of us unconsciously communicate disrespect for and resentment of the human race. If we want to be effective, we must stop that."

Page 247. *Earth in the Balance* was published in 1992 by Houghton Mifflin.

Thomas Berry is the author of *The Dream of the Earth* (San Francisco: Sierra Club Books, 1990).

Page 248. "What then?" is one of many cautionary catchphrases used by the environmental philosopher and human ecologist Garrett Hardin. Hardin's most recent book is *Living Within Limits: Ecology, Economics and Population Taboos* (New York: Oxford University Press, 1993). He is professor emeritus at the University of California in Santa Barbara. I have never met anyone who can talk as calmly as Hardin can about the most difficult steps we may face: the containment of our reproduction and the fact that we still have not developed ways to do so that are both efficient and humane; the restraint of immigration; the regulation of our ways of life to prevent their degradation or destruction. He does not mince words. He marshals them.

Harris's statement comes from his book *Our Kind* (New York: Harper & Row, 1989).